Nick Harkaway is the author of two novels, *The Gone-Away World* and *Angelmaker*, and a regular blogger for the *Bookseller's* FutureBook website.

The Blind Giant

How to Survive in the Digital Age

NICK HARKAWAY

JOHN MURRAY

First published in Great Britain in 2012 by John Murray (Publishers)
An Hachette UK Company

First published in paperback in 2013

1

A CIP catalogue record for this title is available from the British Library

Paperback ISBN 978 1 84854 643 1
Ebook ISBN 978 1 84854 642 4

Printed and bound by Clays Ltd, St Ives plc

John Murray policy is to use papers that are natural, renewable and recyclable products and made
from wood grown in sustainable forests. The logging and manufacturing processes are expected to
conform to the environmental regulations of the country of origin.

John Murray (Publishers)
338 Euston Road
London NW1 3BH

www.johnmurray.co.uk

To
everyone who has ever taught me:
thank you

Knowledge is power, but it is a power reined by scruple, having a conscience of what must be and what may be; whereas Ignorance is a blind giant who, let him but wax unbound, would make it a sport to seize the pillars that hold up the long-wrought fabric of human good, and turn all the places of joy dark as a buried Babylon.

Daniel Deronda

Explanatory Note

Throughout *The Blind Giant*, you will find printed hypertext links (for anyone new to the digital world and thinking about taking their first steps, those are the messy strings of letters and characters.) If you type these into your web browser, you will find yourself at the book's website, where you can share a fragment of the text with friends and invite discussion, or dive into whatever conversations may already be under way. From time to time, you may also find additional thoughts from me or from others on the topics covered in the book: the pace of events is so fast, and the debates so intense, that in the month or so since I finished editing the main text I've seen four or five things I wish I could have included. Some of these have fractionally changed my opinions and others have confirmed them. Thoughts on paper are fixed, but the world moves on.

Contents

Introduction

Nothing Stays the Same

The hardback edition of this book came out in May. I'm writing at the end of July, and things have changed – again. A transistor made of chitosan has just been developed which may hold the key to understanding assorted brain diseases – and to connecting technological devices which use electrons to the workings of the human body. A designer at Airbus is working on a plane which will not be built, but printed, and similar technology will soon be used to manufacture drugs. Researchers at the Mayo Clinic in Rochester, Minnesota, say that they are 80 per cent likely to succeed in growing functional heart tissue from a sample taken from a reporter's bicep. (Unfortunately, it's not all good. Governments continue to assert ridiculous and draconian rights over electronic communications, and the Greenland ice sheet melted at an unprecedented – even terrifying – rate, going from 40 per cent of the surface showing signs of thawing to 97 per cent in just four days.) All the while, computers and phones and RFID chips are appearing everywhere, doing new things, making the world subtly or unsubtly different from how it has been.

Which leaves many of us feeling bewildered (which is to say 'lost in a pathless place') or amazed (i.e. 'overwhelmed with wonder' or possibly just 'driven stupid') by what's happening around us. It's a feeling which is far from historically uncommon. The idea of information overload has been around since the 1970s, and Jean-Jacques Rousseau complained of a similar sense of being marooned by life two hundred years earlier. In his *Reveries of a Solitary Walker*, Rousseau described himself as 'ripped out of the normal order of things'. The more he tried to understand his world, the less he did.

If you're feeling that way now, I may be able to help. Bear with me: the path is a little winding. That's because the typical culture of investigation, especially in countries that speak English as a first language, is geared towards a kind of dissection. If you want to know about a thing, you drill down into it, cut it up, analyse the pieces, describe them in detail, and this will somehow explain the whole. It's a strategy which comes from the early days of natural science, from A.J. Ayer and also from Hegel; a hunt for the genealogy of a thing and an examination of its component parts as a way of seeing its nature. The problem with this method in the context of the Internet and its interaction with our society is that they are more like a mosaic than a rock formation. (Not so coincidentally, one of the first web browsers, which is generally credited with popularising web surfing and hence facilitating the birth of the Web we have now, was actually called Mosaic.)

Looking in Two Directions at Once

This book is about understanding the relationship between us and our technology, which also means understanding something about our relationship with ourselves and the systems we make. It will help you if you find the whole digital discussion utterly alien, because it roots that discussion in the past and in the less technological areas of human psychology, culture and behaviour. However, that's not to say it's no good to you if you're a Lambda calculus badass or a social media guru. This book is about joining up the dots to give you a grip of the shape of the world. If that sounds a little vague – or a bit grandiose – try this: when you travel to a new country, you ask your friends who have been there about it. The experience of being in a completely foreign environment is huge – vast amounts of information and experience come your way all the time, from the smell of the airport and the traffic to the texture of the linens to the flavour of the orange juice and the colour of the sky – and that's before you even talk about the people. So your friends don't try to tell you all that stuff in a list. They tell you stories, which are incredibly compressed, tonal portraits of what it feels like to be there. If those stories are well chosen and well narrated, they actually help. They give you an instinct for a place you have never visited.

This book is longer than those stories, more factual and less poetic. But the job is the same: to convey not just information, but a feel for where to find more and what it may look like. It's supposed to fill the gaps in your knowledge, whatever your specific area is, by showing you where that area touches the others in this convergence.

Drilling into a mosaic may tell you a lot about how the glue was made and what underpins the image, but it won't tell you anything about what the mosaic shows or how the pieces fit together – and how things fit together is the key to this particular discussion. What does deindividuation do to us and how can it be diffused? How is it caused? What will happen to our brains and our culture as we continue to adopt digital technologies into the family spaces of our lives? Why don't we talk about technology the way we talk about art and literature, and why do we ignore scientific responses to questions of fact, such as the benefits of sex education or the relative risks of marijuana and horse-riding? How does Intellectual Property connect with Privacy and why are they important? Is our world really controlled by high economic and structural forces beyond our reach? Or are we simply in the grip of governmental and corporate interests, which combine, intentionally or not, to manipulate and dominate us? And if the latter, how can we take charge?

The Ape that Pokes Things

Digital technology is everywhere; we have brought it into our lives in the same way as the washing machine, the television, or the car. We use it wherever we can, and we are affected by it and by the forces which caused it to be created and shaped the forms it takes – and the forms of our societies. You can't start to understand digital technology without looking at where it touches everything else.

Understanding is important. It's important to us as individuals because if we can't grasp the nature of our world we'll make lousy decisions about it and feel utterly out of control. That feeling in turn has adverse practical consequences in terms of stress, adverse economic consequences because it makes us unwilling to invest, borrow, or lend, and adverse political consequences because it makes us likely to focus on issues immediately touching upon us at the expense of vital but more distant ones. (The environmental situation, for example, has dropped off the face of the political discussion during this financial crisis, something we will doubtless all have cause to regret down the line.)

And understanding is important if you run a business, because your business plan could be brilliant and still founder if it ignores the reality of the world in which it must function. As the splendidly moustachioed commentator Ben Hammersley is fond of pointing out, the practical application of Moore's Law (that chip processing power doubles every two years) is that something which was impossible in 2001 can be commonplace in 2013.

But I suspect that isn't really why we need to understand. It's all true, but I think we need to understand our world the way we need to talk and hug and fall in love. It is perhaps the most human trait of all: we don't have shells, claws or stingers – we have brains. We are evolved to figure things out. That's our evolutionary strategy. It's built in to us. We're the ape that pokes things.

So to reiterate, this is a wide book not a deep one, and that is deliberate. The notes sprinkled through the text are there not to prove my points but to let you do your own drill-down if you need to: they say 'this is where this idea came from'.

Iterative Design

It's also intended to be what you might call an iterative book. The concept of iterative design is very popular in technology circles – it's a business model and a creative ethos in which a company releases a technology early and improves it fast, offering new versions rapidly and doing the final stages of design in the acid bath of public scrutiny and testing – and it's touted as something bold and new. It has also become something of a philosophy, a way of seeing the world: you can't ever get things exactly right, but you can make a statement and amend it in the light of subsequent revelations. Yes, I know: that's essentially the scientific model in a nutshell, but in this incarnation it's got a special cachet for having emerged from a physical process in which all the steps can be seen and the changes understood at the basic level of understanding you see when you spend time with a baby: touch – about which, more in a moment.

So this is an iterative book in the sense that I don't offer it as the defining statement on all the issues it touches. It does have answers in it, but they're mutable, because the world moves on. Sadly – though perhaps happily for my sanity – I can't afford to sit around updating the book every month to keep it perfectly in date and up to speed with my own perceptions of what's happening. It's not that kind of iterative book. But it is supposed to be the start of the conversation rather than the end: a handyman's tool kit of ideas, not a taxidermist's lab of unassailable truths. The conversation is supposed to continue in your head, and online and over lunch. For the moment, at least, the only next iteration of this book I can count on is the one which takes place when the ideas you carry off in your head affect the way you react to the world thereafter.

Regarding Touch

There are several specific points which have emerged from discussions at the Royal Geographic Society, the Bristol Festival of Ideas, the Google Big Tent and elsewhere, which I should add to the text, and my editor at John Murray has been kind enough to give me some space here in which to do that.

Perhaps most interesting to me is the evolution of interfaces which is happening right now and what that means and will mean for our relationship with digital technology. Again, it sounds dry, but it's actually incredibly vibrant and human. When I was first encountering computers in the late '70s and early '80s, displays were monochrome green or brown, and the user interacted with them through the Command Line Interface, so called because you typed in commands at a prompt. Everything was textual – there was no graphical component at all. A very simple command would be something like RUN "PROG.EXE", which would – unsurprisingly – run the program called PROG. EXE. There was no metaphor; you told the machine what to do and it did it. If you got the command wrong, you were told you'd made a Syntax Error and nothing happened. Like many early designs, it made no effort to reach in our direction: we had to learn how to use it, rather than the machine working the way we think. The philosophy of tool-making has almost always been about making a sharp enough blade to do the job. The blade makes no concessions to the frailty of human skin, so you have to develop skill and strength in the hand that directs the chisel. Only relatively recently have we started to make tools which are both ergonomic and protective of the user, and reached the point where chainsaw blades retract when you take your hand off the handle. We could still go further and create saws that wouldn't work outside a given physical area, or that would stop the moment they touched a piece of specified protective clothing. This concept of 'user-friendliness' began to spread, and has not stopped. We began to expect our tools to understand that they were there to help, to have a rather more sophisticated idea of their own place and function.

The next stage in the evolution of interfaces was the Graphical User Interface, the pretty desktop metaphor we all still know. This created a notion of the digital space as separate and special, which is covered in the book, so I won't get into it too much now. The digital culture with which we are familiar, and the societal traits and discussion we have from it, come from this kind of interaction, this metaphor. The digital world was a separate space behind the screen, a neverland reachable through the keyboard and the mouse, but separate, into which we projected ourselves. Crucially, it was sterile. You couldn't really bring anything back with you, so there were no consequences to what you did or said online. As the Net became a venue for commerce, and for more and more people, that changed, but the basic attitude stayed the same.

But in 2010, the iPad came along, and things began to shift. There had been touchscreen computers before, but the iPad was hyped and sold with Apple's typical élan, and connected to the pre-existing ecosystem of apps and content. All that, of course, was owed to its smaller precursor, the iPhone, but sheer physical size made it a different experience. And it was just so easy. Apple sold 300,000 iPads on the day of release and almost 15 million by the end of 2010. The Graphic User Interface was no longer the only way of seeing the digital world.

The Touchscreen Interface does away with the metaphor of cyberspace and makes data something which responds to your fingers as if it was physical and alive. In doing so, it brings data and digital back from their exile in cyberspace and sites them firmly in a humanly comprehensible place, into an immediate 'right now, right here' relationship with the user. The technology is reaching for a more and more intuitive and realistic feel. The next generation of touchscreens will be responsive, able to produce drag to hold onto your finger and mimic different tactile experiences – smoothness, roughness, stickiness, movement, oiliness. This feeling of reality changes at an instinctive level how we see data, and how we think about the digital environment brings us increasingly to the important realisation that there is no digital world. There's nothing special or sovereign about the digital environment, and nothing particularly rotten about it, either. It is – it always was – us. We cannot map out a perfect society online and import it. Nor can we pretend that the bad things about the online world – the crimes, the lynch-mob mentality of newspaper comment pages, the occasional callous disregard for other people – are anything other than human action. If we want to fix the world, we have to do it in the here and the now, not in the play space behind the screen. We have to do it with ourselves. Technology no longer provides a convenient scapegoat.

There is, incidentally, another class of technologies that needs this kind of uplift: the systems we create to make our society work. Democracy, capitalism, justice, bureaucracy – all these are systems which seem to be in the Stone Age of design. They do what they're supposed to do just the way a chisel does; they carve chunks out of the world and shape them. They're equally capable of severing your finger used wrongly. But we no longer think of these things as set in stone. As our digital adventures have given us a new understanding of systems and of text, we've come to realise that what is written is not written for ever. We've come to expect things that are hurting us to stop doing it. And we've begun to recognise in the context of objects made of data that our systems are not separate from us, they are things we make. That being the case, how are these huge structural forces different? They're not. They're us, too.

From which it follows that we have a great deal of work to do.

State of the Globe

Why? Because the world is in a terrible state. I realise that won't fill you with joy to read, but on some level you already know it. Our financial system is broken, made dysfunctional by years of fairy-dust economics and an entrenched culture of short-termism over stewardship which will take painful and prolonged action to root out. Our benign and democratic governments must for some reason treat and trade with leaders who routinely torture their own citizens, and while we dicker about how to fix the global monetary engine, our planet's environment is being overloaded by the ridiculously wasteful and destructive way in which we live. The gap between rich and poor is so vast as to be almost impossible to understand from either end. In so many ways, we are in freefall. In consequence, the collision between the liberal and tolerant ideas on which our democracies are based and the tacit assumptions of overwhelming power and cultural supremacy which ride along with them is becoming more acute, and our rulers are abandoning long-vaunted principles of fairness and the Rule of Law in an effort to compensate. Economic crisis, the exposure of our national misdeeds, a heritage of spin and an almost pathological inability to answer a simple question have reduced trust in government to a sour joke. The 2012 Edelman Trust Barometer measured a nine-point slump in trust across 25 countries since 2011, the largest drop since the project began, bringing average trust down to 43 per cent. The UK was five points below that at 38 per cent. At what point does a government cease to be legitimately democratic?

Unable to make a case to the electorate for the necessary changes on substantive issues of all sorts – having in fact almost systematically degraded the public's ability to hear bad news during the blissful dream of free money that was the Dot Com boom and the Sub-Prime Bubble – our political class is turning to less conventional means of influence. A new book by Richard Thaler and Cass Sunstein advocates the use of 'nudging' – or more formally, choice architecture – to create desirable outcomes. The most obvious example is organ donation. There's always a shortage of donor organs because most people don't carry a donor card. It's not that they don't approve of organ donation, they just don't want to consider their own mortality so they never get around to it. But if you change the formulation of the choice – if organ donation is opt-out rather than opt-in – the same lag plays in favour of donation. Very few people have a substantive objection to donating their organs after death, so the majority probably would not opt out.

It makes perfect sense, and the goal is admirable, but the outcome is to my eye utterly ghastly. Ultimately, nudging produces a population of voters who are never faced with a challenging choice. The wide deployment of nudging creates a culture of people who live in a world of easy decisions – and are therefore ill-equipped to participate in the hard ones, which must inevitably come along as a consequence of valid participation in democracy. Choice is not an inherent quality, it is a skill, and it must be practised to be retained and refined.

Privacy and Big Data

For me, this is where the rubber meets the road on the issue of privacy. The personal aspect of privacy and the creepiness of someone you don't know leafing through your Facebook profile or your Flickr feed are a matter for each individual. The overarching issue of the gathering and deployment of vast quantities of behavioural data is something else again; even comparatively crude studies of services like Twitter can yield surprisingly consistent (predictive) information about mood across the working week. The power of more complex studies, with access to better and deeper data, may prove considerable. We like to think of ourselves as rational deciders, but we can be influenced in one direction or another by irrelevant and trivial things, and in predictable ways. That being the case, we need control of how much data we share, and an awareness of how we are being influenced so as to take account of the effect and balance it in our choice-making. The alternative is an increasingly undemocratic society and one where the basic assumptions of capitalism are undermined – both democracy and the free market depend on a notion of the individual as making choices in his or her own self-interest. If that is not the case – if nudging is deployed successfully and ubiquitously – what we actually have is a technocracy directed not in the interests of the people but the gain of multinational corporations and the unconsidered and uncertain agendas of politicians seeking re-election. If that feels uncomfortably familiar, well, yes – but imagine it raised to the level of seamless perfection: Brave New World wrought not with sex but with consumer goods and personalised news.

As you'll see if you keep reading after that depressing salvo, I'm actually optimistic about the future. I believe our digital tools potentially allow us to take control of our decision-making, inform ourselves and demand a better world – but it will be a choice, and we have to make it.

Goofed

Having said all that, I have a confession to make: I goofed. In the first section of this book, there is a moment where I talk, briefly, about how humans assess risk. It was supposed to be a classic 'on the one hand, on the other hand' moment, but in fact it isn't – I moved the text around, cut the second half temporarily, and never put it back in again, so you have a strange situation where I appear to be suggesting that we are an inherently pessimistic species, or at least a pessimistic society. In fact, of course, the truth is rather more subtle. As with so many other things in *The Blind Giant*, I'm a tourist in the field of risk psychology, and there are plenty of people who can tell you more about it if you're interested (notably David Ropeik, whose book *How Risky is it Really?* is rather fun). However, for the record: we assess risk very, very badly. We have a Negativity Bias, which sees bad events as more significant than good ones, and spends more time and effort processing them. And we suffer from Optimism Bias, which is our belief that bad things happen to other people but not to us – a phenomenon so strong that HM Treasury actually publishes a guide to how to weed it out of your financial forecasts. We also suffer a host of other factors, which interact in our irrational thinking to produce an understanding of risk that is moderately absurd. (I don't play the lottery in part because I feel if I raise my hand for the jackpot I'm also signing up to risk being struck by lightning. The odds are about the same, and once you announce to the universe that you're prepared to play on that field, who knows what's going to happen? I know this is silly and superstitious. Even so.)

To my eye, the upshot is this: we tend to believe we'll be okay somehow, but once something has been identified as an actual, proximate threat to us personally, it comes to be more important than other threats, even if the actual risk of those threats is greater than the one we have identified. In the context of this book, this would explain why people having been told that digitisation is a threat, seem to be running around screaming that the technological sky is falling in on them, when there are so many other, more serious things to be concerned about.

In Sum

This is an area I find fascinating, not least because it's a lens through which I can look at the issues of agency and action in society that are at the core of any attempt to understand human life. The revolutions of the Arab Spring, the riots in London, the arrival of the iPad and the sub-prime crash are all sudden shifts in the perceptions which underpin how we see the world – shifts in the paradigm of understanding. Because I find it fascinating, it's not an effort to stay current with the amazing writing and thinking which is going on, or with the technological developments which are driving these shifts – so I'm relieved to be able to say with hand on heart that *The Blind Giant* is not in danger of going out of date. The ebb and flow of corporations and their products continues, but the issues which underlie our encounter with our tools are, if not constant, at least persistent. This book examines that encounter and what we need to know about ourselves in order to improve the world and feel that we're living well. It is in a small way a polemic. It's also a history, a crystal ball, and a handbook.

And despite being about technology, it's not about machines. It is – and has to be to make any sense – about us.

Nick Harkaway
July 2012

Dreams and Nightmares

THIS IS THE nightmare world, the place where all the bad things are:

A child sits goggled in a chair, senses open to a tsunami of babbling media: violent games, meaningless shotgun blasts of movies and TV shorn of context and plot, semi- and outright pornographic images, musical mash-ups and plagiarized, bastardized art. The child cannot concentrate on lessons in school or build relationships in the real world and is as a consequence completely emotionally shut off. This is all they are interested in: plugging in to a pleasure machine. Real life is boring. The child's health, unsurprisingly, is poor, limbs flaccid and body weak.

The child's parents carry cellphones and rarely make eye contact with one another because they are emailing and texting. Often they sit in separate rooms because they are always connected, trivially, in the Cloud. If they read books on their devices, or newspapers, they do so in a shallow, fragmented and distracted way, partially assimilating content without thinking about it, echoing it without considering it. They don't bother to learn things or try to understand them, any more than the child, because they know they can find everything through search engines. They have long since stopped trying to keep track of what their offspring is consuming, or even what laws are being broken. The monitoring and filtering software they installed a while ago has proven inadequate to restrain or protect junior.

On the other hand, both they and the child are watched at all times by dozens of corporations and banks, not to mention the local council, the police, the government and several intelligence agencies from various nations. There's no reason to suspect them of anything – beyond the endless downloading – but they are watched anyway as a matter of course. Their buying habits, political beliefs, lifestyle, sexual preferences and religious convictions are all recorded. From time to time, a software system somewhere sends them information about a product they will want, and – accurately assessed by the system – they do indeed buy it, mostly without really thinking about it. This places strain on their financial situation, but they are barely aware of that because banks and credit companies are watching their incomings and outgoings and know just when to offer them loans. These loans are now compounded and unrepayable, the interest alone sufficient to tie them to their present social and commercial classification, keep them working hard at the jobs they have rather than risking the job market, even when the terms of their contracts become draconian.

Finally, when stress, poor diet and lack of exercise take their toll, these people become sick, and are treated according to a system of quotas devised by a machine at a healthcare provider. The machine knows that there are various ways to treat them, and selects the one which is an acceptable compromise between patient care and healthcare-provider profit. Actuarial sub-systems calculate the likely length of their lives and encourage them towards habits which will not put too great a strain on the corporate or public purse. There is no discussion of whether this is the best solution from their point of view, because they don't ask. If the machine proposes it, it must be.

Outside, in the city in which they live, everyone is the same. When they meet, they do so in order to video it and put the video online. They live entirely in reflection of themselves. They don't engage politically because they're only really interested in the next gadget. Their libidos are ruined by images of physical perfection and moral depravity which have replaced their natural sex lives. They have become isolated from one another and society as a whole, each living in his or her own technological bubble, opinions reinforced by news articles and clips culled to agree with their prejudices and uninformed preconceptions – of whatever residual political stripe. The problems of the world around them are irrelevant, except where they impinge directly on their own lives, and in these rare cases they often believe bizarre, xenophobic theories of conspiracy to avoid consideration of their own culpability in the way everything works. They are sheep, herded by commercial interests; government is reduced to the role of debt collector, corporate enforcer and policeman.

Through these wretched Eloi move sinister Morlocks: terrorists and child abductors and sexual stalkers whom the police are powerless to identify, so deftly do they manipulate the digital environment. All that open data, shared in exchange for games and trinkets, heedless of the possible risk, makes the population an endless, soft-shelled smörgåsbord to predator entities of all kinds. This in turn engenders paranoia and a fear of the outside world. People stay in more, demand more surveillance rather than less, yield their rights and their privileges in exchange for a delusion of security.

The situation is locked in, self-reinforcing. 'Lock-in' is the bane of technological and systems-based societies, a condition in which a historical choice such as driving on a particular side of the road, made for what were then good and sufficient reasons (allegedly because a right-handed swordsman on horseback would always keep his weapon between himself and an oncoming stranger), is so embedded or buried in subsequent choices and infrastructure (the way we learn to drive, the way our cars are made, the way our roads are constructed) that changing it becomes impossible even if rationally in the modern context it might be better to do so. Thus something is locked in, because while we might wish to break out of it, we cannot do so without also unravelling everything that has been constructed on top of it, and many of those things are hugely profitable and hence powerful and able to defend themselves. They refuse to be undermined, even while the individuals within them might privately recognize the need. The petroleum industry could be seen as the perfect example of lock-in: it and its dependent transport and manufacturing industries fighting tooth and nail to preserve a dominance in world affairs and commerce which must eventually crash, and which in any case is wrecking our planet's ecology.

In this present example, the lock-in is more than usually secure, because unbiased news – through which the people might otherwise come to understand their situation – is all but dead, because no one pays for it. Journalism is balkanized: there are remnants of the old media, paid for by advertisers who demand their own slant on the facts; bloggers whose opinions they cannot separate from the truth; unchecked misinformation and infomercials; propaganda campaigns by oil companies demanding the right to drill everywhere and subsidies to do it; the food industry eroding standards to include more and more high-fructose corn syrup, which suppresses satiation and keeps consumers eating. High-quality film and TV are things of the past; theatre has ultimately become commercially unviable. All that remains is an endless circle of mash-ups of mash-ups, derivative works made more and more so by the multiple layers of meaningless repurposing. Rare new works are not cherished and certainly are not paid for; they are just meat dropped into a piranha tank.

The technofetishism of this nightmare society is such that little by little the actual humanity of the people in it is fading away. Their brains are adapting; they are learning to be aspects of their own machinery. Consciousness itself, abstracted thought and a sense of the individual as separate from the environment – all these are withering away. In the end, at best, all that will be left is machines which remember us fondly. More likely is that the whole of our world will simply slow down and stop like an old-fashioned clock with no one to wind it, leaving a giant junkyard planet rapidly overgrown with weeds.

~

By way of contrast, this is the digital dream world, where everything that could possibly go well, has:

Shining, healthy people move through a sunlit space filled with birds, plants and slick technology. They are very fit, because they monitor their own health and pay attention to what they eat. Informed by a mass of expert opinion and scientific testing checked against the real world in one vast crowd-sourced human experiment, they know the pattern of their own DNA and the risks that are peculiar to them. They take steps to make sure they do not increase genetic predispositions to cancer or Alzheimer's; they work out and eat well, knowing the precise benefit of each effortful hour. They are rewarded for their efforts not only by a longer, better quality life, but also by their healthcare provider, which offers rebates on insurance or tax for a healthier lifestyle. Their employers, knowing that healthier people are happier and more productive, make facilities for exercise available and do not object to their workforce taking the time to use them.

The space around them is vibrant because the city itself is alive: filters and molecular technologies and even micro-organisms have been integrated into the fabric of buildings to clean the streets and the air, making the entire place carbon-negative. Even the stones are networked and augmented to understand the needs of those walking on them, to measure traffic flow and suggest alternative routes in the event of congestion. Each block communicates with the next so that the street knows when it requires repair, when the infrastructure of pipes and cables beneath the ground is failing. Air quality is tested and if necessary improved, and when it gets dark, lights come on so that there are no dark, alarming corners or grimy alleys. The people never get lost, never worry that they've wandered into a strange neighbour-hood, because they know exactly where they are – the city tells them. In any case, there are no really bad neighbourhoods any more. Opportunity, communication and familiarity have made financial and ethnic tensions fade away.

Through this paradise, the inhabitants and visitors walk, greet strangers in the street as friends because – thanks to their always-on, augmented-reality link-up – they actually do know things about one another at first glance. No one has to ask 'Where do you work?' or 'What do you like to eat?' because those facts are discernible, coded on their skin or clothing markers, or just gleaned by software from face-recognition profile tools. Instead, people talk about matters of substance, continuing conversations they've been having online, or finding shared interests to make a connection. In groups, they discuss politics, ethics, science and literature. They are voracious, interested in everything. They remember what they need, but store great quantities of information in digital form – on wearable computers or in the Cloud, the shared digital storage and processing space which is accessible to everyone – for later access and perusal. Detail is always available, but trying to hold it all in the mind is futile and takes up attention needed for actual synthesis and creation – although there are rumours of actual extensions to the brain itself, in a few years.

In the meantime, a casual chat may rapidly lead to a new business venture or an artistic project: each person feels able to exercise his or her talents. There are no barriers to innovation; the culture has adopted an approach which – in the old vernacular – 'comes from yes'. Requests for copyright clearance and licens-ing are flashed around the world, processed under standard terms and agreed immediately so that new sales channels can open, new exploitations of old material can be begun while the energy is there. Digital start-ups happen in a day, are deemed successful and swallowed by larger entities in a week, and become as com-monplace as a corkscrew (or discarded as a nice thought without stamina) in a month. There is no stigma attached to failure, and many well-respected innovators have never created an uncomplicated hit, but their work has led others to produce something brilliant, and this contribution is understood and rewarded as vital. No one is considered a plodder or a hack. Everyone has a role to play.

Even projects that work with actual physical objects can be up and running in a matter of hours, courtesy of 3D printing technology, which allows designers to create a prototype object from a digital sketch in mere moments, printing it in layers with machines costing less than a microwave oven: complex mathematical shapes are easy, and printed circuits and moving parts can be managed by those with the right skills. The time slip between concept and creation has been reduced to hours, or days; true unemployment is low, and no one is regarded as unskilled, because everyone is learning new skills all the time. This climate of innovation and distributed manufacture has produced a thriving, decentralized economy. The 'lottery culture' of the one big score in business has been replaced by a far healthier knowledge that hard work and a good idea will ultimately provide a decent life.

Friendship, too, is easy to come by. Trusting the systems around them and the assessments of those they already know, people are relaxed about making new acquaintances. They see no distinction between friends discovered online and those met in the flesh, frequently converting one form of relationship into another. There is no question of 'digital' and 'real'; this is a society that is quite at ease with the differences between physical and mediated communication, and has learned how to read the semiotics of the second as readily as the first. At the same time, the technology has improved to allow more accurate impressions to form from voice, eyeline and body language when meeting someone online.

Almost the only feature in the social whirl which remains

tricky is romance. You can find someone with matching interests without difficulty, but the precise combination of body chemistry, wit, compatibility and hitting upon the right moment in two lives (or more) is more elusive. Sometimes what look like impossible matches come off, and perfect partnerships go nowhere from the start. It's perversely reassuring, and the subject of a lot of comedy: human love is still essentially as opaque as it ever was. Even so, the divorce rate is down: everyone expresses themselves more freely, sex is less a taboo topic and more something you discuss with a specific group – those who go on and on about it tend to rate nothing more than a yawn – and fewer people make ill-advised leaps into serious relationships, so misunderstandings are rarer. Committed relationships, in various forms, are actually more stable than they have been for decades.

Many administrative and commercial matters are managed from moment to moment – and very few companies or government departments are ever unavailable, at any hour of the day or night – but even now it's easier to have a degree of scheduling so that everyone has a shared sense of time: it helps social cohesion. So midway through each afternoon, the whole society pauses in what it is doing to vote in a series of plebiscites, each individual drawing on his or her own expertise and experience to answer today's pressing questions: a perfect, ongoing participant democracy in which reason prevails, moderated by compassion and goodwill, and the strong, measured centre holds sway. Anyone doing something too engrossing to participate – be it surgery or scuba – need not vote, but frequent abstention is considered odd. No one has to vote on everything, but it is generally accepted practice to vote on issues in which you are disinterested as well as those that directly affect you, because the network of connection and consequence is such that nothing takes place in isolation. With access to all the information in the world, both curated and raw data, people are well able to make informed choices and, through their combined intelligence, solve problems which seemed intractable to the old style of government which relied on notionally expert leaders. No one goes hungry, no one is alone, no one is unheard.

This is the happy valley, the high plateau of technological culture.

~

We are culturally and perhaps as a species predisposed to give more attention to bad occurrences than good ones – possibly because, in a survival environment, from which none of us is many generations removed and through which we all to some extent move all the time – being relaxed about serious threats results in death. A predisposition towards watchfulness is a survival trait. In other words, if you find yourself thinking that the nightmare I've drawn is infinitely more plausible than the happy valley, take a moment to consider whether that's really the case. Both draw on trends and technologies that already exist; both would require significant shifts in the way we live to come true. It's hard to balance a horror and a dream without making the latter look specious or diluting it to the point where it is no longer as positive an outcome as the nightmare is negative.

Detractors of the digital technologies with which we live lament the practice of digital skim-reading, and worry that while it is in its own right a useful skill, it does not substitute for 'deep reading', the more focused, uninterrupted form of information intake and cognition which was common twenty years ago. Hypertext – text with connections to other texts and data built in, in the style of the World Wide Web – is apparently a lousy medium for focusing on what's written in a given piece; some studies show decreased comprehension in readers of a document with links as opposed to those issued with a plain text version, because, among other things, the brain apparently has a maximum 'cognitive load' of a relatively small number of topics which can be held in the working memory at a time. Hypertext, with its multiple pathways, simply throws too much at the working memory, and comprehension and retention suffer. Since the reading brain and the habits of thought which go with it are central to our present human identity, the question of how this affects us is an important one: if our reading habits change – the written and read word being arguably a defining aspect of our cultural evolution and the formation of each of us as individuals – what change will be wrought on us and our world? On the other hand, if we resist that change, will we be unable to cope with the information-saturated environment we have made? Is it a question of losing who we are whatever we do?

Meanwhile, the world we live in – despite being by some measures an extraordinary place – has some serious unsolved problems. Some of these, in specific sectors, are bound up with technology, but the majority and the worst are not – at least not directly. In 2008 we discovered that our financial markets had become so cluttered with bad loans that we'd inflated the system into a – historically familiar – giant bubble, which had burst. It then turned out that we couldn't simply let the sin of hubris punish itself, because the same institutions which created this idiocy were deeply enmeshed in the day-to-day business of living. Banks had to be rescued, because their failure entailed the failure of industrial heavyweights on whom millions if not billions of jobs depended. Those banks were not too big to fail, but too embedded. The fairy-dust economics of the 2000s – in which global debts rose from $84 trillion to $185 trillion (yes, really) – is turning to stone in the cold light of dawn, but by some strange miracle it's still impossible to regulate the sector to preclude a recurrence of the 2008 crisis without instantly provoking exactly that. The social media and even the conventional press buzz with frustration, and the Occupy movement has emerged, an international phenomenon made possible in part by rapid communication and self-identification; but no solutions are obvious yet, and the reaction from many quarters to the

Occupy camps has been negative to the point of alarmingly oppressive.

At the same time, many nations are seeing a decline in manufacturing, and while some thinkers herald this as the dawn of the Information Age and the Knowledge Economy, others are rather more cautious. Knowledge has always been the basis of industry, but by itself, it doesn't actually make anything or put food on anyone's table. As far as I can see – in the UK, at least – 'post-industrial' is shorthand for a finance-based economy like the one which recently imploded so excitingly when we accidentally established that it was made entirely of financial smoke and mirrors. Meanwhile, we face the curious spectacle of Warren Buffett telling the US President that the mega-rich in his country do not pay enough tax, and Google CEO Eric Schmidt agreeing that Google would happily pay more tax in the UK in order to operate here. On the flipside, charities in my home city say they are seeing a rise in homelessness, and some evidence seems to suggest that many of those made homeless are well-qualified people who cannot find enough work to live on.

Overseas, Europe and the US are enmeshed in any number of small-to-medium violent conflicts, in most cases to protect our access to oil and rare earths needed to sustain our mode of living – a mode that is mostly mid-twentieth century, constructed around the automobile rather than the Internet. That petroleum lifestyle is killing the biosphere on which we depend (the only one to which we have access) while making us radically unpopular with large portions of the global population, who feel – not without some justification – that we export poverty, waste and violence and import money and resources. Some of the states in this relationship with us have begun to re-export violence in the form of terrorism, a bleakly ironic twist on conventional economics.

At home, issues of race, religion, sexuality and gender remain poisonous, our governments demand greater and greater rights of surveillance over our lives and wish to curtail week by week the

THE BLIND GIANT

historic freedoms of assembly and speech which have marked our culture's development. Trial by jury, habeas corpus and the rules of evidence are constantly assailed, as is the independence of the judiciary. In the aftermath of the riots which took place in the UK in the summer of 2011, David Cameron vowed that he would crack down on 'phoney human rights', which seems to mean any rights that are not convenient. At the same time, and despite evidence that it was both impractical and counter-productive, some MPs began to call for the government to be able to 'pull the plug' on the Internet and the cellphone network in times of civil unrest; a weird, desperate grasping for centralized power and control which seems alien to a modern government.

Perhaps in consequence of this kind of disconnection, politicians are perceived as mendacious, governmental press releases as spin. The professional political class, in return, describes the electorate as apathetic, or unable to comprehend the issues. The standard response to a public outcry is not 'we'll change the policy' but 'clearly we've failed to get our plan across properly'. In the UK under the Blair government, two of the largest political demonstrations in modern British history took place on consecutive weekends – one against a ban on fox-hunting and another against the Iraq War – and were parlayed against one another into a stasis which meant both could be ignored. More generally, serious issues often go untackled or botched from fear of expending political capital on unpopular legislation in the face of tabloid scorn. Extremist political views are becoming more popular across Europe and in the US as mainstream political parties fail to speak substantively about what is going on, preferring instead to throw mud at one another.

In other words, before we start to look at possible digital apocalypses, we have to acknowledge that the general picture is a lot less rosy than we tell ourselves when we're brushing our teeth in the morning. In fact, we stagger from one crisis to the next, and while we are insulated in the industrialized world from some of them, we are by no means immune. Our prosperity and our civilized behaviour are fragile, our world is unequal and – for billions – bleakly callous.

The opposing extremes I described – total immersion and passivity, and utopian liberty and creativity – are both unlikely. Patchwork is more probable than purity; if the late modern (the term post-modern has a number of meanings in different disciplines, some specific and others irksomely vague, and in any case suggests that we're in some kind of afterparty of world history, which I think is untrue, so I use late modern, which means more or less what it sounds like and doesn't instantly cause me to break out in sociological hives) condition we inhabit has any rules, that must be one of them: everything is muddled together. What is unclear and indeed undecided is which futures will spread out and flourish and which will fade away. But neither extreme is technologically or societally impossible. We live in a time when boundaries of the possible are elastic, while our unconscious notions of what can and cannot be done remain lodged in a sort of spiritual 1972. Unless we can change that, we're going to find the next twenty years even more unsettling than the last. Abandon, please, the idea that no one will ever be able to connect a computer directly with the human mind and consider instead what will happen when they do, and what choices we might – must – make to ensure that when it becomes common practice the world is made better rather than worse.

Only one thing is impossible: that life should remain precisely as it is. Too many aspects of the society in which we presently live are unstable and unsustainable. Change is endemic already, but more is coming. This is for various reasons a time of decision.

~

A word about navigation:

The first section of this book deals with the common nightmares of digitization and attempts to assess how seriously we should take them and whether they really derive from digital technology or from elsewhere. It contains a potted history of the Internet and a brief sketch of my own relationship with technology from birth onwards, and asks whether our current infatuation with all things digital can last. It also examines the notion that our brains are being reshaped by the digital experience, and considers our relationship with technology and science in general.

The second section considers the wrangles between the digital and the traditional world, looks at the culture of companies and advocates for digital change, and the advantages and disadvantages of digital as a way of being. It deals with notions of privacy and intellectual property, design and society, revolution and riot, and looks at how digitization changes things.

The third section proposes a sort of self-defence for the new world and a string of tricks to help not only with any digital malaise but also with more general ones. It asks what it means to be authentic, and engaged, and suggests how we go forward from here in a way that makes matters better rather than worse (or even the same).

More generally: it is inevitable that I will be wrong about any number of predictions. No book which tries to see the present and anticipate the future can be both interesting and consistently right. I can only hope to be wrong in interesting ways.

PART I

I

Past and Present

I WAS BORN in 1972, which means I am the same age as the first ever video game, Pong. I actually preferred Space Invaders; there was a classic wood-panelled box in the kebab shop at the end of my road, and if I was lucky I'd be allowed a very short go while my dad and my brother Tim picked up doner kebabs with spicy sauce for the whole family. In retrospect, they may have been the most disgusting kebabs ever made in the United Kingdom. When the weather's cold, I miss them terribly.

I grew up in a house which used early (room-sized) dedicated word-processing machines. I knew what a command line interface was from around the age of six (though I wouldn't have called it that, because there was no need to differentiate it from other ways of interfacing with a computer which did not yet exist: I knew it as 'the prompt', because a flashing cursor prompted you to enter a command) and since my handwriting was moderate at best I learned to type fairly early on. Schools in London back then wouldn't accept typed work from students, so until I was seventeen or so I had to type my work and then copy it out laboriously by hand. Exactly what merit there was in this process I don't know: it seemed then and seems now to be a form of drudgery without benefit to anyone, since the teachers at the receiving end inevitably had to decipher my appalling penmanship, a task I assume required a long time and a large glass of Scotch.

On the other hand, I am not what was for a while called a 'digital native'. Cellphones didn't really hit the popular market until the 1990s, when I was already an adult; personal computers were fairly unusual when I was an undergrad; I bought my first music in the form of vinyl LPs and cassette tapes. I can remember the battle between Betamax and VHS, and the arrival and rapid departure of LaserDisc. More, the house I lived in was a house of narratives. More than anything else, it was a place where stories were told. My parents read to me. My father made up stories to explain away my nightmares, or just for the fun of it. We swapped jokes over dinner, and guests competed – gently – to make one another laugh or gasp with a tall tale. Almost everything could be explained by, expressed in, parsed as, couched in a narrative. It was a traditional, even oral way of being, combined with a textual one in some situations, making use of new digital tools as they arrived, drawing them in and demanding more of them for the purpose of making a story. We weren't overrun by technology. Technology was overrun by us.

All of which makes me a liminal person, a sort of missing link. I have one foot in the pre-digital age, and yet during that age I was already going digital. More directly relevant to this book, my relationship with technology is a good one: I am a prolific but not excessive user of Twitter; I blog for my own website and for another one; I have played World of Warcraft for some years without becoming obsessive (I recently cancelled my subscription because the game has been made less and less sociable); I use Facebook, Google+, GoodReads and tumblr, but I am also professionally productive – since my first book came out in 2008, I have written three more, along with a screenplay and a number of newspaper articles. I am also a dad, an occasional volunteer for the charity of which my wife is director, and I have the kind of analogue social life everyone manages when they are the parent of a baby; so aside from whatever moderate brainpower I can bring to bear on this topic, I can speak with the authority of someone who manages their balance of digital and analogue life pretty well.

I am, for want of a better word, a digital yeti.

~

In the late 1950s and early 1960s, when my older brothers were being born, the Defense Advanced Research Projects Agency (DARPA) in the US planted the seed of the modern Internet. The network was constructed to emphasize redundancy and survivability; when I first started looking at the history of the Internet in the 1990s, I read that it had grown from a command and control structure intended to survive a nuclear assault. The 1993 *Time* magazine piece by Philip Elmer-DeWitt, which was almost the Internet's coming-out party, cited this origin story alongside John Gilmore's now famous quote that 'The Net interprets censorship as damage and routes around it'. Although DARPA itself is unequivocally a military animal, this version of events is uncertain. It seems at least equally possible that the need for a robust system came from the unreliability of the early computers comprising it, which were forever dropping off the grid with technical problems, and that narrative is supported by many who were involved at the time.

That said, it's hard to imagine DARPA's paymasters, in the high days of the Cold War and with a RAND Corporation report calling for such a structure in their hands, either ignoring the need or failing to recognize that a durable system of information sharing and command and control was being created under their noses. For whatever it's worth, I suspect both versions are true to a point. In either case, the key practical outcome is that the Internet is in its most basic structure an entity that is intended to bypass local blockages. From its inception, the Internet was intended to pass the word, not ringfence it.

The seed grew slowly; at the start of 1971 there were just fifteen locations connected via the ARPANET (Advanced Research

Projects Agency Network). Through the 1970s and 1980s, growth came not from a single point but rather from many; educational networks such as the National Science Foundation Network and commercial ones such as Compuserve met and connected, using the basic protocols established by DARPA so that communication could take place between their users. I remember a friend at school, a maths whizz whose father was an industrial chemist, patiently logging in to a remote system using a telephone modem: you took the handset of your phone and shoved it into a special cradle and the system chirruped grasshopper noises back and forth. Eventually – and it was a long time, because the modem was transmitting and receiving more slowly than a fax machine – a set of numbers and letters in various colours appeared on a television screen. I could not imagine anything more boring. I asked my friend what it was, and he told me he was playing chess with someone on the other side of the world. He had a physical chessboard set up, and obediently pushed his opponent's piece to the indicated square before considering his next move. Why they didn't use the phone, I could not imagine.

Around about the same time, my mother and I went to an exhibition of some sort, and there was a booth where a computer took a picture of you and printed it out, using the letters and numbers of a daisywheel printer, double-striking to get bold text, because the inkjet and the laser printer were still years away. The resulting image was recognizably me, but more like a pencil sketch than a photo. It was considered hugely advanced.

By the time I arrived at Clare College, Cambridge, in 1991, email was a minor buzzword. There were terminals set up in the library for those who wanted to embrace the digital age. I discovered that a surpassingly pretty English student with whom I was besotted sat up late each night using Internet Relay Chat (the spiritual precursor of modern chat systems such as Skype) to talk to someone whose identity I never established who apparently by

turns exasperated and delighted her. I began to think this electronic communications stuff might have something in it, so after
some soul searching I got myself a dial-up account with Demon
Internet and dived into Usenet, the system of discussion groups
which prefigured today's website forums.

Usenet was a motherlode of unlikely facts – and, no doubt,
non-facts – and I should probably have realized the potential
to learn more about my degree course, but inevitably I got
sidetracked instead, pondering a modern revisiting of Alexandre
Dumas's *The Count of Monte Cristo*. Researching supertankers
(in the story, my new Edmond Dantès was going to be first
mate on one of the huge ones), I discovered the diary entries of
a man who had sailed aboard Ultra Large Crude Carriers in the
previous decade as part of what he described as a kind of gay
ocean-going swingers' party. He had only uploaded the diary,
he wrote, because as far as he knew he was one of the last men
left who had really been in the heart of this brief, joyful subculture, the vast majority having succumbed to HIV-related
illness.

The World Wide Web – the combination of images and text
with clickable links which most people mean when they talk
about 'the Internet' – grew from a way of displaying data which
which was created at CERN by Tim Berners-Lee and let out
into the wild in around 1990. In the interest of absolute clarity:
the Internet is a network connecting computers; the World
Wide Web is the system of documents written in the HyperText
Markup Language (HTML) which are viewable through that
network. The viewing of HTML documents is only one of the
things the network facilitates – though, clearly, it is a definitive
one at present. The Web (the term itself feels antiquated now)
was initially just a way of sharing information, enabling users to
connect a particular word or image with a further document; a
logical progression from the Internet's roots as a tool for pooling
scientific information.

It became more and more – and the Internet was used for more and more activities in our lives – as personal computers became cheaper and more common and connection speeds rose throughout the 1990s, allowing for the downloading of more complex files such as images and eventually music and movies. The services and companies we think of now as being an integral part of the digital realm are relatively recent. Amazon.com began in 1995, letting people order through its digital shopfront from what was effectively a warehouse system. In the same year, eBay was born, hosting 250,000 auctions in 1996 and 2m in 1997. Google was incorporated in 1998. The first iPod was sold in 2001, and the iTunes Store opened its online doors in 2003. Facebook went live in 2004. YouTube did not exist until 2005.

This extraordinarily rapid development can create the illusion that the Internet and the aspects of our culture it supports came from nowhere, a feeling strengthened by the metaphor of cyberspace, the notion of a foreign land brought abruptly into existence inside and yet somehow beyond the beige box cases of our computers. Zeitgeist novelist and commentator William Gibson coined the term in 1982, ushering in a new fictional mood (cyberpunk) which, while futuristic, was also noirish, baroque and gritty. Cyberpunk presented the electronic environment as a three-dimensional virtual world which was both beautiful and dangerous, the preserve of a technological elite. Around the same time, the first Graphical User Interfaces – early versions of today's Mac OS X and Windows – began to tempt people away from the command line interface to the desktop metaphor of folders and piles of paper. However flat and simplistic the representation of a desk was, with pixellated images of folders and in-trays, the iconography did its job. In our minds, the space behind the screen was no longer occupied by a cathode ray emitter: the glass was a barrier between us and another place where anything was possible.

That sense of the digital as belonging to another place strikes me as pivotal in our relationship with it. We feel that what happens online somehow does not happen in the real world. It doesn't feel like something which should have real world consequences. The ethos of the Internet and the way people use it is often seen to be in conflict with the dictates of non-digital life, as if the Internet were a kind of perpetual pirate ship circling the globe; a roving rebel anti-nation where normal nation-state rules do not apply. This was shaped in part by Free Software pioneers such as Richard Stallman, who created the GNU project in an effort to resist proprietary operating systems, and who is also a principal architect of the copyleft movement. Stallman's touchstone is the hacker culture of the Massachusetts Institute of Technology in the 1970s, a free-wheeling techno-cooperative mood drawing on the hippie ethos and notions of libertarianism and political anarchism which perhaps bizarrely was underpinned by DARPA. (The word 'hacker' is endlessly misapplied. It means, originally, someone with the technological skill to make devices or software. That it subsequently became a synonym for 'cracker' – one who unlawfully and sometimes maliciously breaks into someone else's computer systems – is an irritation to those to whom it more rightly belongs. A 'good hack' is an elegant solution to a problem, not a successful intrusion.)

Stallman famously resisted the introduction of passwords on the system at MIT, and urged fellow users to change theirs to an empty string (i.e. no password at all) to preserve the open culture at the time, and remains a powerful voice of resistance to the corporatization of and governmental interference in the affairs of the Internet. The important point is this: that from the very beginning, the makers of the digital realm saw it as something different, something which would change the world. The Internet has always been – perhaps was created to be – disruptive, to mount a challenge to the conventional norms of behaviour which have grown up around the inherited structures of the modern world which derive from the history of the last 400 years.

But powerful though the influence of figures such as Richard Stallman may be on our understanding of what the digital realm is and how we should act within it – even among those of us who don't know his name – the notion of a separate space is all the more so. Inadvertently, Gibson, along with Steven Lisberger (writer and director of the original *Tron*, which also came out in 1982) and others who played with the same idea, crystallized the language and the notion of the space behind the screen as another country. That space came to be seen as having very few if any laws, as being outside any country – or perhaps more interestingly in a no-man's-land between countries – and bound by no jurisdiction. For a long time, courts in many states were unwilling to accept jurisdiction over actions on the Internet; it was unclear where an offence might be taking place and under what law it should be prosecuted. Free speech was assumed, and (notoriously) copyright was seen as void by many users – even if it was understood at all. In the 1993 *Time* article, David Farber, then a Professor of Information Science at the University of Pennsylvania, joked to Philip Elmer-DeWitt that the Internet itself should apply to be recognized by the UN as a state – incidentally providing *Time* with a title: 'First Nation in Cyberspace'. Almost everyone quoted in the piece – along with the author himself – refers to the Internet as if it were a physical space. Perhaps the most telling description came from Glee Willis, engineering librarian at the University of Nevada: 'It's a family place. It's a place for perverts. It's everything rolled into one.'

This is the first point which needs to be understood in any discussion of digital technology and its influence upon us: for all that it's almost impossible to discuss the issues of digitization and the adoption of new technology without using the expression, there is no such thing as 'the digital world'. The metaphor of space behind the screen is just that. The Internet is not separate from the physical world we inhabit day to day, it is an expression of it, and of us. All of it – the Internet and the World Wide Web, the social media sites they facilitate, the cellphone network and the twenty-four-hour news channels which rarely have much more to tell us at five thirty than they did at five or four or three – is a part of us, just as the football field, the economy-class cabin of an aeroplane and the green room of a television studio are aspects of our lives. There are simple historical reasons why we tend to think of computer-mediated communications as a separate place, but the separation is a false one. What occurs online is a reflection of what occurs offline, though it often occurs much faster and much more publicly, and it is less ephemeral: the memory of computers lasts as long as anyone can be bothered to maintain it.

Looking back, the enthusiasm and idealism of the Internet's arrival in the public awareness seems similar to the wild, magnificent fantasies of space colonization in the mid-1970s, which dovetailed high science, post oil-crisis resource worries and ecological concerns. NASA design studies and countercultural re-imaginings of human life came together in plans for toroidal space stations and rich, comic-book-style illustrations of cylinders in space, open-plan, park-filled orbitals serviced by a commuter version of the Space Shuttle or perhaps a Space Elevator. The images generated at NASA Ames Research Center are a mix of eco-utopian frontier town and suburban grid-system living, a kind of perpetual space-going America, with the best view in the solar system. It seems that we – modern industrial societies – have a slight cultural claustrophobia, a need to get up and out of our lives and away to 'somewhere else' where life is less restrictive and where the liens of history and existing law weigh less heavily upon us. In 1975 that was space. By 1995 it was cyberspace: the infinite, lawless, playful world behind the screen.

When governments and corporations at last woke up to what was happening and tried to enforce 'real world' laws, it was as if lawyers had walked into private houses during Sunday lunch and started demanding that everyone pay for using the cutlery. The arrival of sheriffs and Pinkertons on the digital frontier was the start of a conflict of law and ideology that continues to this day. The assertion of national and corporate power – often in aggressive ways as officials and business affairs departments raced to preserve their authority and their bottom line – created an online resistance. As well it might; it is very hard, in drawing up legislation to deal with the Internet, to avoid legislating broadly about human life. Attempts to curtail undesirable behaviour which is conducted through the embedded and ubiquitous communications medium of the Net almost inevitably cannot be restricted to a single venue. Legislation about the Internet almost inevitably becomes legislation about everything, because the Net is everywhere.

~

The promise and rhetoric of the Internet as given in the 1990s – when it ceased to be part of the on-campus life of specialists and met the wider world – was of open systems, free speech, individual privacy and governmental transparency. The electronic realm would be the crucible in which the physical one was remade. An untouchable refuge for revolution and experiment, the Net was the venue where anything that was suppressed could be given voice. Creativity would no longer be locked in old corporate patterns but opened up to everyone. The gatekeepers of the existing cultural order – publishers, music executives, newspaper barons – would be bypassed or inundated, and new voices and new identities would find their expression. The ownership of the means of creation, to put it in Marxian terms, would no longer rest solely with established power structures. The digital cottage industry could and would compete with the big boys on equal terms. In 1998 Microsoft's Bill Gates told writer Ken Auletta that he wasn't worried about challenges from regular companies, but rather from someone working on something amazing in a garage somewhere. The right person in the right place, the stories went, could change the world. And it was true, to a point: in 1998 Google was being born, exactly as Gates predicted, and rapidly evolved into a creature to alarm even the powerhouse of Redmond, Washington.

This sense of laws not applying online and the ease of digital copying threw Net users into direct conflict with copyright holders and – in some cases – law enforcement and the courts. The rows continue: the UK courts faced simple disobedience from users of Twitter regarding injunctions against the publication of certain information early in 2011. The company itself went to court in America to secure the right to notify users that their information was being requested by the US government in connection with WikiLeaks – and won, prompting *Wired* magazine to suggest that Twitter's corporate response should be the industry standard to demands from law enforcement and government for secret access to user data.[1]

There's nothing specifically digital about breaking an injunction, of course, but there is a feeling among some Net users that the online world is a special case, a free speech zone, and that in cyberspace it is entirely appropriate to divulge what a print journalist, subject to national laws, dare not. On the other hand, government and legislation have also designated digital communications as a special case, asserting that they do not merit the same kind of protection given to older media. In November 2011 a US judge ordered Twitter to give up the data, despite filings by the American Civil Liberties Union (ACLU) and the individuals named. The ACLU response was trenchant: 'The government shouldn't be able to get this kind of private information without a warrant, and they certainly shouldn't be able to do so in secret. An open court system is a fundamental part of our democracy, and the very existence of court documents should not be hidden from the public.'

In the context of copyright, the famous statement by Stewart Brand, publisher of the original *Whole Earth Catalogue*, has become a motto for those who believe any information once released into the digital wild is communal property, and that creativity – taking place in the context of a shared global cultural heritage – is not uniquely the property of whoever creates, but also of everyone else. What Brand said in 1985 and restated in 1987 was: 'Information wants to be free.' There's more to it than that, of course, and the full quote from his *The Media Lab* is prescient – or, at least, insightful:

> Information wants to be free because it has become so cheap to distribute, copy, and recombine – too cheap to meter. It wants to be expensive because it can be immeasurably valuable to the recipient. That tension will not go away. It leads to endless wrenching debate about price, copyright, 'intellectual property', the moral rightness of casual distribution, because each round of new devices makes the tension worse, not better.

This philosophical clash has become an often vicious legal battle in the real world. The ethos of groups such as the Electronic Frontier Foundation (EFF) and the Free Software Foundation (FSF) (in which the word 'free' means not just 'given away' but also 'ungoverned' or 'unshackled') evolved in opposition to the growing sense among lawmakers and corporations – and, to be fair, some citizens – that the Internet had to be regulated, whether for reasons of security and criminal law or for the purposes of making money. These Internet freedom advocacies are not primarily manifesto organizations, with a list of positive statements in their pockets. The early generation of Internet pioneers didn't need a manifesto, because they all knew what they were doing – indeed, in most cases they knew one another – and so saw no point in articulating what they believed in because they lived it, wrote it and coded it all the time. Rather, although they have clear statements of identity, the EFF and the FSF are in the first instance an attempt to retain and defend a spirit that existed before the Net was big enough to need a constitution, when it was acted and known by all who participated. The EFF, in particular, came in part out of a massively misguided United States Secret Service raid on a company called Steve Jackson Games (SJG), which must rank as one of the all-time law enforcement fiascos; although, in keeping with the sense of the Internet as being ultimately a consequence-free environment, no one actually died.

Briefly, the Secret Service raided SJG and confiscated their computers in pursuit of a document which was alleged to have been illegally obtained from the telecoms company BellSouth. SJG was at the time in the process of making a role-playing game with a cyberpunk tone, which perhaps explains somewhat why the Secret Service agents, having confiscated the company's online bulletin board and files (called 'Illuminati'), apparently decided that they had uncovered 'a handbook for computer crime'. The Secret Service retained the confiscated computers for several months, and finally returned them stripped of much of their data. The company sued, and the trial judge found against the government, determining: 'there has never been any basis for suspicion [that SJG] have engaged in any criminal activity, violated any law, or attempted to communicate, publish, or store any illegally obtained information or otherwise provide access to any illegally obtained information or to solicit any information which was to be used illegally.'

Nonetheless, by that time the company was in dire financial straits. As a result of discussions on the Whole Earth 'Lectronic Link (the WELL), one of the earliest digital communities which is still active to this day, Mitch Kapor of Lotus, John Perry Barlow of the band the Grateful Dead, and John Gilmore, then an employee at technological powerhouse Sun Microsystems, founded the EFF. The Steve Jackson Games case established electronic mail as having the same protections under US law as a phone conversation – a protection which, apparently, has not yet reached Twitter. (Obviously, Twitter is premised on sharing thoughts with a wider audience than a phone call, but that does not immediately mean that the private data of a user should be less well protected in law.)

In other words, the Electronic Frontier Foundation is at root the digital resistance, seeking to preserve the ideals of a digital environment which was still small and built on notions of community and cooperation. Likewise, the Free Software movement was and is a response to the rise of proprietary operating systems and the attempt (presently successful) by Apple and Microsoft to use operating systems as a springboard to dominance over how people access information and view content over the Internet. This is worth remembering as one encounters these organizations, and their central themes: we're not seeing them now in a pure state, but rather as they try to codify a more diffuse ideal of the living Internet in the face of activities by corporate and government power to control, limit, censor and commodify what the key players in the EFF and similar organizations took to be an opportunity to leave behind these kinds of capitalistic, nationalistic and paternalistic ways of being, and seek a better world. The hard part of any revolution begins not with conquering the enemy – the Internet, after all, has become as ubiquitous as any reasonably high-level technology can be in our fragmented world – but with what comes next: the encounter between the dreams of the revolutionaries and the smaller, more specific concerns of the people they think they represent.

The hope, then, was that the free (unfettered, not necessarily unpaid) flow of information would redeem a world staggering along in the aftermath of the greed-is-good culture of the 1980s and the sudden demise of the Cold War as the defining paradigm of our lives. The template for the perfect creative endeavour in this early stage of the commercial Internet was the garage band (a label subsequently appropriated by Apple for their bundled music production software). The idea was a group of musically talented individuals using digital technology to mix their work and the Internet to distribute it directly to the world without the involvement of a conventional industry power structure. There are echoes of this notion in Google's founding, and in the small start-ups that can so rapidly ascend to the digital heights; Blogger, for example, was a side project which birthed an entire culture of online diarists and commentators.

That may have seemed possible in the 1990s; now the situation is more complex and difficult. The massive number of people attempting the same thing makes discovery – making your creative product not just available but known about – rather than distribution, the barrier to success. More, as the share-and-share-alike attitude to content has proliferated, content has either become cheap or free, or it has been shared without permission of the creator. The downward pressure on price is so strong that many have given up charging directly altogether, and propose to make content available without monetary charge either on a simple advertising-funded model, on a merchandizing model where content induces fans to buy related material or hardware, or on a cross-subsidization model which sells the data generated by users as demographic information to advertisers.

Online ads, however, sell for about one-tenth of their print counterparts, because the Internet has an endless supply of advertising hoardings. It turns out that these models require in most cases a huge number of visitors to a discrete website, or a distributed network of sites like a radio-telescope array, each contributing a small share to a larger entity. Similarly, merchandizing sales are not usually a reliable revenue stream. As an example: the Internet has spawned any number of webcomics – short strips of ongoing storylines, some in the comic-book style, others in the older three- or four-panel strip. Of these, a vanishingly small number are known to be self-sustaining, let alone actually profitable. Wikipedia lists a total of twenty-three creators presently reported by third parties to be making money from their work online. The cross-subsidy models, meanwhile, are undesirable in another way: cross-subsidization is essentially a bit of sleight of hand in which a service appears to be free, but is in fact paid in kind.

What is presently emerging sometimes appears to be the opposite of the creative democracy: a centralization of the ability to profit from content, in which hubs such as Amazon, Google and Apple take a percentage of millions of sales and thrive on the creation of an ecosystem of app developers and content makers who rarely break even. It applies in every niche of the online world; one of the most talked about iPad apps of 2011 was *Nursery Rhymes*, by developer ustwo. This storybook app for children had a secret weapon: busy parents could call from elsewhere and read to the children they couldn't be there for in person. The feature inspired all manner of positive and negative comment, the most pointed of which was probably the title of the review at CrunchGear: '*Nursery Rhymes Storytime* reminds you of the blasted lunar hellscape that is your life'. The app went to the top of the charts, and was discussed everywhere. The developer calculated the investment cost at £60k, and the money coming in at £26k – a shortfall of £34k. And that was a popular application; only a very, very few apps will do better.

Apple, of course, profits from every single sale. The economics of the Internet, as presently constructed, do not favour the old dream of small content makers. Instead, they seem to produce an inevitable trend towards consolidation and gatekeeping. Rather than trading the fusty cultural chains of the conventional media for a bright new world of digital cottage industries, we are in danger of exchanging one bottleneck for another. Even the much touted original ebook writers such as the hugely successful Amanda Hocking work through a hub (Amazon) rather than going it alone – and Hocking herself has now signed with a conventional publisher.

The Internet is sometimes heralded as the end of the middleman. In fact, at the moment, it's more like the ascension of the middleman to an almost godlike status – it's just that the old middlemen have in many cases been cut out of the loop. And while aggregate sales of every app, song, movie or book are enormous – and the hubs take a piece of each sale – the individual sales of an individual product may not be enough to pay for its production.

The present Net style of commerce favours the giants – just as the old pre-digital one does – and in some ways, it is defined and created by one in particular.

~

It is pointless to discuss the Internet age and its cultures without reference to Google. The search giant is at the heart of how we use the web, and its rise – not by chance – is coincident with the rise of the Internet as a part of everyday life. It can't be said too often, not just in relation to Google but in general, that there is no set outcome of digital and technological evolution. What we choose now will affect what happens next. The future is in flux, and we are – more consciously than ever before – choosing a path ahead as we choose small conveniences and commercial options. So we should make even quite minor choices about digital matters with some care.

Google defined the Internet we have now by making possible real search. Before Google, finding things on the web was, if not difficult, at best unwieldy. Search companies didn't actually want you to find what you were looking for too fast: their goal was to have you on their pages long enough to advertise to you. Early search sites were portals, hoping to hold your eyes for a while before letting you go. The key property in commercial web design back then was 'stickiness'. At the same time, the order in which searches were displayed was arbitrary or even perverse. AltaVista searches ranked results by the number of times a term appeared on a given page, so a site which featured 'goal' sixteen times was deemed more relevant to a search for 'goal' than one which used it only ten. You can still find, on old personal pages from the early days of the web, buried repetitions of words, white text on white background: 'goal goal goal goal goal . . .' going on and on for hundreds of lines in an effort to attract the search engine's attention. It's one of the earliest and crudest forms of what is today an industry in itself: Search Engine Optimization.

Google, by allowing the web itself to do the work of ranking pages – Google's method begins with letting the number of links to a given site determine how important it is – got around all that, and set itself the task of getting people where they wanted to go as fast as possible, without attempting to detain them for advertising purposes. That efficiency is the core of the Google identity: make it work properly first, then figure out how to make money from it.

That's not to say that the company didn't have advertising at its heart from the very beginning, only that the model then in use was weak and ineffectual and they eschewed it in favour of something cleverer and more elegant: targeted ads based on user data, ads which could monitor their own effectiveness and charge by the click – the moment of conversion of ad space to interest – rather than by an arbitrary notion of the number of eyeballs skating across a page. Google abandoned stickiness for helpfulness, for speeding you through to your destination – in exchange for information about, and ultimately the possibility of a degree of control over, that destination.

Google is the more important because its ethos is drawn from and massively influential upon the culture of the Internet itself (though, like the notion of 'mainstream culture', that means nothing more than the overlapping of a million unique fragments of online subculture). It is the product of that same transformative dream of the early days of digital computing, but has in some ways a clearer understanding of the world and a stronger perception of itself, albeit one that is occasionally strikingly blinkered. Google is unashamedly elitist – you could say 'meritocratic' if you prefer – hiring only the best, keeping itself to itself. The company's mission is to 'make information accessible', and this is in its worldview an unchallenged good. At the heart of an intellect- and skill-driven enterprise, which has raised efficiency and fact-based decision-making to a new height, and which despises intangibles and fuzziness and tricks of the human mind such as marketing, there is a single tenet based on faith.

Google is an island in the Net, a green land of massages and wind turbines and great food, where employees are encouraged to develop their own projects and bring them to the world through Google's own system of godmothering. It is the company which cares about not 'being evil', though it is not always able to avoid the pitfalls of commercial need or mission creep, or the annoying greyness of human life which can suck the clarity from Google's black and white. In many ways it is the model for what a twenty-first-century corporation ought to be: rewarding, protective, collegial, environmentally sound, innovative – and determined to make a moral calculus part of or even central to its decision-making. It is also, ultimately, a faith-based techno-capitalist entity premised on the idea that more access to whatever information exists is better, and that anything which stands in the way of that is old-fashioned and reactionary and should be washed away. This has inevitably brought it into conflict with media content industries which derive income directly from consumers rather than by selling their attention to advertisers – technology writer James Gleick wrote recently in the *New York Review of Books* that the currency of the Internet is not information but attention – and it

will continue to do so. Google is a feature of the digital landscape, a determinator as well as an indicator of how the Internet
culture sees the world.

Google has also been accused of deliberately fostering and
profiting from unlawful use of copyright material, and of wrecking the newspaper industry by taking over the ad revenue stream
on which that industry somewhat depended and by aggregating
the content newspapers were encouraged to put online free of
charge in the 1990s. To some extent, the company seems to recognize its culpability in the fall of newspaper revenues: Eric
Schmidt talked recently about finding ways to pump money into
news. Say anything you like about Google, but do not ever
imagine that the people who work there are stupid. They are
occasionally single-minded, and not immune to error, but they
are among the most intelligent people in the world.

In many ways, Google is a microcosm of the Internet as a
whole: a force multiplier, a facilitator, an accelerator, a feedback
system and a paradigm changer. The start-up incorporated in
1998 by Larry Page and Sergey Brin is now the Behemoth of the
online world. It has radically reshaped the advertising market,
changed the way we get news and weather, and how we navigate. It has been part of the staggering changes in the music
industry, and moved into the world of publishing with the
attempt to secure a deal to sell books online which was so
innovative – and, to some, alarming – that it would have required
an Act of Congress to make it possible. Had it gone through, it
would have called into question one of the basic tenets of intellectual property on which much of the media, including Google
itself, relies.

Where Google treads, the earth shakes.

The fundamental thing about Google, though, often goes
unremarked: the Google project has barely begun. Domination
of search – and, by extension, of advertising – is a means to an
end. Google, at least notionally, views the world not primarily

as a market but as something to be made better. Money, Eric Schmidt once remarked, is just a technology to help do that. It's an oft-quoted maxim of the company's founders that you can't change the users, so you have to change the system, but in fact the goal of Google is exactly that: to educate, to liberate, to inform and to uplift. Ultimately, to *improve* us all. Its founders candidly envisage a world where Google and the Internet are fed directly into the brain; where to wonder something can be to know the answer; where humanity is so thoroughly blended with its own technology that it's hard to see where one ends and the other begins.

This kind of dream is precisely where many people stop paying attention: it sounds too far-fetched to be serious. But you cannot hope to understand Google or the world which is being formed around you unless you are prepared to contemplate this kind of possibility and to grasp that it isn't metaphor, and it isn't *a priori* impossible. It's a technical and an engineering challenge, and research that could bring it about is under way – and in some cases quite far advanced – all over the world. Do not dismiss the notion as fanciful or laughable. It is neither, and the time to ask whether it's a good idea as well as a fascinating one is now.

More mundanely, in the words of Douglas Edwards, author of *I'm Feeling Lucky: The Confessions of Google Employee Number 59*:

> They would build a company to fix large-scale problems affecting millions of people and terraform the entire landscape of human knowledge. They would speed medical breakthroughs, accelerate the exploration of space, break down language barriers . . . they would clear the clogged arteries of the world's data systems and move information effortlessly to the point at which it was needed at exactly the time at which it was required. They would be . . . an information conglomerate on the scale of General Electric.

The dream is Napoleonic, even Messianic. And a faith in that goal is part of the culture. Google is exceptional (genuinely, in many ways it's the template of the kind of company we should beg to have more of). Like the country that nurtured it, it feels it has a special place in the world – and occasionally finds that the rest of the world receives its painful yet well-intended interventions with less than wholehearted cheer.

That perception of exceptional status seems to lead to a kind of blindness or indifference, too. Edwards also tells us that Larry Page thinks frequent flier programmes are evil. Why? 'They incentivise people to take flights that are not the most direct or the cheapest, just so they can earn points.' In other words, frequent flier programmes damage the consumer's ability to assess which flight is the best for them. They mess with the flow of information in the system, corrupt the user's ability to understand what is the best deal. Which to me makes them a lot like cross-subsidized revenues: services such as Google's core search function, which are free at the point of use but take payment elsewhere in a way which is not obvious to the consumer.

So the corporate DNA of Google is in the first instance transformative. It seeks to make everything more efficient and simpler. The practical consequence of this is the cutting out of the conventional middleman – known these days by the more technical-sounding term 'disintermediation'. Google comes into a market, disintermediates someone, and connects the supplier directly – well, through Google – with the customer. On the face of it, that must be a good thing for everyone; or, at least, anyone whose job does not depend on being a middleman. In reality, the fallible, messy human systems known as culture have often grown up around inefficient and unnecessarily complex ways of doing business. Google's Gordian solutions are not always welcome or even necessarily positive. In the long term, it's possible (though not knowable) that Google's effects on the various industries it has touched will be positive – and that seems to be an article of faith with those inside the door. But in the short term what economists call disruption or 'creative destruction', and Google sees as the cutting away of inefficiency, translates in the real world into lost jobs, reduced revenues for huge companies and the slow, painful demise of the newspaper industry as it struggles to deal with content aggregators, the loss of ad sales and the balkanization of its audience.

The company falls victim to an old, familiar failing of visionaries and engineers: the One Big Fix. Google likes to operate at a global level, doing deals in bulk. The Google Book Settlement – which I mentioned earlier, and which is still rumbling on – is a case in point. It's a meandering and somewhat convoluted story, but these are the bones: in 2002 Google began digitizing books in libraries, and in 2004 launched a Book Search service which allowed users to search what it had digitized. As well as the whole of any public domain text, Book Search would display snippets of any work in the database but still under copyright that was relevant to the search. In 2005 Google was sued by several distinct groups for copyright infringement. The cases became a class action – US law allows for the creation of a single suit which is representative of a class of suits and deals with all of them at once – and instead of taking the case to court to fight on the merits of the situation, the parties opted to attempt to create an extraordinary new deal under which Google would create a massive library and retailer of copyright works. Essentially, it was an attempt to gain the right to trade in the majority of books ever written, even or especially those whose ownership was unclear. The Amended Settlement Agreement was rejected on very narrow legal grounds: it attempted to give Google permission to act in a given way *in future*, which Judge Denny Chin ruled was beyond the scope of what the court could permit. The various other objections therefore remain untested.

Litigation and calls for changes in legislation are a fascinating recurring pattern in digital commerce. Because the legal structures of our society have grown up in tandem with the industries they regulate and serve – and which, of course, they also create in the same way that the rules of football create the game – they are often disadvantageous to new arrivals with new agendas and desires. The response of digital businesses, quite often, is to demand a 'levelling' of the playing field which actually entails the destruction of the old business model in favour of one which favours the new paradigm. The Google Book Settlement was one example, but there are others; Google Music, until very recently, was bogged down because the company wanted to negotiate for huge bundles of content where the industry does deals on a one-to-one basis, with different contractual provisions for different artists. Google's energy is directed at large-scale solutions to large problems, grand answers. In physical terms, the company likes to build machines that are visible from space – but much of the world's population still lives in the areas through which these titanic engines must pass.

Efficiency, meanwhile, is an alien sort of god. Human life is in many ways blazingly inefficient. Some rather extreme examples: we spend ages trying to meet people we like, randomly zinging through bad and better relationships, learning skills and habits and empathies that either improve or (sadly) reduce our chances of meeting someone with whom we can be happy. Likewise, we pick our professions if not at random at least with a healthy degree of chance and irrationality. How much more efficient would it be to mechanize, centralize or mediate these processes? Vastly. Is it desirable to do so? That's less obvious.

What effect would it have on us as a society and as individuals to have a vast database of personality types and physical preferences and know that at a certain point the Love Authority would let us know we had a viable match? Would it be acceptable to us to have our future professional life dictated by strenuous testing? People already use dating and headhunting services so it hardly seems like too much of a stretch for these things to become the norm, or to use them retroactively: according to the system, that nice guy you met the other day has a low, low percentage chance of becoming a good husband. Probably best to ditch him. By the way, your dream job doesn't really match your level of competence or education or even your personality. Think again! Or more: surely the traditional methods of child-rearing and care are both inefficient and fraught with poor practices: how would we solve that?

I have unfairly biased the case against efficiency. It does not imply these totalitarian ways of being, it merely creates them if you move efficiency into inappropriate spaces. And yet at the same time, I haven't: the ethos of time-saving and resource-saving runs clear and hard through Google's approach to many areas which are almost as complex and bound up with our society as it stands as these, and while the world may be diffusely 'better' if we accept them, it's not obvious by what mechanism or on what timescale, and nor is it clear what the adoption will do to us more generally. What will we turn into if we accept the premise that efficiency is best? The faith seems to be teleological: blow away the old, tangled nonsense and usher in a new foundation and the world will automatically fall into a better configuration. People will step forward to make it so. Never mind that this seems to my untutored eye to be a little optimistic – break the ugly vase and a new one will replace it – it ignores the fact that the very decision to do that, to tear down what's there rather than phasing it out or improving it, is itself a part of the message.

A company with this kind of weight sets patterns not only by what it does but by the style of its action. Google's internal ethos is notionally fairly flat, anti-hierarchical, cooperative. It's all about fostering creativity, nurturing innovation. The campus has buses, masseurs and chefs. It's family friendly. From the inside, Google is paradise. On the outside, however, it sometimes operates what appears to be a scorched earth policy; the attempt to make a run around the edge of the copyright laws of the United States for the Google Book Settlement may have been intended as something for the greater good, but part of it was the decision to avoid seeking a major change in the law in Congress. Consider that for a moment: this was an attempt to make law without reference to the body elected by the people and appointed to that task by the constitution of the United States. The scale of the ambition is breathtaking. It should also be terrifying.

It's not unusual for companies to attempt to lobby Congress, or national parliaments in other countries. But to attempt to make the centre of law-making, one of the three core parts of the US government, an irrelevance to the reality is to seek to change the nature of that country at a fundamental level. Once again, put that attempt into the context of another brand. Ask what it would mean if the private security company once known as Blackwater were to attempt this, or the oil giant BP. Influencing law is one thing; rendering irrelevant the founding documents of a nation – especially a nation with the economic and military might of the US – is another. But that is precisely the measure of Google's self-perception: a government that isn't doing what Google regards as right is an impediment to progress. A law-making body that has failed, again and again, to produce a reasonable re-evaluation of intellectual property (IP) law (and the US Congress has, sadly, not done well in its attempts to reform IP in a rational way) is simply not worth respecting. Like the Net itself, the company interprets the blockage as a system failure and routes around it.

I occasionally find myself asking if Google is itself a war economy – if it must continue to expand away from its core to support itself, just as expansionist states used to have to – making it the digital image of one of those acronymed organizations that tried to reshape the developing world in the image of the indus-trialized north-west during the seventies and eighties, insisting on westernized, fertilizer-dependent agriculture techniques, industrial harvesting and so on, only to discover that intercrop-ping was more important than it appeared to prevent pests, soil erosion and disease. It seems fanciful, and I dismissed it until I watched Roger McNamee's TEDx talk from Santa Cruz in July 2011.

McNamee, author, guitarist and co-founder of an investment partnership, suggested that Google is overvalued because index search (i.e. Google's kind of searching) has peaked: from 90 per cent of all search activity in 2008 to just over 50 per cent in 2011, the heart of what Google does has been shunted away from its central position. Google's core is undermined by its own success: 'The index became full of garbage. In fact, the entire web became full of garbage.' If McNamee is right, then the energetic expansion into fields other than search is not merely an expression of Google's self-perception, but a necessity. 'What it cannot do,' McNamee suggests, 'is recover its position as the dominant player on the Internet . . . [Google's] form of commoditization has been tremendous for Google and horrible for almost everyone else, and I believe . . . it is over.'[2] In other words, Google has no choice but to apply its engineering ethos in a broader context. Recently, Google has been taken to task by other Internet companies for seeming to privilege search results from its own social network, Google+, over those of Twitter, Facebook, and so on. The offended parties have gone so far as to create software which will re-rank Google results to show how they would look without the apparent bias. If this really does represent a drift away from Google's original central idea – letting the Internet determine the importance of websites – it demonstrates that the company is capable of a radical change of identity, discarding an aspect of its self-perception which one might assume was fixed. It also raises the possibility that this is a retrenchment triggered not by the original ethos, but by a dawning awareness of commercial vulnerability.

Debating the sustainability of Google and the Internet commerce models is a task for a battalion of analysts with access to the company's numbers. For myself, I believe Google is a positive force – just – with some serious institutional blind spots regarding the value of the existing ecosystems of the areas into which it moves. The point is this: that the efficiency ideology of Google and the ebullient creative share-alike culture of the Free Software Foundation, along with the problem-solving, results-based philanthropy of Bill Gates and the idealistic legal-societal battles of the Electronic Frontier Foundation, are brothers under the skin. They all stem from a common root and they share a common idea of better living through technology.

These groups and individuals and their ideas are in fact the children of the Enlightenment – the great surge of science which turned the medieval world into the modern one, and which created, and was created by, a culture beginning to place its faith in reason over religion, and which in turn fell in upon itself when it became apparent that it, too, was ultimately premised on nothing but faith, albeit a faith in reason. This was the original attempt by proponents of technology to transform mankind's lot, and these are its inheritors, for good and ill. It is not only the technology of the Internet that is inherently disruptive, but the heart's blood of the organizations that create, define and deploy it. They draw on a shared ideal of positive transformation, of beating the negative lock-in of inherited inefficiency and unfairness by radical – overwhelming – reshaping. Of all these, Google is the most extreme: arguably the last great Enlightenment project.

And that's where the trouble starts. The disruptive effect of digital technology – and digital age companies – on many industries, and the way in which they are altering how we arrange our lives, appears to produce in many a sense of inundation and panic. That sense chimes with the nightmare image of the networked world in which digital technology has somehow swallowed us whole and made us less than we are. There are various components to the nightmare, some more and some less real. There are concerns regarding the law and privacy; there are economic and commercial issues; there are questions of power and legitimacy and worries about the effect on the brains both of children and adults; but the first layer of fear – or perhaps, at this point, it would be fairer to call it discomfort – about the effect that new media and mobile devices are having on our lives as individuals and as societies is summed up in two words: information overload.

2

Information Overload

INFORMATION OVERLOAD IS a sort of buzz phrase at the moment. I hear it everywhere, the way I used to hear about stress and the work–life balance. To a certain extent, it's just a statement of the modern condition: when people feel the world is getting on top of them, they call that feeling by whatever name is current. I occasionally wonder what they called it in the seventeenth century, when Newton was alternating between science and alchemy and half the population believed that Armageddon was imminent. Was there a term for apocalypse fatigue, the feeling of disappointment and relief and post-traumatic stress which arose from the End never actually arriving? Did people experience culture shock from hearing about the Laws of Motion? It's easy to see this as a sort of paradise syndrome, a complaint for those who have little to complain about, and it's tempting to dismiss it out of hand and go on to the rather scarier claims made about digital technologies. But information overload is not just hot air, any more than stress or indeed the work–life balance. It's just that people often use the term without really asking whether it's what they mean, or where the blame for the malaise truly lies.

The metaphors are almost all about drowning. It seems we are sinking in a flood of information, a tide making it impossible to breathe or to think. While war-on-terror prisoners are bombarded 24/7 with loud, discordant noises and music to stop them sleeping and weaken their grip on reality (one man said it was worse than the period he spent having his genitals slashed in a prison in Morocco, because he could feel his mind slipping away) we have arranged to bombard ourselves, in a much smaller and less aggressive way, with signals which interrupt our thoughts. And there is some justification for the fear that we are somehow intruding on our relationship with ourselves; it *is* possible to present the brain with too much stimulation, to paralyse us with loud noises and bright lights. We tense when we hear sudden thunder, and a flashbang grenade can make even trained combatants useless for a few moments. We can be overwhelmed by options and possibilities, too, from that trivial indecision at breakfast ('What kind of egg? What kind of egg?') to strategic paralysis in a military context (about which, more later). Technology commentator and author Nicholas Carr's concern about distraction in the midst of concentration stems from an experiment showing that reading a hypertext document does, apparently, produce a different form of cognition and consideration from reading a plain text, a form in which what is written is constantly judged, the brain flickering between perception and analysis.

And too much information can be a problem in a less abstruse way, as well: as writer Malcolm Gladwell explains in *Blink*, a very simple diagnostic chart exploring simple criteria is a better guide to whether a patient is having a heart attack than a more profound examination of all the possible symptoms. The chart boils down to a combination of whether the patient has a bad electrocardiogram and is suffering from unstable angina, has fluid in the lungs, and has a systolic blood pressure lower than 100. If the answer to all four is yes, then the patient is in big trouble and needs immediate assistance. Mixed combinations of these factors lead to diagnosis of intermediate or low risk. And that's it. You don't even have to know why these things are significant. You only have to know that statistically speaking, they are. The chart, when first applied at Chicago's Cook County Hospital, turned out to be 70 per cent better at determining when patients were not having a heart attack than even experienced doctors. More important still, it was between 10 and 20 per cent better at spotting patients who were seriously at risk, raising the accurate diagnosis of serious heart attacks from 75 to 89 per cent to over 95 per cent. The problem, it would seem, was that the doctors were simply looking at too many factors, trying to encompass too much.

The advertising industry is well aware of the feeling of intrusion, despite, or perhaps because of, being a major culprit. Advertisements for holidays feature empty beaches and deserted romantic restaurants; cars are sold with ads which set the silence of the ride and the tranquillity of driving in contrast with the chatter and howl of a modern office – at the end of a long day, open roads and wildernesses beckon. Bubble baths and glasses of wine sell chocolate; running shoes are for running alone through the forest, not pounding the treadmill at a gym, though perhaps a majority of us will never take them out of doors. Aspirational imagery is frequently about carving out a space for the self, a space that is defined by quiet.

It's hardly rocket science to say that people – some people constantly and most of us from time to time – feel invaded by telemarketing, meaningless fliers through the door and spam email; by the phone calls from utility companies offering us new pricing plans we don't understand to replace old ones we never got to grips with, which we are assured will save us money and effort but which we are distantly certain will ultimately cost us more in some roundabout way. We groan inwardly at a call from the office which intrudes upon what ought to be our private time; at least, ought to be so by the standards of work and family life which were operative before the advent of the mobile communications device. And we blame, inevitably, the phone which makes the call possible rather than the culture which surrounds our job. The external pressure of communication, of the world which demands a share of our attention, we blame on technology.

The key word is 'attention' once again; there's a battle taking place, in which various media and industries compete for our attention. Leisure time is limited, so obviously assorted media want us to listen to their music or play their game, watch their movie. But at the same time, we each of us have a variety of other slots in which various entities are seeking primacy: banking, phone and Internet connection, TV and so on. Many of these know that they will not get our attention – our focus and engagement – at work, so they call when they know we will be at home. And in doing so they intrude on something very important and fundamental.

~

The feeling of information overload seems to consist of a small parcel of sins, of which the first is noise – and not just ordinary clatter and bustle. It is a noise of the mind, the relentless howl of the exterior world, possible only because technology is an open pipeline into our lives, and more specifically into the hearth: the place which is set aside for the things that matter. The word 'hearth' – the old word for a fireplace, which evokes notions of the duty of a host to a guest and vice versa, and which proposes an almost medieval life of wood ovens and pre-industrial simplicity – has a primal feel which is I think entirely appropriate to this discussion. This is very much a personal, instinctual thing.

It need not be a literal fireplace, but consciously or not we take the notion of 'hearth and home' very seriously. We really dislike anything that threatens the sanctity of the hearth, even by doing something as innocuous as crossing the threshold by phone or email without permission. Ask yourself how annoyed you get about telemarketing calls, or – a step up – how irritating it is to have a guest who outstays their welcome. More seriously, consider how much stress you feel about mortgage payments, or renovations, and, by contrast, look at how many people were prepared to get themselves into vast, irredeemable debt in order to secure a permanent home. Look at the power of the political pledge to enable us to buy our own homes, and at the number of revolutions and wars begun with the promise of land. The hearth is where we do our real living, it is what gives meaning to the hours we spend working and administering. It is our most profoundly personal place, a definitive statement of our identity as well as a component of it. It's our reward: the 'life' part of the work–life balance and the centre of domestic fulfilment. It is – or time spent there is – to some extent the thing preserved by philosophies of 'slow' evolved to combat the hectic pace of modern life. The hearth is where we play, in the broad social and philosophical sense of the word; it is where our humanity is initially learned and ultimately asserted. Intrusion into the private space of the hearth is the most unsettling and unwelcome of invasions.

Except that, in a way, it's not an invasion at all. The hearth, once a very simple, solid thing with discrete boundaries, has been extended into the world. The telephone allows us to reach out; the television allows us to see out; the computer allows us to search, to send messages and so on. We have positioned these things within the compass of the private space, and extended its reach. At the same time, we have made it somewhat porous. We have extended our personal space into the digital, storing images and parts of our history, interacting online. We make common digital spaces with family members overseas, with friends in other locations. We even shop from our living rooms, allowing a limited amount of the commercial world to enter our homes. We have extended the hearth to meet other hearths, and to connect with the aspects of government, media and commerce which are designed to face the private space.

The benefits of the extension are profound; the openness they require is, if not a vacuum, at least an area of low pressure, into which capitalism and administration have naturally flowed. Much of what digital technology does, good and bad, is achieved by a kind of blurring of the lines. We have blurred the boundaries of our most important spaces, and done so deliberately if not knowingly. We now have to learn to control the tide, to push back against the inward pressure. The boundary between the world of relaxing baths, partners and children, dogs, and the hearth and the world of work has become blurred. Distraction shatters focus, and, once gone, it's hard to re-create the fragile entity that is a mood of peace and tranquillity; but even more, to reconstruct the sense of private place and safety. Before ever there was Myspace – the first of the big social networks, which aptly recognized the importance of a bounded personal area online – there was the hearth space, and physical or not, outmoded or not, we need it.

In response to the external pressure, some people simply shut down or refuse to engage. A lawyer who worked in my wife's office when she was starting out refused to hold any meetings by phone at all, and did everything either in person or by letter. These days I suspect that is simply impossible, unless you are sufficiently powerful in your own arena that you are able to define the rules, but how you would get to that point these days without using digital communications I'm not sure. All the same, many people of my parents' generation own mobile phones but carry them switched off, getting them out only to make calls and immediately putting them back to sleep as soon as they have finished. My father in particular has a tendency to do this, often leaving me messages to which I therefore cannot hope to reply. I've likened this to the old children's game of banging on someone's door and then running away, but he remains Luddishly and somewhat joyfully unrepentant.

The interesting aspect of this solution is that while it protects the hearth space by blocking the channel, it doesn't seem to help with the feeling of pressure: in the case of people I know who have adopted this or more extreme strategies (one woman threw her mobile phone into the Thames), the results are the opposite of what is intended. The phone, inactive, becomes an accusation or a harbinger of doom. 'What if someone's really trying to reach me in an emergency?' I turn my mobile off overnight, on the basis that anyone who really needs me at 4 a.m. has my home number. The landline phone is next to the bed. As in most things, I'm midway between the Always-On generation (young Americans overwhelmingly go to bed with a mobile turned on and close to hand or even under their pillows, which according to a 2008 study might have a negative effect on sleep, leading ultimately to ADHD-like symptoms, although a larger experiment a year earlier found 'no support for the notion that the aversive symptoms attributed to mobile phone signals by hypersensitive individuals are caused by exposure to such signals')[1] and the previous one.

But the spectacle of people on buses, in the street, with their children, alone on park benches, bending over their handsets and tapping at the keys – and the awareness that in one's own pocket there's a device very much the same which is even now bringing in messages from friends, colleagues, bosses and commercial entities, 24/7, every week of the year – can create a feeling of oppression. The intrusion of work into the hearth space, of responsibility into the place where professional responsibility is supposed to be shelved in favour of home life, is particularly hard to handle. It's worth noting that the idea that work messages must be answered immediately has more to do with the nature of our relationship with capitalism than it does with our understanding of technology, but, in a sense, that's a dodge: capitalist enterprise will expand to fill the available space, and in any case, the technology and the culture have grown up together. And on the subject of noise, the nay-sayers certainly have a point. Fifty million tweets and 200 billion (yes, billion) emails are sent every day. We are generating more communication now every few days than we did from the dawn of human history until 2003. And much of it – as science fiction novelist Theodore Sturgeon could have told us – is crap.

Somehow, we need to come to terms with the influx; and switching off doesn't appear to be the answer. Refusing to connect is like refusing to open your post: it doesn't solve the problem, it just leaves you ignorant of what's happening, and gradually the letters pile up on the mat.

~

Alongside the sense of intrusion is a gnawing fear that the modern world quite simply contains too much we ought to know, or need to know. It's not obviously a digital issue; rather, it's a consequence of the ethos of factual inquiry which comes from the scientific and technological current in our society. Issues of how we feel are not clear-cut or always entirely logical, but it seems to me that the blame for this aspect of information overload is cast on technology for its place as a part of the scientific family.

And inquiry certainly does yield complexity, because we inhabit a world which is complex. In academic study and practical research we have pushed back the boundaries of ignorance as the Enlightenment promised that we would. In consequence there is so much more to learn in every sphere of life that we either become hyper-specialized or, in choosing a broader spectrum of knowledge, accept that we cannot know everything which is to be known about our subjects. When I was a child, I was told on a museum visit that Sir Isaac Newton was the last man to know the entire field of mathematics as it stood in his time. After Newton, the story went, it was simply impossible to absorb it all. Since then I've heard the same thing proposed about Carl Friedrich Gauss, Gottfried Leibniz, and a half-dozen others. It doesn't really matter which of them – if any – genuinely deserves the title. The point is that no one now can claim it, or anything like it. In 1957 Colin Cherry wrote in *On Human Communication*:

> Up to the last years of the eighteenth century our greatest mentors were able not only to compass the whole science of their day, perhaps together with mastery of several languages, but to absorb a broad culture as well. But as the fruits of scientific labor have increasingly been applied to our material betterment, fields of specialized interest have come to be cultivated, and the activities of an ever-increasing body of scientific workers have diverged. Today we are most of us content to carry out an intense cultivation of our own little scientific garden (to continue the metaphor), deriving occasional pleasure from chat with our neighbors over the fence, while with them we discuss, criticize, and exhibit our produce.

If it was true then that knowledge had outstripped our capacity to retain and process it, it's vastly more so now. Universities complain that they cannot bridge in three or four years the gap between the end of the school syllabus and the place where new work is being done, either in the commercial sector or in Academe. The quantity of information and theory available is boggling, so that on any given topic there may be multiple schools of conflicting thought, each of them large enough to be a lifetime's study by itself. The situation of any project with a broad scope is analogous to that of an artist painting the Alps: she tries to capture the scale of the peaks, the colour of the sky, the appalling drop to the valley floor, but has no hope of accurately rendering the village in the distance or the great swathe of landscape directly behind her back. Moreover, the picture will reproduce only the visual scene, not the scent, the sound, the taste of the air or the texture of the rock. The other senses can only be suggested.

The most egregious example of a glut of complex issues all bound to one another, though, is probably government – by which, inevitably, I also mean politics. Any claim by one party will be furiously rejected by another, and both claim and counter-claim will be couched in terms that are either incomprehensible on the face of it or ostensibly clear-cut but somehow freely interpretable. Worse yet – the final part of the information overload problem – no issue occurs in isolation. Issues which are themselves complex and require complex solutions are connected to others which appear to pull in the opposite direction: political programmes inevitably have to be paid for, creating what appears to be a budgetary zero-sum game in which a positive must be measured against a corresponding negative – the hope being that the consequences of the first will leverage the consequences of the second and we can all go up a level. More often they seem to drag one another down.

At the same time, some or all programmes will have unforeseen and unforeseeable consequences, good or bad. In *Freakonomics*, economist Steven D. Levitt and author Stephen J. Dubner trace the unexpected consequences of incentives and apparently unrelated social policies. The paths they follow are convoluted, but the lesson is that everything is connected – according to *Freakonomics*, the failure of the 'urban superpredator' to appear and make the streets of American cities unsafe in the 1990s can be traced not to programmes of education or tougher juvenile sentencing, but to the legalization of abortion in the 1970s – and while the connections are often unexpected they are powerful and close. The human world is not a loose-knit bundle of strands from which one can be plucked out, but a snarl of cross-connected threads woven together by centuries. Our social systems, after all, are not created by a design team but evolved to cope with changing conditions and forever struggling to catch up.

The only way through the maze might seem to be to go back to the source and try to build your comprehension from scratch, but that's almost impossible; quite often you'd need years even to understand the questions, let alone acquire a full understanding of the opposing positions. And yet without that understanding, how can you decide whether you believe in – for example – proportional representation voting systems? The pros and cons of a flat tax, the national need for a nuclear deterrent, or membership of the European Union? The stakes are so high, and yet the answers seem to be utterly mired in complexity. The broadcast television news was bad enough, but now every social networking site includes feeds and miniature party political broadcasts, debates and opinions about issues local and global which seem to have a direct connection to our lives – indeed, they seem to propose our personal complicity in decisions of which we greatly disapprove. There's an obligation upon us, surely, if the information is there, to inform ourselves about our moral liabilities and act.

And yet, you could spend a lifetime doing so. From fish to cocoa to cars to wood, everything has a narrative, and not all of those narratives are happy ones. That was fine while we could imagine ourselves isolated from ill-doings far away, but nowhere is far away any more. The chain of connection from our homes to the war zones of the Middle East and Africa is horribly short. Once more, the hearth is touched by things which belong in other spaces. The television news brought the Ethiopian famine of the 1980s to the living rooms of Britain. Images of starvation in another hearth space came home to the fireplaces and buttered crumpets of the UK, and the response was huge. But now it seems everywhere is broken, and it's too much to take in, because the net of connection implicates the lifestyles of the industrialized nations in the suffering of others. The hearth itself, which is supposed to be a place of refuge from the world, seems to be purchased at the cost of pain in the world. Every decision – even what fruit to buy, what brand of tea, or whether to eat beef or chicken, what it means to buy from a given supermarket – is part of every other, and all of them seem to have disproportionate knock-on effects in unpredictable places. The simplest questions have acquired nuance, controversy and multiple interpretations. We are at sea.

And the ship has a hole in it. Writers such as Dan Ariely have shown us that we can't even trust our own basic rationality. In *Predictably Irrational*, Ariely discusses how we make irrational choices about pricing in predictable ways: having seen an 'anchor' number, we judge everything against it – even if the anchor is nothing more than a vehicle registration. An absurdly high anchor will cause us to think of even a substantial lower price as acceptable and a normal one as a bargain (many restaurant menus these days have one super-expensive item because it makes the next price down look acceptable).

More generally, some of us desperately seek to block out facts that unsettle us – the same instinct which inspired my friend to lob her trusty Nokia off Westminster Bridge – hence the global and increasingly absurd market for climate change denial. Heralded as heroes are such curious characters as Australian geologist Ian Plimer, whose book *Heaven and Earth* relied for its ability to 'debunk' the idea of global warming on a theory that insists that the sun is largely made of iron. Michael Ashley, Professor of Astrophysics at New South Wales, lamented 'the depth of scientific ignorance' in Plimer's book, 'comparable to a biologist claiming that plants obtain energy from magnetism rather than photosynthesis'. And yet the appetite for such unlikely claims remains unaffected. Huge numbers of us are apparently anchored to an idea of the world the way we want it to be. Recognizing the truth is painful, so we don't. Of course, if you're sticking your fingers in your ears and shouting 'lalalala' about climate change, any number of topics – from ocean acidification to fish stocks to international development – will abruptly become part of your information overload noise problem.

Everything in our world is in doubt, bringing on a sort of lifestyle dissonance – the extended hearth encompasses uncomfortable and inconvenient truths. We are increasingly aware that the food we eat is bad for us; that the money we earn and spend feeds into and comes out of a banking system whose goal is not stewardship but lottery win success, and whose excesses can create and then abruptly annihilate enormous sums; that the planet itself is not a fixed point but a collection of vital systems we are woefully overtaxing; that our national wealth derives not (or not only) from virtue but also from a privileged post-colonial position which we have adeptly exploited, but which now brings us danger and violence; that our governments sell or facilitate the sale of guns, execution drugs and manacles to states whose actions we publicly oppose in exchange for the oil we need to continue the cycle.

Every action of our lives carries a tacit burden of complexity; and digital technology possesses the ability to bring it to the forefront: to report it live, to bring to our notice obscure but poignant crises, to connect us to matters far away and make the problems of people we do not know seem close. Objects can be tagged (virtually or physically), their narratives made explicit, the stories of those who created them in sweatshops can be hovering at your shoulder as you buy. Your neighbours are no longer the people who live next to you but whoever you talk to online; people who share your interests and dreams may as well be in Karachi as in Paris, London or New York. The evictions of the Occupy Wall Street protests have made global villains of heavy-handed police officers who a few years ago would barely have been remembered six months later by those they arrested. If you had been following a Pakistani IT contractor named Sohaib Athar on Twitter at around 9:30 pm GMT on 1st May 2011, you would have read his grouchy discontent about loud helicopters over his house. Athar didn't know it at the time, but he was tweeting live coverage of the US raid on Osama bin Laden's Abbottabad compound.[2] What would have been, as recently as 2005, a military action in a foreign land, became something happening just down some-one's street.

In a digital world, nothing is simple any more. The world is slippery and hard to pin down. Everything is out of control.

~

This feeling that we're not in the driving seat of our own lives – of discomfort with a world that is rushing past us, with the pace of change and with the impossibility of affecting its course – is not new. Anthony Giddens wrote in *The Consequences of Modernity* in 1990 – safely before the digital avalanche began – that many of us have a sense 'of being caught up in a universe of events we do not fully understand, and which seems in large part outside of our control'. A decade earlier, American doctor Larry Dossey coined the term 'time-sickness' to describe the effects of the increasingly rapid pace of life in the 1980s. Dossey's work isn't viewed with unalloyed approval by the medical community, but that doesn't change the fact that he identified a perception that 'time is getting away, that there isn't enough of it, and that you must pedal faster and faster to keep up' which resonated – and continues to resonate – with a lot of people.

Ten years before Dossey, Alvin Toffler wrote about it as 'future shock', which he defined as 'the shattering stress and disorientation that we induce in individuals by subjecting them to too much change in too short a time'. This phenomenon has existed as long as I've been alive, and I suspect you can find it in every decade. I remember, when I was at school, seeing a tablet from an ancient civilization (I think it was Sumer) lamenting that things were better in the old days when children really respected their parents. Perhaps it's inevitable, an artefact not of changes in society but in the life of commentators: we start out young and rich in leisure time, then form stable relationships and get proper jobs, then have children, and gradually have less and less time devoted to ourselves and more to external – if beloved – things.

Of course, if events are increasingly complex, or if their complexity is increasingly apparent to us through better access to information, seeking understanding of them would be increasingly time-consuming and difficult, and hence, also, gaining control of them.

Giddens also discusses theorist Jean-François Lyotard's idea that the post- or late modern era is what follows the collapse of grand narratives, over-arching notions of human development and the human place in the world which have been our context for as long as humanity has been capable of abstract thought, but which are vulnerable to the inquisitorial mentality of Enlightenment analysis. Ask enough questions about a grand narrative, and it comes down to a viewpoint, rather than a fundamental truth. Religious prophecies, Marxist historical materialism – even the Enlightenment itself, with its untested and unfalsifiable belief in the idea that rationality and science would lead inexorably to a better world – have given us ways to locate ourselves in the universe, to understand what we are. With them gone or fading, we have nothing left between us and the raw world. We are like a man who has worn orange spectacles for years, and, removing them, has discovered the rest of the spectrum.

It's worth considering the idea that we look at the digital technologies we have made and blame them for the changes in our society because we need a fresh narrative. The Cold War which provided a backdrop in my early life gave way to the War on Terror, perhaps itself an attempt to create a simple, bi-polar worldview. But the War on Terror is problematic, fraught with the discovery of our own ill-doings and undermined by the invasion of an unrelated nation – Iraq. Worse yet, even a cursory examination of its causes takes the investigator back into the real-politik compromises of the Kissinger era, when we chose to endorse strongmen over democrats who might lean towards Moscow, and when we backed the mujahideen in Afghanistan against the Soviets, incidentally creating the basis of many of the organizations which today are opposed to our versions of democracy. The iconic image which undercuts the storyline we are encouraged to accept – that Bad Men came out of the desert and did Bad Things to our Free World – is the now-infamous picture from 1983 showing Donald Rumsfeld shaking hands enthusiastically with Saddam Hussein.[3]

The world we live in is governed not by a single narrative, but by a multitude, a Babel of opinions and priorities, of manifest destinies and lofty goals, corporate agendas and private conspiracies. And it is the nature of the Internet and the social media realm that they reflect this. They are not a separate place, but a statement of our world's identity. The bewildering complexity of the Internet and of our communications is a map of us, and the fact that it seems to intrude is as much because we have reached out to the world as because the world has come to us.

The feeling of information overload we have – in some ways quite understandable, because the world is more complex, richer in conceptual information than ever before – is derived not from digital technology, but from our encounter with a world whose patterns and tides are increasingly apparent to us through the lens of that technology, and which carries a weight of history and increasing complexity which we are now beginning to appreciate. It's not that computers made the world more difficult to understand. It's that the world – which, yes, is shaped in part by our technology and our scientific understanding – is difficult to understand, and now we know. As we extend ourselves into the world, we are vulnerable, and we need to develop coping strategies. But we need to be there, because the alternative is a hermetic, head-in-the-sand existence which refuses to engage with real problems and lets them pile up.

That being the case, what are the real battlegrounds of the digital world and the society which sustains it?

blindgiant.co.uk/chapter2

3

Peak Digital

THIS IS THE High Baroque period of the digital culture. Everything that can be is being digitalized, the weight of commerce and received wisdom (at least some received wisdom) asserting that this is progress, and very much for the best. Digital technology is going into everything: water bottles, car keys, pets and running shoes. You can wire your house so that it can report to you on its energy use, humidity and security. You can buy a library of digital books, and query the author directly via Kindle's built-in @author feature. Queues form outside Apple's flesh-and-blood stores for the release of each iteration of its products as if Megan Fox and Jack Nicholson were working the red carpet. Users become tribal over iOS (Apple's mobile system software) and Android (Google's competitor with the smiling robot face): which is better, which is faster, which ecosystem is more authentic? We habitually replace our desktops every three to five years because the capabilities of the new machines are so far in advance of the ones we have (whose capabilities most of us do not use) that the software no longer fits into the impoverished motherboards of the older computers.

We're like the proverbial man with a hammer: every problem looks like the kind you can solve by hitting things. Commercially and culturally, we are herded towards shiny consumer devices – and stampeded, it sometimes seems, to new formats that replace last year's new format, accumulating a plastic and silicon junk-yard of defunct devices and those infuriating proprietary chargers, none of which fit other almost identical products, each of which costs some ridiculous amount of money to replace when you leave them in a hotel.

It is not sustainable.

We live in a world of finite resources, and our digital toys and tools entail, just as much as the auto industry, our dependence on petroleum from unstable and oppressive regimes, and rare earths from what are presently called 'failed states'. A fine example of the latter is coltan, the mineral from which we derive tantalum, a material vital for the production of electronic capacitors and hence for mobile devices and computers. Coltan mining has been implicated in strife in Congo since the 1960s. A UN report from 2004 states: 'Illegal exploitation remains one of the main sources of funding for groups involved in perpetuating conflict.' The report is accompanied by a stark triangular diagram: coltan exploitation, conflict and arms trafficking are locked in mutual facilitation. The centre of the triangle is simply 'impunity/insecurity'.[1]

Consumer electronics, it would seem, are like blood diamonds, and our hunger for them, twinned with our unwillingness or inability to change how the system feeds horror upon horror, allows the continuation of appalling violence in Congo. Understand that the prevalence of rape in eastern Congo – as a weapon of terror, not as a civilian crime – was adjudged the worst in the world in 2007. A UN report from May 2011 acknowledges that very little progress has been made in stemming the violence in the region, and described the levels of human rights abuse as 'alarming'. The term 'failed state' suggests misleadingly that 'failure' is a static thing, a noun. It's not. It's a continuing action – and it's ours at least as much as it belongs to the inhabitants of the region. The incidental price of Congolese coltan for the world is apparently local atrocity. This is precisely the sort of information that streams into our extended hearth from the digital, connected world. The right answer, obviously, is not to ignore the information, but to solve the problem – and the only way to do that is to begin to take ownership of the consequences of our trade.

If the humanitarian cost of the consumer digital culture is not enough, the onrushing peak oil crisis and the environmental situation surely must give us pause. There are still, of course, those who don't accept the reality or seriousness of anthropogenic climate change. Theirs is a position for which I have great emotional sympathy, but as far as I can tell it's scientifically bankrupt. The climate is changing and the consequences will ultimately be dire. Even if that were not the case, the acidification of the oceans is damaging our food supplies. On a purely practical level, it is clear that oil is finite and therefore is at some point going to run out, and within a humanly comprehensible span of time. If we're not at peak oil – the moment at which supply begins to drop away as new fields are harder to reach and reserves are depleted, while demand continues to rise – then it will come within a decade or two, bringing inevitable shocks to the global economy and to our way of being. (The debate about peak oil is endless and circular and no one who is not a petrochemical geologist can truly assess the various claims. However, the occasional signs and portents we are allowed to see clearly are not good: in February 2011 a US diplomatic cable from the WikiLeaks cache appeared to suggest that Saudi Arabian oil reserves were 40 per cent smaller than had been believed; HSBC warned in May the same year that we may have no more than fifty years of oil left at current rates of consumption.)

The always-on consumer society which idolizes digital goods is probably not stable in the longer term – at least in its present incarnation. We had a sobering warning in 2008 with the collapse of the sub-prime bubble, but we seem determined, most likely because it means getting richer on paper by doing nothing at all, to repeat that mistake. The latest area of experimentation with new financial instruments is the global food market: having seen what happened with property – as with nutmeg, tulips, South Sea shares and tech stocks before – we should all be rather unhappy about that.

Thus, it might be fair to say that we are living in the peak digital era: the brief and impetuous flowering of digital technology during which we inhabit a fantasy of infinite resources at low market prices (because the other costs are concealed, just as – according to Raj Patel, author of *The Value of Nothing* – our economic and agricultural system conceals the genuine cost of a fast-food burger priced at a couple of pounds; the real cost may be in excess of a hundred).[2]

And beyond that, truth be told, fashion is fickle. For the moment, digital technology is cool – at least up to a point. But it's been the new new thing for a while, and there are newer things eyeing the throne. What if you could swallow a pill and change the way you smell, make your skin sweat beads of gold? Well, perhaps you can. A Harvard biologist and an Australian artist have announced that they are developing an orally administered perfume which responds to your body's state of excitement and your genetics to produce a unique scent. And DNA is about to go DIY. To do DNA sequencing, you need access to a PCR (polymerase chain reaction) machine. They used to be expensive. Now, however, you can get a basic PCR machine for $600. With that kind of price tag, home biohacking becomes a genuine (and yes, somewhat alarming) possibility. Sure, you need a computer. But honestly, given the choice, which would you say was more exciting: writing code for an iPhone app, or for your goldfish or yourself?

Finally, the mood in digital technology seems to me to be about seamlessness and integration. There's a shift taking place from devices that do things to devices that connect you to the Cloud, to digital shopfrontage, to services. The trend in design is for minimalization and integration: it's all about making the technology vanish into the background, leaving us free to work with the data, the content. Apple's iPhone is not primarily a phone – that's just one of the things it does – but a portal, a shop-front for the company's massive media resources (or, rather, for the company's role as sales agent for any number of digital items it does not actually produce). The drive is towards removing the sense of mediation from computer-mediated communications, to integrate systems so completely that the hardware vanishes into the world altogether, leaving people, and an environment of manipulable information. When you notice your user interface, that means something has gone wrong. The physical world is being connected and integrated into the digital one, and vice versa. After a certain point, that very ubiquity guarantees a loss of the gloss of digital technology. It becomes a standard tool, and it's hard to get anyone – except a specialist – excited about a power drill or a winch.

I'm not suggesting that either fashion or energy problems will mean that we reject the computer – although if we really manage to deplete the planet, that could yet happen. Rather, digital tech-nology will probably replace other, more resource-intensive options in some arenas, such as business meetings. As the cost of aviation rises and video chat technology improves, it seems likely that more and more business trips will go virtual. But at the same time our relationship with digital is already changing from awed to bored, and as we stop thinking about the technologies of the Internet and the mobile phone as new excitements, the systems they are part of and which have evolved around and on top of them will congeal. Hallowed by habit and buried under layers of commercial, governmental and social systems, things will be much, much harder to change. We will reach digital lock-in, and any bad habits and poor choices will be entrenched, just as our present ones are.

The outcome of the tug between our love affair with digital technology and these various stresses – and others – acting on them probably won't be clear-cut. As I see it, the polar opposite possibilities are digital ubiquity, in which every house and car is wired and almost all transactions, social and financial, have some digital element; and a retreat from digital technology into other areas, effectively brought on by economic factors such as the price of oil and rare earths and the advance of biotech. I'd hazard that even in the first case, we might still see a move away from the fetishization of digital technology, because it's hard to fetishize the commonplace. Ubiquity could come to mean invisibility; a seamless integration of the digital world with the physical one in which objects report and can be queried for information about themselves, and buildings, vehicles and furniture go out of their way to be more agreeable to those who use them. Writer and futurologist Bruce Sterling coined the term 'spime' for an object which has a digital existence in this way, and whose history can be traced through the Internet, showing its location, point of origin, its journeys.

As more and more objects can be accessed in this way, or can communicate information to people nearby as they need it, the physical world and the digital one become more thoroughly intertwined. After a certain point, the oddity would be an object which belonged to the class of things which could reasonably be expected to communicate – a car or even a dustbin – but which could not. That point is closer than it seems; any number of items theoretically could already respond to a local request for information if they were set up to do so, and in fact we're also tagging ourselves in this way, reporting our statuses to Facebook and geotagging (i.e. appending a GPS location to) many of our online interactions. Some tools allow us to do these things in real time: Apple's new iPhone includes a 'Find My Friends' feature which allows users to let their friends check their physical location. There are already services which remind you to act in a given way based on your device's understanding of your location in the world (for example: 'buy milk' if you're at the market).

But more likely, to my eye, is a hybrid outcome, an uneven

patchwork in space and context. Hybrids – consequence of the interaction of two different strands of thinking and style – are common in our connected world, though you could argue that all the really interesting advances and fashions emerge from the encounter between two or more existing entities to create something new. A hybrid in this case would look a lot like now, only more so. In some countries, some objects would still be digitally inert, while everything else would be wirelessly reporting. In others, privacy laws or practical concerns would prevent full uptake. Some people would disable the system for their devices; others would deliberately feed in bad information. Some cultures and subcultures would simply shy away from digital technology, or disconnect it from the Net. Whatever happens there, however, we are at this moment picking the basic tenets which will define our understanding of our interaction with digital technology – at least in the mainstream. Should technology be 'free' or commercial, 'free' or surveilled? And, not unrelatedly, what about us?

It seems to me that we need to move towards our technology and get a better understanding of it, and how we work with it and where it comes from and where it takes us. I'm not worried that technology damages us; I'm concerned, sometimes, that the logic of our technologies – physical and systematic – takes us to places we do not need to visit and leaves us there.

~

The human animal is a really cool piece of technology. If you have the chance to go and see the notorious *Body Worlds* exhibition whenever Gunther von Hagens next rolls it through your town, you should: it's not the macabre and ghoulish spectacle it was made out to be when it came to London in 2002. Rather, it's the first chance I ever had to appreciate the mechanisms of the human body as extraordinary. In most people's lives, the only experience they have of the body's interior landscape is traumatic:

a broken bone or an operation. The whole thing is frightening. Even pregnancy scans can give you the willies – especially as the fictional backdrop for all these moments is TV shows like *House* and *ER*, in which everything seems to be fine until you start bleeding from the eyes and it turns out you have a variant form of kuru which is transmitted in goldfish urine.

But the human body beneath the skin when nothing is wrong is hugely impressive and, while squishy-looking and flesh-coloured, also beautiful. (It helps enormously not to have a soundtrack suggesting that the eye-bleeding is about to start.) Von Hagens is often criticized for putting plastinated human cadavers into positions suggestive of athletic leaps or games of chess, but in my view that simply showed them as what they were: human bodies. It wasn't disrespectful; if anything, it was the opposite. This was a tribute to how amazing we are. I remember particularly a running man, the muscles and tendons which would have been moving his foot frozen in place by the plastination.

All of which is an obvious preamble to what ought to be an obvious point: there are advantages to analogue technologies and to biological ones. Digital is just one of a string of options that all work, and our present fascination with it has as much to do with skilful marketing and pricing as it does with the technology itself. It is often the most convenient (especially at the moment, where digital is spreading into new arenas in an effort to join everything up), but not always. Sometimes, digital gear isn't as good for a given job as something else – although that's a perception that can sometimes raise eyebrows. By way of example, if you asked me to choose what sort of communications gear I'd take into the wilderness for a prolonged trip, I'd want a clockwork radio in there. A satellite phone, of course, is a hugely impressive bit of kit, but if something goes wrong with it I'm stuffed. With a clockwork radio, I might be able to take it apart and reassemble it – especially if there was a manual. Not so the sat phone. I won't be popping down the mountain for a new SIM and a soldering iron.

Digital technology is not durable: batteries run out, chips need fairly narrow conditions to survive, circuitry suffers from static, from dust, from moisture. Printed paper books are fragile, but not nearly as fragile in some ways as the ebooks presently being touted to replace them. Archiving artworks electronically implies the continued existence not only of digital society but of the formats and knowhow to preserve the electronic infrastructure. Analogue systems have their place. Less complex systems can be more effective in a given situation, and sometimes it's not helpful to get real-time updates and try to centralize decision-making.

The most acute statement of this truth was probably the 2002 Millennium Challenge, a US military exercise pitting the tiny tinpot nation of Red against the mighty forces of Blue. The challenge was planned in 2000, and Red was no doubt conceived as a generic Middle Eastern nation with a nod towards Iran, though by the time the exercise took place it was pretty clear that it was a dry run for a future invasion of Iraq. Saddam Hussein, it would seem, was the only person not really paying attention, because if he had been, the face of March 2003 might have been rather different.

Commanded by a retired marine officer, Lieutenant General Paul van Riper, Red eschewed technological communications and used motorcycle couriers, sacrificing speed of communications for security. Van Riper launched a surprise attack against Blue's fleet, coordinated apparently by an audio signal concealed in the muezzin, and sank most of Blue's vessels. The situation was so desperate that after a while the Blue fleet was 'refloated' and van Riper himself was essentially removed from command so that Blue could win second time around.

Blue's systemic problem, it later emerged, was literally that it had too much information. Van Riper, knowing he couldn't hope to communicate in the field with his commanders in real time without those messages being disrupted or intercepted by Blue's forces, had given his men a great deal of leeway within the basic structure of his plans. They were therefore able to react locally and in sympathy with one another, if not actually in concert except where some major signal united their efforts. Blue, meanwhile, had a vast array of sophisticated information-gathering equipment which was used mistakenly to re-direct forces during the battle in real time. This meant Blue was constantly trying to cover all the bases, paralysed with a glut of data which must be interpreted and accounted for. Blue was also assuming a parallel command and control structure in Red's forces, spending resources blocking transmissions, and presumably also trying to extrapolate a coordinated over-arching plan from the individual initiatives of Red's distributed decision-making apparatus.

In other words, Blue was over-thinking it.

Although the first Walkman – the device which ushered in the age of portable music, beginning with cassette tapes and moving on to CDs and MP3s – belonged to Sony, the chief mover in the fetishization of the digital device since the turn of the century has been Apple, whose sleek, minimal designs have been masterfully injected into the consciousness of the high street with a mix of music, wit and supremely seamless functionality. Apple's devices are not simply objects. They are gateways, leading to Apple's liveried spaces in what is increasingly called the Cloud (only the US National Security Agency seems to use the term 'cyberspace' any more). The Cloud is a vague collective noun referring to computers in any number of locations running services that can be accessed remotely. Google offers email, document storage, translation, search and a great deal more in the Cloud. Apple customers can buy media content with a single click. The next episode of a TV show, the next album, the next book is only ever a few moments away.

Apple's Cloud presence is replicated in its steel and glass outlet stores: a perfectly predictable and stylized shopfront which performs with a minimum of fuss. In 2000 the Canadian design guru Bruce Mau described a selling environment in which 'the brand identity, signage systems, interiors, and architecture would be totally integrated'. The point was the blurring of information and physical reality. The first Apple Store opened in May the following year – and then something else happened which was absolutely unexpected and appalling.

I can't begin to unpick the interplay of the iPod's launch in October 2001 – a month after the 9/11 attacks – with the slow, painful retrenching of American self-perception as being on top o' the world. It seems facile, in the face of the falling towers, to wonder whether a small white box full of music became a part of the climb back out of the pit. And yet, if not music, what else do you fight horror with? It may be nonsense, suggested by the simple proximity of dates, or it may be an important part of the US relationship with the iPod – and, hence, everyone else's too. Apple's decision to go ahead with the launch must have been an almost impossibly hard one to make, but it was, in hindsight, the right one. Digital music went from being another format which might not catch on – like the MiniDisc player – to being the default format for many, myself included. Apple's gizmo ushered in a new era of technology that was hot and cool at the same time, and – probably not coincidentally – set the stage for the arrival of multi-purpose pocket devices such as the iPhone, which in turn make possible the degree of integration of physical and digital space we're now seeing, while at the same time opening all of us up, in our homes and our persons, to the tide of information that so upsets some of us.

The rise of Apple, along with Google and Amazon – the latter two both begun in the 1990s but attaining titan status in the same decade – has brought us here, to a place where everything seemingly must be digitized, from libraries to shopping to medicine to streets and maps. The combination of functionality and cool has made each new advance – the latest being Apple's Siri voice interface, which allows users to ask their phones questions in ordinary language and receive a spoken answer rather than engaging through a screen or keyboard – a must-have item, a consumer product and an identity statement as much as a simple tool. Some aspects of human life – a small number, but an increasing one – are now inaccessible without a smartphone. Our relationship with technology is no longer that of tool-user and tool; it is more complex and emotional. We replace things more often than we have to, and long before they are worn out, so as to be in possession of the latest thing, the cutting edge. (Although it's fair to point out that our brains factor our habitual tools into our self-perception, so the connection between a craftsman and his awl has always been rather more profound than appearances might suggest.)

There is now such a thing as an 'unboxing' – indeed, on YouTube you can watch videos of people removing their new technological gear from its packaging. Writer Neal Stephenson describes one of his characters revealing a piece of kit in his novel *Snow Crash*; the experience is quasi-sexual. We have, in every sense, fetishized our technology.

We are also, as a culture – the Western world, from Berlin and Paris to Los Angeles and on to Sydney – somewhat addicted to notions of apocalypse. Perhaps it's because we're also prone to lock-in; a crisis brings the opportunity to change the rules, to impose resolution on issues that otherwise simply fester. Politicians know this: witness the Neo-Conservative advance planning for a crisis that would allow the Republican Party to reshape the United States' political landscape, which was then perfectly enabled by the unforeseen horrors of 9/11. In an apocalyptic scenario, all the usual rules can be re-examined, often to the great advantage of political leaders from one camp or the other.

In the present digital moment – the pre-crisis, perhaps – the lock-in hasn't set in across the board. There are still conflicting platforms for ebooks, for music; still conflicting operating systems, each representing a different philosophy and conferring power and responsibility on different groups. This is, obliquely, an extremely political situation. Governments and corporations are fighting it out with one another and with rebellious groups like Eben Moglen's Freedom Box Foundation (which exists to bring uncensorable communication and government-proof encryption to the general population), and while various administrations in Europe and the US have arrogated to themselves the right to trawl through digital communication in search of various sorts of crime, those laws have not yet been thoroughly tested. It's not clear who will own the technological landscape in different areas, although the time window is closing. We don't yet need an apocalypse to change the rules, because the rules themselves are even now being defined, sometimes knowingly, sometimes not – by us. We are making the landscape, not watching it form.

It's one of the most frustrating attitudes I see in my occasional side job as a commentator on the publishing industry's conversion to the digital age: the natural tendency of large corporations appears to be to wait until the smoke clears and a leader emerges, then seek a deal with that person. The infuriating point is that publishing – like many other so-called 'old' industries – can't afford to take this approach this time. It needs to have a hand in defining what happens, because otherwise it will likely be cut out.

The same is true with the rest of us: we can't just sit back on this one and wait. The world is being made – or, rather, we, collectively, with our purchasing power and our unthinking decisions, are making it – and we have to choose to be part of that process, or else accept that what emerges from it may be a cold thing constructed not around human social life but around the imperatives of digitally organized corporate entities. It may not happen that way on purpose, but the combination of commercialization, government involvement, litigation and societal forces – and the trajectory of digital technologies themselves as a consequence of what's already happened – suggests to me that what takes place over the next few years, and what is happening now, will be definitive of how we approach and understand this area for the foreseeable future. To explain what I mean by that, I'm going to have to make a brief detour into the relationship between science, technology, society and the individual.

~

Marshall McLuhan famously asserted that 'the medium is the message'. His meaning in essence was that the content of a given medium was irrelevant; the technology itself carried with it consequences that could not be denied or altered by what was communicated.

McLuhan's perception – aside from being the kind of sweeping statement beloved of the Enlightenment and its ultimate modern prophets – is true only as far as it goes. A technology does, of course, shape society around it, but it is also created by that society in the first place and the lessons taken from it are inevitably filtered by cultural perceptions and understanding. It's not just a praxis, in which ideas become things, but an ongoing, reflexive process in which each generation on one side of the reification divide yields a new generation on the other.

More simply: technology is derived from science. Science is the underlying knowledge; technology is what you then go ahead and do with that knowledge. If you have the science for television, do you create and implement a surveillance nation of closed circuit TV cameras, broadcast soap opera, or improve medical endoscopy? Your cultural bias will decide. (We've chosen to do all three in the UK. With the exception of the last one, it's doubtful this strategy has greatly improved our lot.) Society, of course, is then influenced by the technology it has created. In *The Wealth and Poverty of Nations*, David Landes discusses the impact of what he calls the first digital device – the mechanical clock.

The mechanical clock is obviously not digital in the sense of being electronic. Rather, it relies on a 'regular . . . sequence of discrete actions' to mark time in equal portions rather than following the flow of the natural day. Until it was developed, time, as experienced by humans, was fluid. In Europe, the churches marked the passing of time in each diurnal cycle with a sequence of masses, but the 'hours' were evenly distributed between day and night, no matter what the time of year. They therefore grew shorter as the winter came in and longer in high summer. Time was also centralized, up to a point: the local bells tolled the hours, rather than each individual person or household possessing the means to measure time. There was a time to wake, to trade, to sleep and so on, and all of them were announced by the tolling bells.

On the other hand, as Europe grew more populous and boundaries overlapped, time inevitably varied from place to place – from parish to parish – resulting in disputes. The invention of the mechanical clock, as with the arrival of mechanical printing, diminished the authority of the Church, allowing others to measure and set time. In effect, it also made possible the style of payment which for Karl Marx was typical of capitalism: payment by the amount of time worked, rather than for the product of labour. The mechanical clock, in displaying or creating time as we understand it today, has influenced our understanding of work, and of the length of our lives. In allowing calculation of the longitude it also facilitated the growing naval and mercantile power of Europe, and in cutting the day up into fragments, it paved the way for Newton, Einstein and the rest to examine space and time and uncover the connections between them.

While we're on the topic of Newton, it's worth observing that even science is somewhat influenced by the dominant societal perspective, however much researchers and theorists themselves seek to avoid it. Newton apparently drew the idea of gravity between planets from his study of the alchemical notion of the attraction of souls; he was culturally ready to consider gravity in that particular way before he began to do so. If he had evolved his understanding of gravity from a different background, would he have seen its function differently, providing us with a different aspect of the interactions of gravity with the rest of the forces at play in and creating space and time?

So as we look at the relationship between society and digital culture – a distinction that is in any case pretty hard to make in any other than a rhetorical way, digital culture being an aspect of society, not an invasion from an alternate reality – it's worth remembering that they make one another, and things that are attributed to the digital realm very often are actually just more blatant examples of things that are happening all over. The reason this book even exists at all is that our modern world seems to be completely permeated with digital devices and digitally mediated services and it can seem as if all the machines are taking over, or, at least, as if we're being changed for good or ill without really seeing how this is happening. I'd say that wasn't right: we're changing, for sure – and we always have and we should hope that we always will – and some of those changes are contingent in their form on technology.

But that's not to say that technology is the root of what's happening. It isn't. We are, as part of a cycle of development and change. And that false separation of us from our technologies – whether those technologies are physical ones like the iPhone or satellite television, or mental and societal ones like investment banks and governments – lies at the heart of a lot of what makes us unhappy and afraid in our world. One of the great benefits of digital culture is the growing awareness that we are not separate from one another or from the institutions we have made to do things for us. We are our technology. We just have to reach out and take charge of it, which is vastly easier to do when you know there are 200,000 people thinking very much the same. Twitter isn't about letting your favourite movie star know that you day-dream about him when you're brushing your teeth. It's about knowing what everyone else is thinking throughout the day and seeing your own opinion resonate – or not – with a large group. And from that knowledge can come a campaign to save a TV show, or a student protest, or a revolution.

Technology, used in the right way and with the right under-standing, makes us more who we are than we have ever been. It has the potential to allow us, not to take back control of our lives and our selves, but to have that control in some degree for the first time ever. Hence, this is a moment of decision – a moment we have been moving towards for a while. We have to choose to take control.

blindgiant.co.uk/chapter3

4

The Plastic Brain

I N 2011 BARONESS Susan Greenfield told Britain's House of
Lords that she feared the immersion of children in 'screen life'
could be detrimental to their development. She also expressed a
more general concern as to what our relationship with digital
technology was doing to us as a society and as individuals. As
Professor Greenfield explains it – behind the title Baroness is
another, more conventional one: she is Professor of Synaptic
Pharmacology at Lincoln College, Oxford, and a specialist in the
physiology of the brain – the structure of the individual human
brain is determined by genes, environment and practice. Who
you are accounts for a certain amount, then it's where you are
and what you do with yourself. The degree to which we can
control the first two is questionable – but not so, the third. That
is directly affected by how you spend your time, and her fear was
and is that the use of digital technology in our society is potentially harmful. One of her chief concerns is that we will become
'all process': that we will cease to connect events in a narrative
and live from moment to moment, gratification to gratification.
Another is that our social interactions will suffer, becoming per-
formative – done in order to be reported – or inauthentic, geared
to the screen and not the flesh.

In some ways it's a familiar worry: when I was younger, it was
suggested that television would turn us all into human lab rats
endlessly pushing the 'pleasure' button. In others, it's a far more
serious notion, proposing that we may accidentally climb back

down the ladder of brain evolution to a new version of pre-literate culture and existence while we outsource our serious thinking to machines, remembering things by storing them, letting machines – or, rather, software running in machines – make administrative decisions about utilities, tell us what to buy and what to like, what political parties best represent our interests, who to talk to and who to be friends with. Professor Greenfield is at pains to say that her concerns are theoretical rather than based on strong research evidence, and indeed that research is precisely what she proposes the government should undertake.

In the same vein, Nicholas Carr (like Sven Birkerts in *Gutenberg Elegies*) warns of the death of 'deep reading' – the focused, single-tasking, immersive style of reading he remembers from the days before the intrusion of the Internet. He feels that we are passing through a shift in the way we think, and mirrors the concerns expressed more gently by Dr Maryanne Wolf (Director of the Center for Reading and Language Research at Tufts University) in her book *Proust and the Squid*, that this shift in how we live and work will change the architecture of the brain itself, and thereby alter what it means to be human.

It sounds dramatic, but the brain is a versatile and even to some extent a volatile organ. It does, even in adulthood, alter its shape to take on new skills and abilities at the cost of others. The phenomenon is called 'neuroplasticity', and it is actually – to a layman's eye – remarkable. By way of example: the anterior hippocampus – the region associated with spatial memory and navigation – of a London taxi driver, seen in a magnetic resonance image, shows pronounced enlargement.[1] Taxi drivers learn the streets and the flow of traffic, and that learning is reflected in the actual physical structure of their brains. In fact, whenever you learn a new skill, the brain begins to devote resources to it. Practice may not make perfect, but it does increase your aptitude for a particular task by building the area of the brain responsible for executing it.

Perhaps the most extreme example – if not in terms of neurophysiology then certainly of practical application of the brain's adaptability – is an American man named Daniel Kish. Kish is something of a phenomenon himself: born with a cancer of the eye, he has been completely blind since before he was two. He functions to all intents and purposes as if he can see, however – riding a mountain bike, identifying different objects at a distance, moving with confidence through space – by using echolocation. Kish actually clicks his tongue and uses his hearing – his ears are biologically ordinary – to receive a signal telling him where he is and what is around him. He has learned to interpret this so accurately that he can weave through traffic on his bike. He cannot, obviously, use this skill to read printed text or perform any other task specifically geared towards perception using light. On the other hand, his perception is not restricted to the normal field of vision. He has also passed on the skill to a new generation of echolocators; this is not something specific to Kish, however remarkable he may appear. It's an ability you can learn.[2]

Having said that, it is important not to overstate the extent of neuroplasticity. Steven Pinker, author and Johnstone Professor of Psychology at Harvard, points out in *The Blank Slate* that 'most neuroscientists believe that these changes take place within a matrix of genetically organised structure.' However impressive the flexibility of the brain, there are limits. 'People born with variations on the typical plan have variations in the way their minds work . . . These gross features of the brain are almost certainly not sculpted by information coming in from the senses, which implies that differences in intelligence, scientific genius, sexual orientation, and impulsive violence are not entirely learned.' The question is how far the smaller changes within the brain can take one's identity before the brick wall of genetic structure is reached.

The issue for Carr, Greenfield and others is that we may unknowingly be moving away from the very development that made us what we are. Reading is an act of cognition, a learned skill that is not native to the brain. We are not evolved to be readers. Rather, the brain reshapes itself to meet the demands of the reading skill, forming connections and practising it – just as you'd practise throwing and catching – until it is instinctive. You begin by spelling out words from letters, then ultimately recognize words as whole pieces, allowing you to move through sentences much faster. That moment of transition is the brain reaching a certain level of competence at the reading operation – or, rather, at the conventional reading operation, in which the reader consumes a text that is inert. Ostensibly, at least, traditional text cannot be re-edited on the go and contains no hypertextual connections that might distract you from concentrating on what is there and incorporating the information in it into your mind, or imagining the events in a fiction.

Text in the age of digital technology is somewhat different. It is filled with links to other texts, which the reader must either follow or ignore (a split-second decision-making process that, according to Carr, breaks the deep state of concentration that is at the core of the reading experience, however briefly). Worse, the text is in competition with other media in the same environment – the device – so that email, phone calls and Twitter can interrupt the smooth uptake of what is on the page; and that's not just an issue for anyone who wants to read a thriller without losing the thread. Reading – not in the cultural sense, necessarily, though that's no doubt a part of it – has had a profound effect on us as individuals and therefore on our societies.

The evolution of reading and writing, in concert with our own, seems to have triggered a subtle but vastly significant change in what it means to be human, allowing a greater sense of separation from one's own knowledge and a greater sense of the individual self. Some thinkers suggest that written language defined a new age of the singular individual, where before our thought was more immediately experiential and our sense of self was fuzzier, more identified with the group. Written and read thought allowed us to see ourselves and our ideas from the outside, and began the long journey to technological society. What, then, will happen to us if we abandon it?

Apart from anything else, a recent study by researchers at the University of Buffalo suggests that reading increases empathy – or even teaches it. On the one hand, the experiment is slightly alarming: reading Stephanie Meyer's vampire novels causes you to identify more closely with words like 'blood', 'fangs' and 'bitten', which seems to imply that readers are empathizing with the indestructible and tortured undead; but I did that when I was fifteen and it doesn't appear to have warped me too much. On the other hand, it seems that what is learned is the forming of an emotional connection in general rather than the creation of a connection just with those characters.[3] What isn't clear – I suspect because it's outside the scope of the study – is whether this is a consequence of reading specifically or of concentrating on a narrative in any form. Does this effect not occur with film or video game narratives? Perhaps not: those forms are apprehended directly through the senses rather than being taken in cognitively, so maybe there is a difference. Then again, perhaps there isn't. But the spectral possibility that reducing the amount of simple, disconnected reading we do might also reduce our capacity to empathize is worth spending some time and government money to rule out.

~

This kind of concern – like many others in the digital debate – is familiar. Plato records Socrates inveighing against the notion of mass literacy, reportedly worried that if the population could read and write, they would cease to bother to remember. Their thinking might be jeopardized, too, as the new technology of writing created in them a kind of false consciousness, a simulated cognition derived from what they read rather than a real one produced by consideration of the issues from first principles. It might seem outlandish – except that it's exactly the same as the one we're discussing now – but if some modern notions of our brain's history are an accurate depiction of what happened, then Socrates was absolutely right. He was even right to imagine that the nature of thinking would be fundamentally altered by literacy. But he was wrong – at least superficially – in his dire prediction of a society made ignorant by letters.

Indeed, the development of the modern mind – and perhaps even our modern concept of individuality – can in some ways be seen as starting with the written word. Abstracted thought, reflected in the new medium of letters, is one of the defining characteristics of the world we inhabit today. And, as you will know if you've seen a showman memorize a deck of cards in a few seconds or heard an imam who does not speak Qur'anic Arabic recite the Qur'an from memory, we can still learn the trick of extreme memorization. One way to do it with a deck of cards is to make a narrative out of the numbers and images as they pass by, telling a memorable story rather than trying to retain a random slew of numbers. (In the case of the Qur'an, Islamic tradition holds that the language is so perfect, proceeding directly from the divinity, that the verses are uniquely memorable and impossible to counterfeit.)

The ability of the brain to acquire new skills is phenomenal, but neuroplasticity is not exclusively a blessing. It's also the key to any number of bad habits, bad personality traits and some addictions, and – like technology itself – it's subject to a sort of lock-in, where pathways become so well-trodden as to be hard to vary. (That said, even the most ingrained habits can ultimately be overcome and replaced with new ones.) The fear expressed by critics is that long periods of time using computers will cause the brain to adapt itself to the demands of the digital world rather than the real one – or, I suppose, rather than the one that is not inherently structured around digital technology. Instead of learning to respond to cues from face-to-face interactions, people will become used to dealing with text: a profound distinction, as sense inputs are handled in a different area of the brain from cognitive skills. More, human interactions until now have featured enormous amounts of tacit communication in the form of body language, tone, eyeline and even scent. There's a great deal going on that is not conveyed by the technology we have now, which is why online poker players do not generally make the transition to the in-person gaming table without some problems: the in-the-flesh game is more about tells and giveaways, subtle personal indicators of confidence or bluff, than it is about knowing the odds.

Furthermore, runs the objection, digital interactions require – and hence promote – different mental skills; in general, memory is less important (Socrates would not approve) because information can be cached, searched and recalled in the machine. Nicholas Carr makes reference to a scene from the life of Johnson, where the good doctor identified two types of knowledge: 'We know a subject ourselves, or we know where we can find information upon it.' What interests me here is the definition of the first sort of knowing. Conventionally, in the traditional textual way of learning, we learn, if not by rote, by acceptance of authority. We acknowledge the primacy of the teacher and take in not only the information they impart but also their value judgement of it, their perception of its reliability and context. Students are encouraged to consider the biases of reported facts and sources after taking them on board.

It seems to me, though, that the digital environment fosters a far less trusting approach. It is not in the first instance important to know what some guy called Nick Harkaway thinks about the facts, but rather to figure out what they are and then consider whether Harkaway's opinions are significant or useful. Rather than learning by rote from a single source, Carr's 'power browsers' are assembling their own narrative from a variety of sources.

It's both pre-emptive de-spinning of material – we live in a world where almost nothing is not spun – and the creation of a personal viewpoint rather than the incorporation of someone else's.

For those who fear this shift, the gap between the digital and the traditional is profound: Birkerts, seeing reading as an act of translation from the act of looking at printed text to an immersion in the flow of ideas and narrative it conveys, wrote that print communication is active, requiring close engagement from the reader. More, the communication between reader and author is private and disconnected from the world – a kind of perfect connection degraded only, presumably, by the inevitable incompleteness of the acts of transmission and translation; no writer is so good as to convey meaning without room for misunderstanding, and no reader so empathic as to receive what is written without further mistake. Physical reading is also measured in a physical journey through the book, page by page, and a temporal one from beginning to end which is in accordance with the human experience as it is lived.

By contrast, digital communication is inherently public, part of a larger network. Information can be taken in passively, or interacted with, neither of which is the same as the self-created immersion of the traditional form. The order of digital text can readily be rearranged, hypertext allowing different paths through a document. A greater emphasis is placed on impression and impact than logic. The branched, lateral nature of digital text affects how it is received, which is not similar to the way we live through time, but more like the rapid, convoluted succession of images and events in a Tarantino movie. That may make it less suitable for reading a conventional fictional narrative – in which case the publishing industry will either be relieved to find paper books still sell or appalled as conventional written fictions cease to be part of the culture – but it's not clear to me what it means for non-fiction. It suggests that books are no longer read so much as they are filleted, consumed and repurposed.

As a writer, I find myself wondering whether the traditional version of the author/reader relationship is truly so private as Birkerts believes. All reading takes place in the net of human interaction: literary critics have argued for years about the extent to which the experience of reading, say, Charles Dickens is altered by the numerous film adaptations and references to his work in popular culture. Reading *A Christmas Carol* after having seen Bill Murray play Scrooge is not the same as reading it beforehand. More, books are – and have long been – discussed in literary salons, in book groups and around the family table. Books exist to be experienced and that experience is not complete until it is shared; we're a more profoundly collaborative species (though perhaps not culture) than we generally imagine. It seems to me that the inherently connected nature of the digital realm that Birkerts talks about is not so much a difference of type as a difference of speed. The pace of analogue discussion is slow, and the number of people involved in the conversation tends to be limited by physical space. Digital, by contrast, allows the same comment to be seen, considered and discussed by an unlimited number of participants at one time. Everything moves faster. That, of course, does make the experience different – but it doesn't make it entirely foreign.

I also question the linear nature of human experience that Birkerts leans on so hard. Our memories are intensely selective. You probably don't remember brushing your teeth every morning and evening this week in great detail. Each of those moments most likely blends into one general recollection of slightly uncomfortable, humdrum mintiness. Similarly, you tend to allow the details of your commute to fade away each day. You may even drift off while it's happening. Albert Einstein once observed that relativity was to be found in the fact that putting one's hand on a hot stove for even an instant seemed endless, whereas a long time spent with an attractive woman seemed to pass impossibly quickly. Our experience of time is more like a movie – maybe even a choppy, disconnected one – than we generally acknowledge, and our subsequent memories are edited by us so that we recall the important bits and leave the dull parts behind.

For Carr, the consequences of our love affair with digital technology are clear. He points to a 2008 study by Professor Gary Small of UCLA's Memory and Aging Centre. 'Book readers,' Carr explains, 'have a lot of activity in regions associated with language, memory, and visual processing, but they don't display much activity in the pre-frontal regions associated with decision making and problem solving. Experienced Net users, by contrast, display extensive activity across all those regions when they scan and search web pages.' Reading a hypertext page is a constant process of evaluation and judgement as well as comprehension; a cycle of reading the text, seeing a link, evaluating the likely level of interest at the other end of it, judging whether or not to click on it, then returning to the origin text (or not). The problem is that that moment of evaluation, however brief, apparently kicks the brain out of the immersive mode of reading. Societally, we are spending less time reading conventionally, and hence less time in the cognitive space that Carr is anxious to preserve.

If this is true, it seems to be partly a matter of choice; the simplest solution, if you're concerned, is to read a text stripped of links, and to take pains to make space in your day for uninterrupted reading. Other solutions exist for work; for a while now, some writing software has included the option of a kind of 'quiet room' – a working environment that shuts off access to the distractions of the Internet. If it transpires that the brain is rewiring itself away from traits we need as a consequence of digital technology, and this is detrimental to the way we live and think, surely that high-powered evaluation and decision-making skill we will have acquired will help us to see the obvious remedy: a balance of modern text, complete with connections, and the more traditional variety without them.

If necessary, in future, we can pick different production tools and different media for different tasks. In a sense, I've been doing exactly that in preparing this book, switching between Scrivener (the writing software I use for work) and a pen and paper, reading some items online or on a digital reading device, and others on paper. If neuroplasticity is sufficiently extreme as to put the architecture of the human brain and the mode of living we currently have under threat or strain, then we can simply change it back. The time frame Professor Small noticed was measured in days, rather than months, and neuroplasticity flexes in both directions. An early experiment by Dr George Stratton, detailed at the Third International Congress for Psychology in 1896, involved wearing special glasses that inverted the wearer's vision. After a few days, the brain adapted, and the wearer was able to see and move around as normal. Removing the glasses then caused a confusion akin to putting them on in the first place, but, again, the brain was able to re-train in less than a week.[4]

For adults, then, this isn't such a problem. Once we know we need to, we can simply re-learn a necessary skill. After that, retaining it becomes a question of going to the reading gym to resist the spread of nasty mental flab. The problem is more serious with children becoming adapted to digital rather than analogue modes of living. Will they develop a desire to create a habit of 'deep reading' they've never experienced? And if so, how? Or does it become a matter of parents insisting on it in the same way they insist on dental hygiene?

That discussion aside, it pays to remember that these changes in the brain would be specific to an individual. They would not be passed on genetically, and they would not occur in places where digital technology is less common. In order to gain dominance in a society – to become the basis of a new form of society – they would have to be supported by a perfect lock-in of social and political norms. That's not impossible; if a given way of being appears more attractive than available alternatives, it will be adopted. It's not so clear that such a state would be stable, though, especially if it resulted in a society that was unable to relate to itself, distracted and fragmentary and consequently unable to innovate or to produce work at a high economic level – unless such a society became in some way useful to a financial cycle. In that case it might be perpetuated.

All the same, it seems implausible to me, given the patchwork nature of the world in general and individual societies in the specific, that the negative effects of digital technology could become entrenched to the point of affecting us on a species-wide basis. My original nightmare scenario would require a number of unlikely events to occur in perfect synchrony: the adoption of digital technology across the globe; social pressure to abandon other pursuits and concentrate on the screen derived, probably, from a financial and manufacturing system that could function and thrive in such an environment; cheaper digital devices and fewer disposable digital devices and software; a global diminution of interest in sport and religion; and so on. Vastly more likely in my opinion in the long term, if we don't take steps to avoid it, is the emergence of a world like the one depicted in Ernie Cline's *Ready Player One*, in which a global underclass lives in poverty and privation made somewhat endurable by access to an online game. Our present way of living lends itself handsomely to a sharp division between haves and have-nots, and I don't see any obvious block to the creation of a class of workers lulled by the opiate of the Internet.

But even if that is true, it need not be permanent. It will be a created and a volatile situation. We'll have the opportunity to go back, and the means. The question is whether we will choose to do so.

~

One of the other accusations made against digital technologies is that they foster depression, attention deficit disorders and other mental problems; but while computer games, online or not, have for years been scored in some magazines (and subsequently, of course, online) on a scale of 'addictiveness', and while some users report themselves as addicts, the notion of 'Internet Addiction' as an actual condition remains in doubt. There are various clinics that will help you to beat it, but the *Diagnostic and Statistical Manual* – the standard reference document of mental medicine – does not unequivocally acknowledge its existence. Many doctors argue that it is in fact a symptom of other, underlying disorders, and should be treated as such.

In 2007 Dr Vaughan Bell of King's College, London, wrote in the *Journal of Mental Health* that although there were studies showing 'pathological internet users' reporting lower self-esteem, greater depression and suicidal impulses, loneliness and withdrawal, it was hard 'to infer a direction of causality, and it is just as likely that anxious, lonely or depressed people might attempt to alleviate their distress by seeking online resources for entertainment, interaction, and sexual gratification.' Bell also notes that while an initial study in 2001 found a small increase in loneliness, a follow-up found the reverse. It may also be that already extroverted people report greater involvement and connection from Net use, and introverted people report greater loneliness. In other words, the Internet on one reading is an exaggerator of pre-existing tendencies, rather than a push in a particular direction.[5]

Regarding ADHD, Sir Ken Robinson, the renowned educationalist, expresses strong objections to medicating children for ADHD on the scale presently common in the US and increasingly common in the UK: 'Our children,' Robinson said at an RSA talk in 2010, 'are living in the most intensely stimulating period in the history of the earth . . . And we're penalizing them now for getting distracted. From what? . . . Boring stuff.' Moreover, children – and indeed adults – presently exist in a world where they are the subject of a sophisticated assault on their senses intended to attract their attention, that being, of course, the primary currency of many business models in the digital age. Attention has been studied, codified and tested; the desire to return to a given activity – be it playing Farmville or watching reality TV – is the yardstick by which many companies now measure success. In other words, until education and daily life, especially in the workplace, are enlivened by these kinds of considered, supercharged, attention-grabbing strategies, or until all parents are able to be ridiculously fascinating to children and teenagers (good luck) a certain amount of attention drift is going to be inevitable.

One of the most necessary skills in a time when information is all around us is the ability to pick one topic and follow it through the noise. That skill may well only be gained from having to do it; the question then becomes, of course, one of motivation – or parental engagement. And indeed, as Nicholas Carr concedes, there is evidence of some gains in this area; he points to a study that showed that British women searching online for medical information were able to make an accurate judgement in seconds of whether a given page contained useful information. Consider, for a moment, the general applicability of the ability to sort fluff from gold in the world we live in.

At the same time, what the detractors of digital media see in social networks and digital technologies is not what I see: Susan Greenfield's description of 'screen life' is a lonely and empty one in which users of Twitter post statements about themselves in an endless quest for almost existential reassurance that they matter; they act only in order to record the action and share it. They emit trivia in an endless, pointless stream of self-cataloguing and sub-gossip, from the moment they brush their teeth in the morning to the moment they fall asleep again. They exist to see themselves reflected, and live in retreat from physical socializing, and from a sense of self. It's the beginning of the nightmare world; and yes, if it's emerging from our interaction with digital technology, that would represent a kind of modern version of Henry David Thoreau's statement that most of us live lives of quiet desperation.

According to this picture, the arrival of a new medium has allowed us to stop being so quiet about our horror, and scream it instead into a strangely comforting void that echoes it back to us and tells us we are not alone. I don't see, incidentally, that that would be so damning a statement of Twitter. If its sole function were to soften the crushing weight of human pointlessness, that would be fine by me. (I shouldn't be flippant: if the picture is accurate, the relationship between human brain and machine in this context is actually an echo chamber causing a kind of atrophy, a shrinking of the self.)

There's no suggestion, incidentally, that computer use is like smoking – that it is an inherently bad activity that will cause you to develop negative symptoms however you use it. Rather it is a question of balance. Anything that comes to occupy a dominant position in a person's life may be problematic, be it a computer or an exercise regimen. In this case, the suggestion is that social media are displacing 'real' interaction, and the gratification of interacting with a computer, be it browsing or playing games, is displacing more fulfilling human activity. The negative effects on a person's life of a game like Everquest – a precursor to the ubiquitous World of Warcraft which was sometimes referred to by players as 'Evercrack' for its compelling quality – seem to detractors to be a cause for concern just as much as anything more regularly thought of as addictive or damaging.

But that isn't the character of, for example, Twitter as I've experienced it. First of all, the information that someone on the other side of the world is brushing her teeth holds no interest for most of us. Such a stream of drivel would likely be met with silence at best. More, though, while Twitter was originally conceived as a micro-blogging site – the input box still invites you to tell the world what you're doing right now – it has become in

the hands of its users something different. Far from being a collection of disconnected individuals yowling into the night, it's a
sea of communities, loose-knit but very engaged and very real.
There is research that suggests that users of the Internet and social
media sites are less alone than otherwise, and that Facebook, for
example, is a tool for the maintenance of relationships rather
than a replacement for them.[6] Twitter, in my life, is also a place
to seek, receive and impart information and ideas regardless of
frontiers.

If that last phrase sounds familiar, it's because it comes from
Article 19 of the Universal Declaration of Human Rights.
Twitter, after all, was part of the revolutions in the Middle East
in early 2011. It wasn't the reason they happened, but it was a
factor. The idea that it is primarily a vehicle for banality seems
a little ungenerous.

I use Twitter as a research tool and as what my wife describes
as my 'office water cooler': in breaks between bouts of work, I
can bring up my Twitter page, send out a few goofy messages,
discover what the wider world is thinking about (I follow the
feeds of a large number of people, many of whom hold opinions
I think are silly, wrong-headed or even just obnoxious) and
exchange a few good-natured jibes with fellow writers, publishing folk or whoever happens to be around. I ask questions like
'What was that military exercise where the US had that marine
guy who handed the conventional forces their heads on a plate?'
and a few moments later receive the answer. In other words, I
don't feel a need to tell Twitter about the detail of my life; I do
sometimes report on myself, but not endlessly or (I hope) tedi-
ously; I share ideas, seek answers, encourage others, occasionally
assert dissent. I don't need to be reflected – in fact, I want to
encounter difference – although, yes, from time to time I'm glad
of the reassurance that comes my way from my peers.

If I'm distracted by it, that distraction is generally a profitable
and useful moment of relaxation before I re-enter the hugely

enjoyable yet exhausting state of concentration that I go into for creative production. I want to know that there are other people in the world beyond the walls of my office, and talk to them before I try to finish a chapter. I am aware, however, that this is not typical, and there are others who do use social media to avoid contemplation of a frightened, diminished self, but the same can be said of other activities more generally considered 'wholesome' such as sports, socializing, watching theatre. As with so many other human activities, whether social media are 'bad for you' seems to depend a great deal on the pre-existing circumstances of your life, your emotional and psychological well-being.

In Japan, there is a word: *hikikomori*. It means 'withdrawal', and signifies a group of people who have literally closed the door on the outside world and gone into seclusion. They are mostly but not by any means entirely young men – according to the *New York Times*, 20 per cent of them are female – and they often communicate only via computers or phones. *Hikikomori* have issues of self-disgust, but also feel the world pressing in upon them, observing them (paranoia is often seen as an indicator of issues of insignificance and powerlessness). The American writer Michael Zielenziger has likened the problem to post-traumatic stress, while others have compared it to anorexia: the leading Japanese researcher, Dr Tamaki Saito, suggests that it begins with a desire to 'stop growing up'. Interestingly, the Japanese do not link it causally with digital technology; instead, they see it as part of a wider malaise, and some argue that it is cultural rather than purely psychological; in other words that it is not a mental illness, but a strange reaction to a situation that – if only in a certain light – makes a kind of sense.[7]

It's hard not to wonder about that in the context of the riots in London and the rest of the UK in the summer of 2011. Those ugly outpourings were described at the time as 'pure criminality', an explanation that carefully explains nothing. Depending on who you talk to, Japan is only just recovering from one or even two 'lost decades' resulting from an economic crash precipitated by an investment bubble – a national trauma. As the European economy dances along the edge of collapse and Britain's banks look nervously at their continental liabilities, it's not unreasonable to ask what form a sense of hopelessness might take in the United Kingdom after a twenty-year dip in prosperity. And would we (do we) blame our own *hikikomori*-equivalents on the Internet rather than looking more deeply?

The word people use for someone who chooses not to socialize much is 'introverted', or sometimes 'introspective'. But introspection, the cognitive consideration of the self, is one of the things detractors of the digital realm are concerned may be slipping away in a tide of stimulation and chatter, casualty of a dependence on seeing oneself reflected in the eyes of others. Certainly, it's not inconceivable that individuals might suffer this, though I question whether society as a whole is likely to do so (unless society as a whole has always done so). Moreover, this is a perception which relies for its weight on the idea that we must be whole and complete as single individuals, and that our self-perception must come from within from a kind of interrogation and self-scrutiny tied to the capacity for abstract thought derived from the relationship with text. It's an idea that pervades the objections to social media and the world of hypertext (as opposed to static, printed text): that self is a private journey, and humans are individual and alone.

For what it's worth, that idea probably also lies at the root of the individualism in our financial services which has recently produced some unpopular results. But it's not necessarily an accurate perception of what it means to be human. That question requires a little closer examination, which we'll come to. In the meantime, file under 'uncertain' the notion that any of us ever develops our sense of who we are *without* constant reference to the people around us.

That's not to say that the use of digital technology doesn't have consequences for how we work, and, indeed, how we think. A study by Assistant Professor Betsy Sparrow at Columbia University, reported in *Science* magazine, found that we have incorporated the possibility of Googling answers into our mental model of the world; our brains assume the possibility is there and don't bother to store for longer-term retrieval facts that we know we can get through a search engine. Google has taken its place among our tools and become part of our way of thinking. However, the study also found that if we know in advance that we won't be able to access those facts, we tend to remember much better. It seems we still have the option – and the trick – of remembering information.[8]

The issue with digital technology is not that interaction with it inevitably is good or bad, or has a particular effect, but rather that some effect is likely – just as it would be if you spent a great deal of time shooting basketball hoops, listening to music, or tasting fine wines – and the nature of that change depends greatly on the way you approach the interaction; in a very real sense, mood is a significant factor. If you choose to be passive or are predisposed to passivity, the technology can work with that, and you will practise passivity and get good at it. If, on the other hand, you approach your Internet use actively, you'll get better at being intellectually and emotionally engaged. It seems that the introduction of digital technology into a given arena strengthens and makes obvious patterns that were already present.

So why do some people see digital technology – or perhaps any technology – as a malign force?

And, conversely, why do others become so irate at the very notion that anything to do with the Internet could be bad?

~

The answer to the first question lies, in the UK at least, in a culture of public discussion that is to some extent hostile to science as a cultural force and as a political influence. Media coverage of science issues is always looking for an angle; precisely what the original documents and researchers, bound by notions of objectivity and accuracy, are in general seeking to avoid. Splashy headlines about the dangers of vaccinations are more interesting and emotive – and draw more eyeballs – than quiet explanations of why you cannot get flu from the flu shot (answer: because the shot does not contain a complete virus; it would be like running a car with two-thirds of the engine missing). A case in point is the issue of whether the swine flu vaccine can cause Guillain-Barré Syndrome, a nerve problem that can be painful and lead to paralysis and even, in extreme cases, death. The syndrome results from a given number of cases of influenza, but some studies seemed to show that there was an increased incidence when using the vaccine. Headlines in the UK were frantic: the *Daily Mail* went with 'Swine flu jab link to killer nerve disease'.[9] Actually, there was no clear link, and the largest subsequent study of data appeared to show a slight drop in the incidence of Guillain-Barré in those vaccinated.[10]

Part of the problem is that we have few models in mainstream cultural life that interpret the way the world is, what it may become, or how we arrived at this point, with reference to science. The focus of culture – of theatre, fiction and art – is on personal, interior journeys and emotional and moral truths. These are what might be termed 'eternal human stories'. It's odd, but the science that played its part in bringing us here, and the technologies and ethos that go along with it and which create the world we inhabit, are oddly unrepresented both in these eternal stories and in public intellectual discourse. The classical Greek myth of Prometheus, the thief of fire, and the story of Icarus, which is in some ways the counterpart narrative, are re-told from time to time, but almost always as tragedies of over-reaching. Science is the place from which trouble comes; solutions derive from the human heart, with its capacity to balance the excesses of the brain.

In government, the situation is if anything worse. Science – providing as best it can statements of truth – is but one part of a decision-making process that must also satisfy or at least take into account the wild and inaccurate received positions of MPs and pressure groups. The tired anti-sex rhetoric of religious conservatives shades inevitably into a stout-hearted denial of compelling evidence that sex education reduces STDs and teen pregnancy, and for some unfathomable reason this denial of reality is not grounds for de-selection but for celebration. In the twenty-first century we still have elected leaders who choose policy on the basis of what they wish were true rather than what is known to be so. I've heard this called 'policy-based evidence-making'; our politics, endlessly negotiating and compromising, has no space for the exigencies of the scientific world, so science often seems to carry the can, on the one hand for having the temerity to report facts that are unwanted, and on the other for generating technology that proves – as any widely adopted and significant technology must do – disruptive.

To make things worse, much of the scientific world is apprehended only by cognition. The truths of atomic structure and gravitation are not perceptible to human senses. Our natural understanding of the universe occurs at the human scale, where objects are made of solid chunks of matter, heat is heat rather than molecular vibration, and the sun rises (rather than the Earth rotating to reveal our star where it has always been in relation to our planet). Einstein's world, in which our velocity affects our mass and the flow of time around us is different from that around a body moving more slowly, is a strangeness almost no one considers in their day-to-day lives. It simply makes no sense, so we don't see it. The weirdness of quantum theory, in which information appears to travel backwards through time and a cat may be both alive and dead until an observation is made, is – in so far as it intrudes on our notice at all – a fictional device, a thought experiment or an opportunity for humour.

And yet, projects to construct the first quantum computers are under way even now, and so far seem likely to succeed. If they do, the world will change again, as processing becomes ridiculously rapid and previously imponderable mathematical problems can be dealt with in minutes. The practical upshots will be an end to current methods of cryptography – which are used to secure everything from credit card transactions and diplomatic communications to air traffic control – and a huge boost to biological and medical research, not to mention physics. Climate modelling will get better, or at least faster. The list of things we cannot do will once more get shorter. And yet, almost no one is thinking about it, or, at least, not aloud. Has the Department of Health considered the budgetary implications? Has the Chancellor discussed the issue with the Governor of the Bank of England? If they have, they surely have not done so publicly. Why not? When these developments happen – if they do – the results will shunt us into another series of shifts in the way the world works, and we'll have to adjust. It might help to see them coming up over the horizon.

They don't talk about them, because we as a society are unprepared for the discussion. Where for a while no one could be considered well-educated without a grounding in mathematics as well as literature, biology as well as music, some time around the early 1900s the perception changed – at least in the UK. F.R. Leavis, in reviewing H.G. Wells, argued that Wells should be considered a portent, a type, rather than a proper writer. Leavis also pre-echoed part of today's angst about information technology: 'the efficiency of the machinery becomes the ultimate value, and this seems to us to mean something very different from expanding and richer human life.' That distinction is in my view fundamental to the discussion here: Leavis makes a separation between machinery, and by implication mechanisms and logic, and 'richer human life' which is achieved elsewhere.

The writer and physicist C.P. Snow retaliated that the

mainstream intellectual culture was 'behaving like a state whose power is rapidly declining'. The mood got worse from there, with Snow asserting that there was a growing schism between 'feline' literary culture – which he felt was redefining the term 'intellectual' to exclude figures like Ernest Rutherford (generally considered the father of nuclear physics) but include T.S. Eliot – and scientific culture, which was 'heroic', and heterosexual. Leavis replied that Snow's pontifical tone was such that 'while only genius could justify it, one cannot readily think of genius adopting it'. He went on to clarify, in case any scientists in the room might have missed the point, that he considered Snow as 'intellectually undistinguished as it is possible to be'.

Leaving aside Snow's evident homophobia as an ugly aspect of his time and a sorry anticipation of the hounding of Alan Turing after the Second World War, the spat has resonance today. The present literary establishment's relationship with science is profoundly uncomfortable, and literary fiction predicated on science is rare, perhaps because any that touches upon science is liable to be reclassified as science fiction, and therefore not 'intellectual'. *The Time Machine, Brave New World* and *1984* are all strikingly important novels, and all of them are pretty clearly science fiction, but it can be hard to get anyone to acknowledge that out loud. The science fiction aspect is generally dismissed as 'the least important part'. Time has washed them, acknowledged importance has removed the uncomfortable trace of genre. And try telling anyone that *Cold Comfort Farm* – a novel written in 1932 about a near future some time after a 1946 war with Nicaragua, in which everyone communicates by video phone – is science fiction. Most people I talk to about it don't remember the setting at all; it's as if it just can't possibly be there, so it never was.

When Jeanette Winterson wrote a novel with elements that could be tracked as science fiction, she had to fight a species of rearguard action against mutterings of uncertainty and disapproval, giving a rationale for including these taboo topics. She told *New Scientist* magazine in 2007:

> I hate science fiction. But good writers about science, such as Jim Crace or Margaret Atwood, are great. They take on science because it's crucial to our world, and they use language to give energy to ideas. But others just borrow from science and it ends up like the emperor's new clothes, with no understanding of the material. But you shouldn't fake it because science is too important, it's the basis for our lives. I expect a lot more science in fiction because science is so rich.

Which sounds to me rather severe: the element of play, of wonder, that characterizes much science fiction and which brings science into the living world rather than making it something that can only be observed at a great distance, is missing.

Consider this rather different perspective: the writer Neil Gaiman, as a guest of China's largest state-approved science fiction convention, wondered aloud why China had changed its mind about a genre it previously discouraged. (Science fiction, among its many other evils, has long been a way for cheeky dissidents in any country to express political, social and sexual ideas that would otherwise get them locked up.) Gaiman was told that China had researched the innovation powerhouses of the United States, and discovered that the common factor among all the companies of note in the technological arena was simple: people in those outfits read and were inspired by science fiction. So now China was encouraging its own people to read it, too, in order to become a creator of new technology rather than just an industrial powerhouse turning out tech products for the United States.[11]

The dispute doesn't begin with Leavis and Snow, of course; it's the clash of two competing interpretations of life. On the one hand, you have the Romantic movement, which is fundamentally mystical and seeks meaning in peak experiences and considers all that is important in life to be poetic and irreducible.

On the other, you have the Enlightenment, which believed everything would eventually be explained by science and reason, and promised a world founded upon clearly understandable principles of rational thought. Neither church has ever been able to deliver entirely, and the present situation is a typically modern compromise, a kind of patchwork in which both sides achieve primacy in a circumscribed arena: politics and daily life are generally governed, in those regions where the influence of these competing ideas is felt, by a sort of watered-down rationalism that is most pragmatic, and which makes room for anti-scientific balderdash if it appeals to the popular perception. Appeals to idealism – a Romantic trait – are shrugged off as impracticable and naïve so that business may continue as usual. Culture, meanwhile, is owned by the mystical Romantic thread, suitably embellished with borrowings from psychoanalysis and science where appropriate, but still fundamentally touting a notion that some experience cannot be codified, it must be lived, and any attempt to replicate it is not only doomed to failure but more importantly a fundamental failure to understand the world.

And yet so often, our majority culture doesn't talk about the sciences at all, seeing them as an irrelevance at best, and a distraction from real human truth at worst. This is a fundamental error. We as human beings are not separate from our tools or the environment we make with them. We are not separate from one another. We are individuals, yes, but individuals defined in part by our relationships with others and with what is around us. The investigation of the inner self is vital, but it is not comprehensive as a statement of who and what we are. We need to learn to speak the language of science and follow its logic, to incorporate it into our understanding of what is real and above all what is meaningful. It is definitive of our world, like it or not, unless we intend to drift back to pre-Pasteur medievalism and die at forty with no teeth. It is part of the human condition, in some ways definitive of us as creatures, that we reshape our environment, that we seek understanding of the universe – for control, yes, but also as part of who we are. We make our world, and any discourse of culture that ignores that aspect of us is as false as one that affords no importance to the interior life.

Which leaves my second question: why do some people react to any suggestion that the Internet and its related technologies may not be an *a priori* good as if it were a violent attack?

blindgiant.co.uk/chapter4

PART II

5

Work, Play and Sacred Space

I F OUR TROUBLED relationship with science is partly to blame for the willingness of some to project the modern sense of confusion on to devices that emerged after that confusion had already settled upon us, what about the almost religious zeal with which others defend digital technology? The answer to that question is actually more interesting to me, because I think it goes to the heart of the Internet's role in the human world and the relationship that currently exists – as well as the one we desperately need to forge – between ourselves, our society and our tools.

Between 1980 and the millennium, the Internet became a play space, an 'anarchistic electronic freeway'. Looking once more at the 1993 *Time* article, it's noticeable that both of the things mentioned by Glee Willis – family and sex – are private matters, things that belong to the home and the individual, not the state. They are aspects of the hearth, the personal space I discussed earlier, governed not by sternly codified laws or regulations (unless something goes very, very wrong) but by feelings of natural fairness, desire and emotional reciprocity. They are both venues for relaxation and non-cognitive satisfaction: for immanent, biological living. You could argue that that kind of living is what the hearth is, or is for, and the first online communities retained that ethos. They were, in the philosophical sense, naïve: they were unconsidered, did not spend a huge amount of time examining their own meaning. They were just made up of people living, sharing experiences, helping one another, falling in love, rowing and fighting, and so on. In other words, many of the first colonists of the digital realm – those who arrived just after the frontiersmen from MIT – weren't there for professional reasons. They did not erect a shopfront, because there was no one to sell to. They were homesteaders, and they extended the hearth into the online world, and they did so mostly not for intellectual interest, but because it was fun. It was a strange new thing, and they went about it playfully.

'Play' is a small word that describes a very big concept. Some of the time it denotes something children do more than adults, an unstructured babble of changing fantasies and improbable imaginings. In fact, we traditionally define the arrival of adulthood as the end of freedom to play, which can make the conventional education system into the slow banishment of creativity, as the urge to turn ideas and wisdoms upside down and shake them is cut away and replaced with homogenized thinking. But play is much more than simply what you do to pass the time while you're waiting to grow up – and it's more than just a disguised form of learning, too. Renowned Dutch historian Johan Huizinga asserted all culture was partly a form of play, and enumerated a number of qualities that he felt play possessed, among them that it is separate from the everyday 'real life' both in location and in duration, and that it is not connected with material reward. The digital environment initially met both of these criteria, and even now many of the activities that enliven it – social media sites, blogs, games and user-generated content on YouTube – are free.

Huizinga is not the only one to place great importance on play. Psychoanalyst Jacques Lacan and critic Roland Barthes both used the concept of *jouissance* ('enjoyment') to denote something somewhat similar, though *jouissance* has more than a hint of the erotic: the word also means 'orgasm'. Karl Marx and Ayn Rand (an alarming pairing) both proposed that the basis of unhappiness and iniquity in human society was the subversion or appropriation of the creative urge by malign entities – although they both characterized that creative urge as an urge to work rather than to play. For Marx, looking at the working conditions of the late nineteenth century, 'malign forces' meant capitalism. For Rand, a refugee from Soviet Russia, they meant socialism. Both urged forms of revolution as a proportionate response to the violation of the fundamental human need to create. Creativity appears to span the gap between working and playing – or, rather, it seems that creation as an activity is not interested in the final fate of the product. More, both work and play can drop into a focused freedom of the mind, what psychologist Mihaly Csikszentmihalyi would call a 'flow state' in which labour becomes a function of identity and an expression of it: a route to contentedness through a state somewhere between meditation and intense concentration.

The Internet was staked out early as a play space, a place where there was no need for the conventional rules of society because there were no physical consequences to what happened there. Safety was guaranteed, because the only thing happening online was words. That being the case, the entire digital enterprise could be governed by nothing more stringent than guidelines. Free speech was assumed. The whole concept was an experiment, an opportunity to do things right. The Occupy camps around the world, with their group decision-making, quasi-collectivism and barter culture, are drawing on the same ideals. It's not just protest, it is an actual, simple attempt to organize society in a different way.

The hearth space, with its uncodified rules and informal ethos, is set against the professional world outside the home, where the rules are made to govern not a single family but every family. Laws are an attempt to set down justice in a form that can predictably be applied across thousands of non-identical cases, to counter patronage and favouritism. Professional personas, meanwhile, attempt a similar thing: one person functioning as a tax inspector is supposed to be identical in effect to another. There should be no difference: the identity of the individual is submerged beneath the role. The same is true in a corporate situation: ideally, an employer wants to be able to send any given employee to perform a particular task for which they are qualified and know that the result will be the same. The space outside the hearth is owned by systems – interlocking collections of rules performing the functions of government and commerce, acted by human beings. Balancing the demands of these two worlds is how most of us spend our lives: making sure we spend enough time working to sustain our home lives; making sure we spend enough time with our home lives to maintain them and enjoy them while not losing our jobs.

The playfulness of the Internet, of course, remains to this day. YouTube videos made for fun (often to a very high standard) and LOLcats proliferate. Interesting to me as an author is the playfulness of language that has evolved out of digital technology: the variations of English that have come out of the new media are often zesty references to typing errors that occur when you're trying to play and type on the same keyboard. My favourite is the verb 'to pwn'. It means 'to rule' or 'to achieve a crushing victory' (appropriately, since Huizinga wrote extensively about the play of chivalric conflict). It has a sense of utterly unashamed jubilation, even gloating, but it's also used ironically, with a knowing nod to how silly it is. It has both transitive and intransitive forms and obviously isn't intended to be said aloud. It's a typing joke, inaccessible to the ear. In fact, it relies on the layout of the QWERTY keyboard. The evolution of the word, I think, is relatively straightforward: typing quickly, 'I won' becomes 'I own'. A new use of 'own' arises, meaning 'to win with extreme prejudice'. A further slip of the finger generates 'I pwn'. What's significant is that it has been adopted – infused with lexicographic life.

Every time I run across a new one of these, it reminds me of

Patrice Leconte's delightful 1996 film, *Ridicule*. In the movie, which is essentially about barbed wit and its capacity to ruin lives in the eighteenth-century court of Versailles, there's a moment that stops the breath: Charles-Michel de l'Épée, the originator of sign language, makes a brief appearance at court. In France at the time deafness was seen at best as a form of mental retardation, and when de l'Épée presents his students, the nobles are vile to them. The game changes completely, however, when one of the students makes a snappy comeback in sign language. When asked to translate, de l'Épée responds that this is impossible. The joke cannot be rendered in words.

The Internet, too, has its own humour, sometimes coarse, sometimes almost embarrassingly lyrical. But you have to see it for yourself. I can tell you that the sunset over the Barrens is gorgeous, too, but you won't understand unless you climb one of the hills Blizzard's designers created for World of Warcraft, and sit down and watch it yourself.

All of which comes down to this: the part of us that plays – the deep, strong playfulness of creative adulthood and of the hearth – has come to understand the Internet as being a venue for play. Yes, it is also used to do work, but the way our interaction with the Net and its technology has evolved has made it primarily something that is used creatively, humorously, playfully – even where it is pressed into service by the professional world. The divisions between worlds are blurred online, and intrusions occur in both directions (look how many companies complain at the amount of time employees spend on Facebook). The prevailing ethos of those who created the protocols that underpin the Internet even now – people like Richard Stallman and John Gilmore – was a libertarian one, in so far as it was consciously articulated at the time. The share-and-share-alike culture of researchers and scientists is at its heart. The Free Software and Open Source movements that created GNU and Linux were about making things that were needed and contributing them to the community without charge. David Farber described it as Marxist, but it might be more accurate to call it genuinely anarchic – and it has anarchism's uncertain relationship with the notion of ownership.

Still, when proprietary software systems such as Windows came along, Stallman and others resisted them and tried to create alternatives so that users need not be locked in to the systems of one company. Microsoft and Apple spawned a resistance movement that persists to this day, but by the time they arrived on the scene, the basic character of the electronic world was to some degree already set: it was an environment that did not need or acknowledge rules, a place separate from normal society, where there were no consequences and almost anything was possible and allowable. It was a refuge.

People had set the Internet aside as a play space that belonged to them, and not to the exterior rule-driven world – and there are very few of those left. So when someone suggests that the Internet may be bad for you, or that what is happening online is a problem for the economy, or any number of other things, they're not threatening to take away a pleasurable vice or a useful tool. They're trying to take away one of the most important venues for being what we are – playful, creative, communal creatures – that has ever existed. That space is regarded as home territory by a very primal part of the self. So it's hardly surprising that the reaction is negative in the extreme.

~

We draw lines as a matter of course. We make a separation in our thoughts between private and public, professional and personal, family and friends and strangers, Like Us and Not Like Us. We draw lines in time – birthdays, anniversaries, festivals – and lines in space such as borders and property boundaries. We separate the world into chunks so that we can understand it and control it, or at least predict it. People crossing from one chunk to another without permission alarm us: a work colleague reading our personal journal, or someone jumping over the hedge into our garden. We delineate different spaces that we reserve for certain purposes – churches, sports fields, bars, bathrooms – and we don't like it when someone uses those spaces for other purposes, such as playing football in a church or music in a library. Spaces have purposes, and so do times.

The introduction of a governmental, corporate or legal perspective into a play space feels like a gross intrusion, or, worse, a simple mismatching of concepts, like demanding perfect adherence to the rules of international professional soccer at an under-nines Saturday afternoon kickabout. On the everyday level, it's the guest at dinner who won't shut up about immigration policy while everyone else is talking about television, sex or sport. It's the arrival of parking regulations in our favourite side street. And, inevitably, the same feeling of mismatch applies for many to the belated attempt to force Scandinavian file-sharing anarchists to obey copyright law, bolt a conventional paid-for business model to the age of digital reproduction, or curtail the assumed (but never legislated) freedom of expression in the online world.

Social media services such as the newly arrived Google+, and to some extent also Facebook and Twitter, replicate this sort of partitioning. You can determine who you share information with – at least notionally, and at least up to a point. The desire to keep your parents from knowing what you did last night, or your friends from seeing your baby pictures, is respected by the software. On the other hand, Mark Zuckerberg, Facebook's creator, told David Kirkpatrick (author of *The Facebook Effect*) that having two identities for yourself was an example of a lack of integrity. In Zuckerberg's worldview, it seems, the days of this kind of separation are numbered – if they aren't over already. The various partitions, Zuckerberg appeared to feel, would collapse in on one another, leaving a stew of subcultures and fractions all jumbled together, all able to see one another, and no one would be any the worse for it.

That perception is not entirely disinterested. Zuckerberg's company has an immense paper value – investment firm General Atlantic put it at $65 billion in March 2011 – and a large part of that is the notional value of all the customer information in the network. That information, properly analysed and deployed, could allow the kind of targeted selling companies are only able to dream about (and, ultimately, the kind I proposed in both my opening digital scenarios, as well). If Facebook users started to defect *en masse*, though, either by ramping up their privacy settings or moving to other social media services that allow more perfect control of data, the company could deflate rapidly – a fate familiar to watchers of (and investors in) Internet companies. Facebook needs its users to feel easy in their minds about sharing, and to decide that integrity of the sort Zuckerberg talks about is something they believe in and relate to; or, at the very least, don't hate.

Meanwhile, everything you do online – and increasingly in the outside world, because between your GPS-enabled mobile phone, your credit card and the many CCTV cameras that cover a great portion of the urban environment of many countries, there's not much difference any more – leaves a trail of breadcrumbs. That trail not only leads back to you, it actually draws a picture of who you are. It might not be one you'd wish to recognize or to which you'd want to own up in public, but it will be in some ways strikingly accurate. It may even be more accurate on some levels than your self-perception. Over time, and with broad access, that accuracy approaches what Google CEO Eric Schmidt might call the Creepy Line. Schmidt told the Washington Ideas Forum in October 2010: 'With your permission, you give us more information about you, about your friends, and we can improve the quality of our searches. We don't need you to type at all. We know where you are. We know where you've been. We can more or less know what you're thinking about.'

I said at the time, and I still feel now, that 'creepy' is not a line. It's a no-man's-land, and any time you approach it, you're already in it. Google's StreetView program strikes many as well into creepy territory, for all that it's useful and unthreatening when it's a view of someone else's street. In Germany, where the notion of privacy is more powerful than it is in the UK, the government has constrained Google to allow citizens to assert a '*Verpixelungsrecht*' – a right to blur images of their homes on the StreetView service. It's a made-up word created to express a right that Germans feel they have – and which, in truth, many of us assume we have or wish we had too – to control the degree to which their personal spaces are casually snoopable. The extended hearths of Germany have the protection of their government.

Schmidt at least understands that not everyone wants every aspect of their lives to waterfall together online, although his solution to the problem is novel and perhaps a little tongue-in-cheek: in an interview with the *Wall Street Journal* in August 2010, he suggested that in time it may become customary for a person to take a new name on reaching adulthood in order to disown youthful errors on social media sites and make a new beginning. As a cultural what-if, it's fascinating. As a genuine strategy, it's hopeless. It only requires one person to connect the two identities for the whole thing to go up in smoke, and the idea that, for example, future employers would abide by the restriction on peeking is wishful at best. The information on a standard CV is more than enough to find out who you were, as well as who you want to be now. (I also can't help but feel I'd want to change my name about once every ten years or so just to disavow some truly bad fashion choices.)

The sense of violated privacy is partly the sense of one sphere of life having entered another without permission; the inappropriate application of type B rules to behaviour that took place within a space governed by type A rules. Or you could see it as the application of the working world to play. There's a blurring of the lines – a common phenomenon in situations where the digital world is heavily involved in our lives. In reaching out to the world through social media, we have extended our grasp and made ourselves available to a great webwork of personalities and information. We have extended ourselves into informational space, and we are richer for it in many ways. But in reaching out, spreading our memories into digital formats and storing them outside our physical hearths, in servers accessible from around the world, we have also weakened the borders of our personal space, and as we extend into the world, so, inevitably, the world reaches out towards us – or even into us: at least, into the new spaces of the mind where we have located our external selves, and through them into the private spaces that we guard more jealously, but which, until recently, we did not need to fear might be exposed from without.

I say 'we' although there is a school of thought that says that the generations after my own feel less and less that this is the case. I'm not sure that's true: I don't think privacy is ever a primary issue in a political campaign, any more than a triumphal speech about voting reform and electoral methodology is likely to win you an election (alas). But the desire for privacy arrives when it is breached, not before; until the first time you feel intruded upon, or are denied a job because your Facebook page is too rowdy, how can you know you need it? Privacy is an issue when you want to be respectable, when you don't wish to advertise your sex life, when you want to be alone and contemplative – things that happen somewhat later in life. I don't imagine I cared much for privacy when I was nineteen. I do care about it now. So, yes, I believe that 'we', people in general, retain certain expectations about how our data will be handled, and who will be able to handle it, even if those expectations are unawakened until they are trespassed against.

More specifically: on some level, we feel that the information we create in response to the world, or which is created as a result of our passage through the world – digital or not – falls by natural right under our control. It is our choice who sees it, or whether it should be retained, sold or destroyed. The law feels much the same way, and much of the endless boilerplate text on social media sites is a contractual agreement in which we use the service in exchange for access to that information. Facebook and the like are not free. They are paid for in data about us, but our relationship with personal data is still in flux. We don't yet understand the consequences of it, or even really have a feel for what it is. It's become popular among some technologists recently to refer to laptops and data storage devices as 'exobrains' – an external place to keep information that is nonetheless part of the person in question.

In preparing this book, I've made copious use of a service called Evernote. Evernote is a scrapbook that allows me to see something and make a note of it either by dictating a voice note, typing, photographing or clipping it from a web browser. It is, I suppose, a digital prosthetic that allows me to go far beyond the normal limits of the cognitive load of my working memory without dropping a stitch. When I need to go back to a topic, I type in a keyword and the service produces the items I wanted to consider, allowing me to weave them together with what I'm working on. I am literally using Evernote as an extension of my memory; my brain has no doubt included it in its metamap of my capabilities, considering Evernote a part of me. Here, however, US law at least begs to differ. An electronic device is not presently acknowledged to be a private thing, and is subject to search without cause or a warrant at ports of entry.

Increasingly, though, our information is part of our lives and our identities, even when detached from our persons. Amazon and assorted libraries have historically resisted requests from law enforcement to know what people are reading. Google has fought demands for access to search histories. Twitter has gone to court to avoid handing over user data. Information about us and created by us, we feel on an instinctual level, still belongs to us and in some way is still part of us after we have moved on. Our digital footprints are not (should not be) public unless we say so. And on the face of it, at least, digital corporations agree and understand. In part, no doubt, for the historical reasons we've already talked about, many of the founders of these companies are averse to government scrutiny. The general tenor of hacker culture is anti-government. But not always anti-corporate, or, at least, not against the use of information gleaned from customers to make very large amounts of money. (It also has to be acknowledged, as Misha Glenny points out in *Dark Market*, that a certain amount of leeway exists in the relationship between large digital corporations and the US government; the US considers Google a strategic asset. Google's Trust and Safety Manager is a former agent of the US Secret Service. This is not to suggest that Google would ever compromise its legal responsibilities to its customers, or that employees of the company would supply data to the government for which they should have to obtain court orders. Rather, it is to observe that while Google's public posture is of rakish defiance of authority – a posture that perhaps looks a bit odd now that the company is a global titan – it seems not implausible that where necessary and permissible, Google tries to be a helpful corporate citizen of the nation where it was born.)

The practical reasons for our desire to sequester information are obvious, if not always entirely honourable. Eric Schmidt again, back in 2009, told CNBC: 'If you have something that you don't want anyone to know, maybe you shouldn't be doing it in the first place.' Well, true; it's probably a lot easier to get caught out having an affair now than it ever has been. On the other hand, Schmidt's posture is massively entitled, the response of a wealthy white male in one of the most protected nations on earth. A moment's reflection shows why he's wrong: it's not impossible, for example, to find shelters for battered women by reverse engineering data. There are many things people do that are legal, even admirable, that require a fog of, if not deception, at least uncertainty to take place without negative repercussions. Face recognition software now being built in to social networking sites has the potential to expose all manner of secrets, from Romeo and Juliet-style relationships to undercover police operations, unless individuals are allowed control over their data. And the appetite for Internet spaces that are not premised on the exploitation of vast amounts of personal data exists: the start-up network Diaspora, constructed in response to a statement by Free Software guru Eben Moglen in which he described conventional social networks as 'spying for free', [1] received $200,000 in funding through Kickstarter (an initiative that allows companies to seek funding directly from the public) and is gathering momentum even as this book is being written.

A desire for privacy does not imply shameful secrets; Moglen argues, again and again, that without anonymity in discourse, free speech is impossible, and hence also democracy. The right to speak the truth to power does not shield the speaker from the consequences of so doing; only comparable power or anonymity can do that. More practical and more disturbing, there is a much used quotation regarding the value of privacy in troubled times – and when are times anything else? – that is attributed to Cardinal Richelieu in the seventeenth century, though it may actually have come from one of his agents: 'If one would give me six lines written by the hand of the most honest man, I would find something in them to have him hanged.'

Privacy is a protection from the unreasonable use of state and corporate power. But that is, in a sense, a secondary thing. In the first instance, privacy is the statement in words of a simple understanding, which belongs to the instinctive world rather than the formal one, that some things are the province of those who experience them and not naturally open to the scrutiny of others:

courtship and love, with their emotional nakedness; the simple moments of family life; the appalling rawness of grief. That the state and other systems are precluded from snooping on these things is important – it is a strong barrier between the formal world and the hearth, extended or not – but at root privacy is a simple understanding: not everything belongs to everyone.

~

One of the areas bringing strife to digital politics is the battle over intellectual property, or IP. It was my point of entry into the issues of digitization, and one of the first things I realized was that measures to 'enforce' IP online almost instantly cease to be about IP and become a discussion of total online surveillance. I think there's an absolute error of priorities there: I am not willing to solve the problem of people not wanting to pay for work I've done by demanding an Orwellian eyeball peering through every keyhole. It's a ridiculous misunderstanding of what society is for and what privacy and – though it's unfashionable to talk about it in the UK – freedom are worth. Without the former, you cannot have the latter.

I also feel that there's a forlorn sort of desperation about the hardline copyright fight. I mentioned Misha Glenny's *Dark Market* earlier; the book deals with a structure of non-public websites and Internet venues that trade in illegal goods and services – some of them frankly vile. The 'dark web' is hard for law enforcement to penetrate, sophisticated and elusive. The commodities bought and sold through it are the stuff of serious criminal enterprise, espionage, terrorism and ghastliness. It remains active. Does it genuinely seem likely that we will be able to crack down on copyright violation when we have been unable to prevent the ongoing commission and facilitation of far more serious crimes online? Will we, in the name of profit and Mickey Mouse, throw away more privacy and accept more surveillance and intrusion than we have accepted in the search for stolen nuclear materiel? It seems highly unlikely; and if we did, I would not count it much of a victory.

I don't think it's a coincidence that privacy and intellectual property are major battlegrounds in the shaping of our digital environment, but I do find it odd that so many privacy campaigners are also uncomfortable with the idea of IP – even though I absolutely see how they arrive at that position, given the draconian measures lawmakers are being asked to adopt by angry content industries. I also find it bizarre that the IP lobby is willing to trash the idea of a right to privacy and even call for massive intrusion. To me, the issues are closely related. Privacy and IP share to my eye a common conceptual basis, and the problems that they both face in the age of digital reproduction are problems in common.

Intellectual property is the idea that information belongs in some way to the person who formulates it. IP law is drafted somewhat differently in different countries, and it should be acknowledged that while I think the principle is sound, the implementation and use are in some cases objectionable, aggressive and counterproductive. Conceptually, however, I believe it's hugely important.

Lawyers break IP into three parts: copyright, patent and trademark. They are absolutely not mutually interchangeable, having distinct applications. Copyright applies to written and recorded original work: this book, for example, is protected by copyright. Derivative works are also protected, so you can't simply read the book aloud and charge money for recordings. However, if you did make a recording, some rights in it would rest with you: I could not come in and take it for my own use without your permission. We'd have to make a deal, and agree some kind of split. Or, of course, I could read the book aloud myself, and require your recording to be destroyed.

Patent is for mechanisms and chemicals; it has a much more limited lifespan, and a more arduous registration process. It is the rule by which drugs companies prevent others from reverse-engineering their products – and, some would argue, keep prices artificially high. In the past, drug research was hit and miss and very expensive, so pharmaceuticals manufacturers argued that they had to cover their costs. Recently, however, advances in computing and genetics have begun to change that.

Trademark is the stamp you see on official merchandizing and designer clothes. It restricts use of, for example, Gucci's logo to Gucci clothing and products and anyone licensed by the company. It's an origin mark. It also prevents anyone except the Walt Disney Company from using Disney's famous characters in toys.

It's worth noting that some, including Richard Stallman, contest the grouping of these three ideas under a single banner. To Stallman's eye, the various aspects of what is commonly called intellectual property have only a superficial similarity, and the conflation leads to errors of comprehension and logic. It's true that under the US construction, for example, trademark is enacted under a different part of the constitution from copyright, although the law was originally created under the same clause and subsequently struck down and then re-created in a new venue. The US perception, however, is far from being the only one.

In fact, the rationale behind intellectual property of different types varies from country to country. In some places, it is regarded as an inherent right, a moral right, derived from what in the UK is called 'sweat of the brow'. Some people, both pro- and anti-IP, see it as something that comes out of the act of creation. In the case of those who resist IP, this leads them to deconstruct the notion of creation, to represent it as a manner of synthesis. They argue that all creativity is in fact derivative, that in consequence nothing is 'original', but draws on a collective intellectual heritage and is therefore common property. (I can't shake the feeling that accepting this assertion ultimately entails a belief that we are all owned outright by the group from birth to death, and that anything we have must be yielded up on request to others, an idea I deeply mistrust because it seems to feed straight into writer Ursula Le Guin's Omelas dilemma, in which a perfect society is sustained by the effective torture of an innocent.)[3]

In the US, by contrast, the basis of IP law is notionally utilitarian: it is a financial inducement to creators to make work, secured by Article I of the constitution, authorizing Congress to 'promote the Progress of Science and useful Arts, by securing for limited Times to Authors and Inventors the exclusive Right to their respective Writings and Discoveries'. That basis seems to me a *post facto* rationalization, a way of coding for something that appeared right but which was a bad fit for the legislative ethos presently in the ascendant; the consideration was derived from British law, but the British thinking behind it was unpalatable, perhaps because it was British, or because it happily appealed to intangibles where the US was to be a rational enterprise. It certainly doesn't stand up well to the modern world or to the copyright wars in which large companies fight to retain control of long-running franchises – essentially to avoid having to come up with new, brilliant, competing works. More interesting to me is the notion – which I believe prevails in German law – that a creative work is an extension of the creator's identity or person into the world.

Whatever its jurisprudential basis, we mostly encounter copyright in the digital realm in negative ways: rules telling us not to share songs, download movies without paying for them, and so on. Very often, efforts to enforce the rules are more obnoxious than the rules themselves, especially to those who are trying to obey the law. Digital Rights Management software can make perfectly legitimate actions impossible and when it glitches, which alas it does, can shut down altogether entirely sanctioned use of purchased media. But IP is also what prevents a photographic shop (or, these days, a photographic website such as Flickr) from selling my holiday snaps to a tour company for use in their brochure. And as citizen-creators become more common – as more and more people have at least some presence on social networks – it becomes a way of preventing an unwelcome entity from turning playful production into a profit centre without permission: in June 2010, for example, it emerged that the UK's *Sun* newspaper had had to scrap a football competition it was running that made use of thirty-two football blogs, some without permission.[4] The *Sun*'s coverage of the Hillsborough Stadium disaster in 1989 in which ninety-six people died was wrong-headed and accusatory, and is remembered among Liverpool fans as an unforgivable bit of media thuggery. Naturally, therefore, some bloggers on the football scene wanted nothing to do with the paper. Contact with it would have represented an invasion of their space by an unwelcome force. Copyright was the legal lever that allowed them to push back against the *Sun* and assert – as the German perception would have it – a right of identity.

The concept of IP or something like it is only going to become more important, rather than less, as we embrace new technology. In a world where the human genome itself is legible to us, for example, who owns the rights to our DNA? A few years ago it would have been ridiculous to worry about it, but now it's merely far-fetched to ask: if I were to collect DNA from someone I found attractive, say from a hairbrush, and have it combined with my own and placed into a viable human egg, would I have committed some sort of violation? What if I didn't bother with my own and simply had a clone made of the object of my desire? Or, more immediate: suppose my genetic make-up is in some way valuable, as was that of Henrietta Lacks, whose tumour became the HeLa cell line from which are derived nearly 11,000 patents (I use that number not as a measure of financial but medical value)? Should Lacks have been entitled to some compensation, even if it was only palliative care, for use of that line? Should a government have a right to step in and acquire DNA that is thus beneficial, so preventing an unscrupulous person from holding back the cure for some appalling disease in the name of vast personal profit? Or should the individual be protected from claims by the state to own the body and genetic map of a human individual? It's important to ask these questions now, before they're pressing. If we have to answer them in haste, we may not like the outcomes.

Less dramatic, perhaps, but liable to cause considerable perturbation and tumult in the commercial world: advances in 3D printing – making objects by rapidly 'printing' or extruding layer upon layer of material in a pattern controlled by a machine – will soon mean some objects can be created from digital templates using a printer that can be run from a car battery and which can make all the necessary parts to replicate itself. In other words, increasingly complex physical objects (the latest iteration of the RepRap 3D printer can incorporate basic printed circuits into its products) will soon be reproducible with almost the same ease as digital files. The technology can in theory use plastic refuse – old fizzy drink bottles – and could bring fairly high-tech manufacturing to remote locations. Is there a mechanism for paid-for printing? Should there be? Many people already put templates online for communal use, in the Free Software tradition. Others will wish to exact a payment for the work in creating and testing their objects. How should we view that request? When the discussions of ownership that are now restricted to the digital arena start to touch upon conventional manufacturing, what does that mean for our economic assumptions? And what should it mean?

Walter Benjamin wrote that 'Even the most perfect reproduction of a work of art is lacking in one element: its presence in time and space, its unique existence at the place where it happens to be.' But in the digital context, this is of only limited help; in the first place, digital objects do have a history of physical presence, though it's one we choose to ignore because it boggles our human scale perceptions somewhat: an existence as electrons arranged to hold information, which could actually be a very loose description of us, too. On the other hand, in the conventional setting, some artworks – and some objects – now never have a physical existence until they are reproduced. A little while ago (like quite a lot of people I know) I fell in love with the artwork of Sydney Padua's *Lovelace & Babbage* web comic.[5] Tentatively, I got in touch with Sydney and asked her about the originals. I had it in mind that I might try to persuade her to sell me one; but, of course, she draws the entire thing digitally. The brushstrokes and pencil lines are all intangible, and there has never been a fragile A2 sheet taped to an easel that I could have on my wall. (Instead of buying a drawing, I found a friend: as ever in my experience, the downsides of digital living were outweighed by unanticipated benefits.) So how would Benjamin find its 'unique existence'? But at the same time, would anyone (or at least, anyone not of the persuasion that original work is impossible) seriously deny Sydney's authorship of a unique piece of art just because pencil never touched paper?

No. Intellectual property, more than ever, is a line drawn around information, which asserts that despite having been set loose in the world – and having, inevitably, been created out of an individual's relationship with the world – that information retains some connection with its author that allows that person some control over how it is replicated and used.

In other words, the claim that lies beneath the notion of intellectual property is similar or identical to the one that underpins notions of privacy. It seems to me that the two are inseparable, because they are fundamentally aspects of the same issue, the need we have to be able to do something by convention that is impossible by force: the need to ringfence certain information. I believe that the most important unexamined notion – for policymakers and agitators both – in these debates is that they are one: you can't persuade people on the one hand to abandon intellectual property (a decision which, incidentally, would mean an even more massive upheaval in the way the world runs than we've seen so far since 1990) and hope to keep them interested in privacy. You can't trash privacy and hope to retain a sense of respect for IP.

~

Walter Benjamin wrote about art in the age of mechanical reproduction in 1935. The fear that machine-made objects are less real, less virtuous than those created by human hands reaches back further, to Victorian-era John Ruskin and his espousal of the gothic as an expression of the human soul. It's very much what you'd expect if creation and making really are central to being human. In the digital age, this question becomes one of pattern versus presence: a digital recording or live online connection versus the physical presence of a person in a room (or the physical presence of an artwork). Those who dislike digital interactions often assert that computer-mediated communication is different from and lesser than physical meeting.

If you're the right age, you may also remember the scene from *The Matrix* in which Laurence Fishburne sits back in a leather chair and skewers a bewildered Keanu Reeves with his gaze. All around them is a charred cityscape, a civilized world made ash. Fishburne wears black sunglasses that have no arms and so are affixed to the bridge of his nose; his voice is resonant with truth and a kind of menace. He says: 'Welcome . . . to the desert of the real.'

The Matrix came out in 1999; it was far from being the first film to suggest that the world we live in is an illusion, but certainly one of the most enjoyable. The uneasiness of the idea – that everything around us is fake, that at any moment someone may come along and show us the world rolled up like a scroll (to borrow from the Bible) and the real truth behind it all – flows through a lot of recent popular movies. *Memento*, *The Truman Show*, *Inception*, *Unknown*, *Dark City*: all of them are premised on some variant of the idea that the world as we understand it is not real. The idea has even been proposed as a literal scientific truth; the logic is that any universe capable of supporting life will eventually evolve technological life able to simulate a universe. Within a simulated universe, cultures will emerge that are similarly able, and so on and so on in an infinite regress of simulations. If there is only one physical universe and a potentially unlimited number of simulated ones, the chance that we are living in the original and not one of the simulations becomes vanishingly small.

Whether there's an underlying sense of worry about what's real – and I would say that there is, and that it derives in part from a sense not that the physical world isn't real but that some of our interactions are somehow not immanent, fraudulently mediated by cognition rather than directly experienced through our senses – we are in our everyday lives at pains to distinguish between things that are real and things that are not, and especially in our encounters with digital technology. Commentators – particularly those who are not in favour of digital media – are at pains to distinguish between 'real life' friends and those found and pre-dominantly encountered online. And, looking back at *Proust and the Squid* again, it seems to me that there is a difference: online friends are primarily understood through text – at least initially – which makes them friends you know cognitively before you know them through your senses. Your relationship is mainly thought-based. I'm not sure what that means in everyday terms, except that you don't have a physical sense of them, don't know how they move or smell or any of the other characteristics that, fairly or not, consciously or not, influence how we relate to people. For some, that makes life easier: there's no risk of being rejected on shallow physical criteria or having to explain or announce disabilities. I met someone when I was playing World of Warcraft and conversed with him on and off for months and never realized he was deaf until he told me; well, obviously: in the textual context it simply wasn't relevant.

But at the same time, when you talk only through text, you fail to receive any number of cues and signals. Text can be starkly emotionless, can appear unsympathetic, hence the desire to create simple textual signifiers of emotion – emoticons. They may not be subtle, but they do, at least, let you know when someone is teasing you where a flat line of text might simply look cruel. It's one of the most painful aspects of autism spectrum disorders, and one of those most likely to lead to difficult and distressing situations – memorably highlighted in Mark Haddon's novel, *The Curious Incident of the Dog in the Night-Time* – that those affected are sometimes unable to interpret facial expressions.

Physical communication goes a lot further than the face, though: the techniques of kinesic interview are about establishing a rapport with a subject by adopting similar postures – or pushing them away using aggressive stances, and so on. It's surprisingly easy to unsettle and even frighten a conversation partner by forcing yourself to communicate wrongly. Most people have at one time or another encountered someone who appears to be talking past them to empty space. We've all also been discomforted by someone who stands too close or stares too long. We've become cross because someone won't make eye contact, or suspected a friend or family member wasn't listening because they weren't making the small, affirmative noises we use to keep a conversation going. We have a lot of these minor cues, and if you depart from the narrow window of normal behaviour by even quite a small amount, people will find you rude. Stray too far and they will assume you are drunk, or mad.

But you don't get these things online, except as they are conveyed through text. The *New Yorker* cartoon has it right: online, no one knows you're a dog. Except that, in fact, there are some ways to tell things about people through text; there is a language of context that goes with Internet discourse. Email addresses, for example, can yield basic or even fairly complex information if you know how to read them: a .edu suffix means an American educational institution; .ac.uk means a British one. A Gmail address is generic, but a Gmail address with a common name without numbers – john@gmail.com – suggests a very early adopter of the Gmail service, someone who was already immersed in the Net in 2004. Apple's paid-for addresses have changed from mac.com to me.com, so someone who still uses a mac.com address is probably older than twenty-five and a little bit stubborn (like me). Other domains such as aol.com and .gov addresses tell other stories. Other services – blogs and Twitter pages – can have similar clues and cues.

Initially, you register these things consciously, but as with reading – and probably body language – the observations rapidly become almost unconscious. Just as a church can be read (although not perhaps to the degree implied by Dan Brown's *The Da Vinci Code*) and clothes convey tribal messages about status and mood, so a Twitter profile tells you something about the style of engagement of a user and who they are. I tend to assume that people who have many followers but choose to follow very few others, for example, are essentially disengaged and have not really understood the inherent contract of a level social playing field that Twitter implies.

It's interesting also that the University of Buffalo study[6] I mentioned earlier suggests that it's possible to empathize quite genuinely with fictional characters in text – well, yes, we all knew that, but it is now scientifically sound as a supposition – which in turn implies that a genuine emotional bond can be formed with a person via digital media. Again, when you spell it out, the first reaction is: well, yes, of course you can. But if that's the case, then what's the hang-up about the reality and authenticity of online communication? It's different, yes, and we should be alert to that difference and aware that we're exercising the cognitive part of the brain rather than the bits that deal with offline life. But it's hard to see why it should be thought of as lesser.

There is, though, a definite tendency to consider anything that happens in the offline, analogue world as real and authentic (a sense that probably owes a certain amount to the early adoption of 'IRL' – 'In Real Life' – by Internet communities such as the

WELL) and anything that happens online as unreal and probably inauthentic. I think partly this is because we are fundamentally analogue creatures; we are not cognitive homunculi riding in the control room of a giant fleshy robot, much as we occasionally imagine that we are. The sense of sight being in the head, along with the ears, nose, mouth and brain, sometimes gives us an exaggerated sense of the extent to which the 'I' is vested in the uppermost 13 per cent of the body. It's not true. We are tactile, physical creatures, our moods and perceptions created by our whole bodies (in one experiment – and I love this, because it's utterly alarming – researchers found that 'people whose frown muscles had been frozen with Botox took longer to read sad or angry sentences than they did before receiving the treatment').[7] The direct apprehension of things is really what persuades us they're real. We say 'I wouldn't believe it if I hadn't seen it with my own eyes' despite knowing that our eyes can be deceived by half a dozen tricks. We court the dissonance when we go to see professional magic shows; we know the magic isn't real, that it's a trick, but we enjoy the sense of bafflement and impossibility.

As the world embraces digital things, though, that simple posture – online fake, offline real – becomes more problematic. We've already looked at relationships mediated by the machine, but it goes beyond that. Online objects such as the currencies of various virtual worlds have real world value, for example; they represent work, time spent and are (artificially) scarce. Gold in Blizzard's online game, World of Warcraft, can be bought on a black market from gold sellers who obtain it by hiring cheap labour, often in South-East Asia, to sit and play the game for hours to accrue the virtual currency. WoW gold can be moved around the world and traded for conventional money such as euros or dollars. Items inside the game have a value in WoW gold, and in effort, and hence also in money. Some virtual universes have experienced in-game con tricks, thefts and so on; all part of the game, and yet at the same time also the removal of real monetary value from one person and its transferral to another person. How should we think of these events? And how should we think of the transfer of a digital Vorpal Sword between users in different countries if it has a value in real money? Is it subject to import tax?

But it's also important to ask whether there is any reason to assume that the more natural mode of communication – face-to-face – is inherently the superior one. The mediated form of communication allows people to express themselves from behind a translucent barrier. The mild anonymity of the Net frees many. The lack of consequences can make people bolder, less inhibited about seeking friendship. Casual meetings are easier, and interaction can yield more serious relationships: a genuine meeting of minds. I cannot help but wonder whether the suspicion of this kind of meeting (an idea celebrated until it was actually possible, and now regarded with scepticism) derives from that same cultural perception I described earlier which sees the mystical journey, which cannot be expressed in words but must be experienced immanently, as far more important than the cognitive kind.

I believe that a balance is necessary: I think there's much to be gained from satisfying the various aspects of the human self. But I think it's mistaken to say that one is superior to the other, just as it's ridiculous to claim that fish are superior to birds. An ostrich under thirty foot of water is in trouble, yes, but so is a tuna on a mountain top. Each of them in its element is immensely successful. In the context of human life, though, we need both access to the immanent experience, through our senses, and the chance to think, read and analyse with our cognitive selves. Pattern and presence are both significant, and the reality is that in our own internal context they may actually be indivisible.

~

The issue of pattern and presence is also part of the wrangles over copyright. When I was ten, commercial content like music was indivisible from the medium on which it was purchased (usually vinyl, although cassettes were the coming thing, much derided by music purists as low-fi) and people never really considered – and companies never sought to educate them – whether they were paying for the physical object or for access to the content via a storage medium. That confusion was thrown into sharp relief by the arrival of tape-to-tape machines and the dawning realization among record companies that people were taping songs from the radio. In the popular perception, when you bought a copy of an album, it was then no one's business what you did with it. You could see this as a notion of 'exhaustion of rights', but I think that's over-complicating it. Purchase carried an item from the public world of rules and exchange into the private world of the hearth. Once brought into the hearth, the object was then subject to hearth rules, not public ones. If you chose to use your vinyl as a coaster, the record company could not come in and tell you that was wrong. Why should they do so if you then chose to record that album on to a cassette so that you could listen to an inferior recording on your new (enormous) Sony Walkman? It was none of their business what you did in your private space.

That discussion was never properly resolved: the kind of legislative clarity that would produce some kind of sanity seems to be completely beyond elected assemblies: the process almost immediately becomes a festival of self-interested lobbying and ridiculous demands, and those of us who are neither red-toothed zealots of IP protectionism nor freevangelists seeking a world where intellectual property is deemed to be held in common go unheard in the din.

The problem is that the content industries as they exist (or possibly as they existed until recently, although the change is far from wholehearted) are largely premised on the idea that their products are both rivalrous and excludable, i.e. that an item that I have cannot also be possessed by you, and that it is relatively simple to prevent me from getting access to it in the first place unless I pay. This set the scene for a showdown. On the one hand, content licensees and vendors – who are often, by the nature of the industries involved, not content creators – set their teeth against the reality of the present day, namely that it is simply impossible, in any reasonably private and democratic society, to police content to the degree that would be required to secure intellectual property absolutely; on the other, organizations such as the Pirate Party are apparently unable or unwilling to outline a way for creators to make a living in a world where their primary skill no longer produces anything that can be sold. (I interviewed Andrew Robinson, then leader of the Pirate Party UK, for FutureBook in 2010. I asked him how creatives would make a living in the new world.[8] He replied: 'This is an interesting point, is it the job of politicians to look purely at what is morally right or wrong when making laws, or should we also be expected to devise new business models to replace ones that have been made obsolete by technology? In a way, it's odd that the Pirate Party is expected to extrapolate our moral position into business practices; however it's very easy to do so. Simply put, the middlemen will have a much smaller role, and the public will deal directly with the creators of content. File sharing will be understood by content creators as an indispensable source of free advertising.' Which is interesting, but still doesn't tell me specifically how anyone earns a crust in an environment where people don't feel they need to pay for content.)

In the meantime, the popular understanding of what is and is not okay, either legally or ethically, is confused by the shouting, and rests on knee-jerk reactions and inaccurate perceptions. For example, many buyers of books believe that the bulk of the cost of a paper copy is physical and therefore reason that the electronic version should be massively cheaper. While there are considerable savings in the production of an electronic book, and many publishers have yet to take full advantage of the digital workflow, it's also true that a large part of book production cost is human: paying editors and writers and so on. So yes, you are indeed paying for intangibles, but those intangibles are people. Moreover, the high price of an ebook during the period of the hardback publication is nothing to do with the physical cover – obviously – but a tariff for early access, something that publishers have failed to communicate largely because the idea of explaining pricing decisions to consumers remains alien: the old media industries are not at all used to having to make a case for themselves. They are continually playing catch-up.

The most recent example of this in my life is Amazon's free ebook lending system, where the company 'lends' readers one ebook at a time for an indefinite period. In fact, in many cases, Amazon is buying the ebook from the publisher at full price and passing it on without charge to the consumer. The only reason I can see for doing this is to create and corner the market in ebook lending, then turn around to publishers and demand terms for access to a thriving industry. In other words, Amazon is purchasing itself yet another arena in which to be massively dominant. The problems with companies owning a given market outright are too obvious and well-known to enumerate, but that is potentially the price to the consumer of the 'free' ebook scheme.

While some may feel ambiguous about paying for pattern – the most common interpretation of 'information yearns to be free' these days is that anything that can be digitized should be given away – almost everyone now uses their own pattern as currency. We trade our personal data to sites such as Facebook in exchange for services that are notionally free at the point of use. But in fact, they're not. The currency of the Internet, as we already know, is attention. Facebook is not free: you pay for it with your data, which is then traded on to get attention – and not just your attention, specifically, although ads will be targeted and tailored directly to you, but the attention of the group or groups you represent, the cross-referenced, modelled, Platonic you.

The peril of this kind of 'free' lies in the clouding of what's actually taking place. What price would you put on your personal data if I just flat out asked you to sell it to me? Obviously, some of it is relevant to the security of your bank account and your credit card, so you might have to go to the trouble of changing your pass phrases, a considerable aggravation. Then there's the creepy factor: the idea that I might plug you into a machine and learn secrets, or just truths, about you; that I might then be able to influence you in subtle ways to do things you might feel weren't really in your interests. I'd know details about your friends and family by implication, too. So for comparison: what value would you put on Facebook's service if you had to pay for it directly? A pound a month? Ten? You surely would not expect to pay more for it than you do for your broadband connection. Let's set an arbitrary figure of £200 a year, which seems astronomically high to me. Is that value lower or higher than the price you'd put on your personal data, considering what might be done with it?

Beyond the point of individual discomfort with the exchange of information for services is the issue of what happens to a market where the whole point of most pricing strategies is to prevent the consumer from getting an accurate understanding of what a product costs relative to what it is worth. Our economic system, and indeed our version of liberal democratic capitalism, rely at root on the admittedly overstretched and tarnished notion that the market makes good decisions about price based on the collective, rational self-interest of those buying and selling. If one side of that equation is deprived of information – deliberately and for the express purpose of preventing them from making decisions as they otherwise would – the paradigm of our society is broken; weight and influence are accorded to products that are not the best they could be, and to the companies that make them. The deliberate creation of pricing strategies that occlude the reality of the transaction undermines the basic assumptions of our system. (You might say: 'Fantastic! We're undermining the system from within, man! We're letting the inherent contradictions of the machine tear it apart!' In which case, great. But you need to have a plan for how to prevent the eventual collapse of the machine from killing a lot of people.)

It's something we don't often consider, but in our kind of society, buying is voting. That's to say that the decision to purchase your groceries from, for the sake of argument, your local Tesco is an endorsement not just of your nearest supermarket and their stock, but of every action taken by the Tesco company anywhere in the world. Every purchase made at Tesco increases their turnover, raising their profile, and therefore also their influence in any lobbying they may undertake. It also represents a lost sale to their competitors large and small, because you won't go and buy food for that week from them and you would have had to buy food somewhere. As the company's market share increases, Tesco is able to be more robust with suppliers, too, demanding better rates. For the company it's a virtuous cycle; for others, that's not so clear.

It may mean that the Tesco style of doing business becomes the only viable one, a complaint made about chain supermarkets in general quite often in connection with the revitalization (or destruction) of local community town centres (a government report commissioned in 1998 found that 'when a large supermarket is built on the edge of the centre, other food shops lose between 13 and 50% of their trade').[9] The savings created by economies of scale may be balanced by intangible or hard-to-measure costs, either environmental (as goods are moved to central depots and then out again around the country) or social (as small grocers and local businesses fail to compete with the giants around them). They may not be local: the buying power of major chains can affect the national markets of other countries. Farmers needing to meet a price point may seek and receive greater subsidies from the government, further unbalancing the already bizarre economics of global agriculture.

If this seems familiar and grindingly depressing, of course, it is. This is the problem of connectedness we discussed earlier: how is it possible to encompass all these variables and arrive at a right action that is also one you can actually carry out and live with? It may sound great to refuse to buy from supermarkets, but it can involve considerable extra effort and expense, and even then, you aren't guaranteed to have done the right thing. But note well: this isn't a problem resulting from digital technology, but rather from the nested structures of globalization and the inherited consequences of empire and colonial history. That's not an instruction to hang your head in shame because you carry a European or American passport: rather it's an acknowledgement that the issues are complex, that they did not spring from nowhere, and that they are locked in and hence hard to deal with in a positive way. All that's changed is that our technology has begun, inevitably, to make us aware of them, and of the reality of the faceless people around the world and two doors down who suffer in consequence of them.

~

There's another aspect to the discussion of services that are notionally free at point of use. When you pay for a service in personal data, you aren't a consumer. You are not, as media theorist Douglas Rushkoff observes pointedly, Facebook's customer.[10] You are the commodity in which the company behind the service trades. Rushkoff suggests that users fundamentally do not trust Facebook, because they know there's a tension between what they want the service to do and what the service provider needs from it. And it's certainly true that in my experience of using the service, it is set up to avoid giving me perfect control of my data. When the new Instant Personalization service was rolled out recently – a service that allowed Facebook to pass data to partner websites to allow them to customize their services for Facebook users – it was impossible to switch off before the service went live. In the run-up to the launch, the option to disable Instant Personalization was visible (buried deep in the site's somewhat arcane privacy settings interface, where many users never venture anyway) but not alterable. To turn it off, you had to wait until after it was switched on.

Being a consumer, a customer, implies a measure of control over the nature of the relationship. The provider of a service sets out to please the customer; unhappy customers generally mean that a company is doing less well than it could. Customers assume – and receive – a certain level of care. The service is set up to make things work well for them. The commodity, on the other hand, gets the minimum necessary attention to keep it in a marketable state. More, companies will always try to get more and more out of their resources; it's the natural momentum of capitalism. Perhaps the best way to change your understanding of who's on top in the context of companies that use this business model is to compare them with livestock farms. The farm animals might imagine that they are the beneficiaries of the farmer's efforts. Pigs get mash and a place to live; cows get open fields, barns when it's cold and plenty of hay. They even get medical care and, in extreme cases, massages. They are, of course, not the customer. For some of them, this will become apparent when they are brought into a narrow pen and emerge as sausages. For others – cows on dairy farms, for example – the prognosis is less stark. They will simply live a life of ease from which others will profit.

It's impossible, in this society, to go through life without ever being treated as a commodity. And it's not as if commodification renders a person powerless. I'm writing this page in the week of 4 July 2011. The *News of the World* newspaper, founded in 1843 and with a circulation in April of 2.6 million, will cease to exist on Sunday. The reason: the massed disdain of the British public. The paper has been caught hacking the mobile telephones not just of celebrities and politicians (an invasion of privacy that interested the readership only in passing, and which was by and large settled by out-of-court payments) but of murder victims and their families, possibly compromising evidence in ongoing investigations and – in the case of Milly Dowler – causing loved ones to believe that she might still be alive. The final straw was the discovery that the paper had also intruded on the private grief of the families of dead British servicemen. Campaigns appeared, on Facebook and elsewhere, boycotting the paper, and advertisers withdrew. What was a going concern a month ago is now a ruin because the readers used their status as a commodity and simply refused to be sold any longer. The shockwaves from this very public self-destruction are still bouncing around: there are rumours of investigations in the United States, and the Murdoch news empire is for the moment greatly weakened.

In the general run of things, however, power flows in the opposite direction: in tiny, essentially useless amounts from each person to a central pool where storage and analysis can transform it into money and significant influence. We tend to assume that that power is benign, especially in the case of Google, whose playful animations, goofy logo and renowned 'Don't be evil' motto have made it the most trusted commercial brand in modern history. We cannot assume that that will always be the case. Google is, after all, a corporate entity, subject – impossible as it may seem now at the height of its strength – to takeover, and to changes of policy. Or to being broken up; Google has brushed up against anti-trust legislation any number of times recently. If you feel comfortable with Google having all that information, let me ask again whether you feel equally happy with it in the hands of News International (the parent company of Fox News), the agri-giant Monsanto, or BP?

Accepting commodification has other downsides, one of which is that it probably contributes to a phenomenon called deindividuation, which is a strange and powerful thing I'll come back to later. Another is what Eli Pariser writes about in *The Filter Bubble*: the creation of a bubble of information that confirms what you want to believe is true. When you're a commodity, it's in the interests of those who sell you to streamline you, make you more predictable and thus a more appealing target for marketing. Pariser's warning is compelling and important: increasingly, the search results I see online are different from the ones you see. Google results, since 2009, are personalized according to various datapoints the company has about you when you search. The broadest ones are things like physical location, but your search history is a factor, too. As Pariser puts it, as of 2009, a search for a contentious topic like 'proof of climate change' will return different answers for a sceptic or an environmentalist. The danger is that our online interactions become not so much an encounter with the wider world, but with our own preconceptions: a feedback loop that simply confirms everything we want to believe.

That's a problem for more than just research. It implies the gradual segregation of society along pre-existing lines of entrenched opinion. Rather than a broadening of debate and interaction, it suggests a fossilization – and that's a disaster – another degrading of the collective ability to make good decisions on which our democracies rely.

One of the grand benefits of digitization is the ability to tap into the phenomenon known as 'the wisdom of crowds'. Tasks that are difficult or tedious for an individual or a small group can be tackled by a crowd in a short period of time. Crowds can be inventive and powerful problem-solvers. The most dramatic instance of this recently – though it's not quite a classic example – has been the production of an accurate model of an enzyme by players of the online game Fold.it. The Mason-Pfizer monkey virus retroviral protease that had eluded scientists for fifteen years was successfully modelled in ten days by gamers working in teams and against one another.

The idea that groups can solve problems has become a commonplace: the idealized expression is the 'guess the weight of a cow' game mentioned in James Surowiecki's book *The Wisdom of Crowds*. An issue is placed before the group (the weight of a cow at a county fair), each member of which brings to the problem their own unique perspective and expertise (farmers, vets, butchers, fishermen, children, cooks and so on having different perspectives). The amalgamation of their thoughts is performed mathematically (by averaging or a more complex approach such as Bayes' Theorem, the bad guesses at either end of the spectrum cancelling one another out), and very often the end results are excellent to the point of being spooky. It would be reassuring to think that our parliamentary systems work this way, but they don't. Crowd wisdom is fragile, and requires quite exacting conditions of behaviour to be met or it goes very, very wrong. Participants must not communicate with one another too much. They must think about the issue, rather than hewing to an established ideological or theoretical position. The process of haggling and horse-trading that is central to the political arena is disastrous: personalities and popularity skew the results. Habit and tradition are fatal. Debate and consensus can be ruinous: the system needs your raw response, not what you arrive at after an hour talking to someone you find attractive or intimidating, and certainly not the position you adopt if you're offered a cabinet post in exchange for supporting someone else's position. Recent research in Switzerland suggests that too much discussion can 'promote information feedback and therefore trigger convergence', resulting in overconfidence in false beliefs.[11]

In other words, personalized search results actually have the potential to wreck our ability to make good decisions as a group before we ever have a chance to exercise it. This is the kind of technology that might make the difference between the dream world and the nightmare: it has the potential to create an increasingly ignorant population basing their decisions on decreasing amounts of information and greater and greater amounts of shared opinion. Worse, it may actually limit our ability to come up with new ideas. Many researchers believe that creativity is stimulated by the collision of ideas from different arenas or schools of thought, the clash creating new perspectives, narratives and solutions. Inside the filter bubble, the likelihood of that kind of collusion is vastly reduced. And so, too, is the possibility of coming to understand the point of view of someone radically different from oneself.

One of the great promises of the Internet, that it would introduce us to people unlike ourselves, is shorn away in favour of a tight, suburban circle of prejudices and comforting nonsense. It's a massive false step. But at the same time, perhaps it shunts us away from asking questions of search engines and back towards other people. Services like Twitter, where you can essentially put the power of the crowd to work for you directly, unmediated by Google's algorithms, can also answer questions and, if you choose, you can include among those you follow people who infuriate and challenge you. Human beings – as the Fold.it experiment shows – can achieve remarkable things by being human to the greatest extent possible. Twitter, if you elect to use it in a way that opens up your world rather than shutting it down, will also point you to the news stories you might otherwise miss, the opinions you don't share, the values you don't endorse. But that decision comes from you. As with much of this discussion, it is a matter of choice: a consequence of your own decisions about who and what you want to be. But to make that decision, you first have to be aware that it exists.

blindgiant.co.uk/chapter5

6

Tahrir and London

CHOICES AND THE Internet were at the heart of the news in the UK in 2011. The revolutions in the Middle East – now called the Arab Spring – and the riots that kicked off in London in the early summer both spoke to questions of identity and to the role of digital communications media in life and politics. Both were trumpeted as the product of a new connected age, impossible without the mobile phone and the Internet, and I think it's clear that they would not have happened as they did without those technologies. But what happened in either case, and why, is unsurprisingly a little more complex – and nuanced – than the news industry and the political commentators acknowledged at the time.

In mid-December 2010 Mohamed Bouazizi, a Tunisian fruit seller brutalized by police, went to the local governor's office in the town of Sidi Bouzid and set himself on fire. He died eighteen days later. His action marked – perhaps triggered – the beginning of revolutions not only in his own country but across the Middle East. At the time of writing, the outcomes of several of them are in doubt. The most well-documented for my purposes, and perhaps the most complete – though revolutions stand or fall not only in their moments of high civil unrest but also perhaps more so, later, when the conflicting drives, needs and political agendas of the revolutionaries must be matched and melded into something that resembles a state that caters to all – is Egypt.

Egypt's revolution, in early 2011, crystallized around a similar event: the killing of Khaled Said in June the previous year, allegedly because he had evidence of criminal activity by police. A local act of wickedness became symbolic of the status of every citizen. This is a classic revolutionary pattern: in an environment saturated with discontent but held in stasis by force and fear, one more thing precipitates a transformation, a sudden and massively powerful shrugging off by the population. Iconic images and narratives of oppression become universal experiences, shared references telling a story of sorrow, desperation and anger.

The Boston Tea Party is perhaps the standout of the American revolutionary narrative. In the context of the Russian revolutions of 1917, the most famous such rallying point must be the mutiny on board the battleship *Potemkin*, immortalized by Sergei Eisenstein's propaganda film of the same name. The mutiny, which was part of the failed uprising in 1905, was triggered when members of the crew were threatened with punishment for refusal to eat food containing maggots. As with Mohamed Bouazizi and Khaled Said in their countries, the situation aboard the *Potemkin* resonated with the whole of Russia. In the 1917 February Revolution that eventually toppled the tsar, food was – inevitably – back at the heart of popular discontent. Russian casualties in the First World War were in the millions, the weather had been appalling, and with so many young men away fighting, famine was imminent. Soldiers mutinied when ordered to suppress demonstrations largely composed of women demanding bread and peace. The *Potemkin*'s maggots were a perfect metaphor for the state of the nation.

The Egyptian revolution is relevant here because Khaled Said's name became a totem first of all on Facebook: a page was created which asserted that 'We are all Khaled Said'. As the crisis grew and grew, it happened live on Twitter. The activists and citizen journalists of Egypt and their supporters overseas used Twitter to get news out all the time, to let one another know what was happening, to coordinate on the fly – until they were face to face and no mediated communication was necessary. They used Facebook to gather and – somewhat – to coordinate. Above all, perhaps, they used social media to let others know that they existed, that they shared outrage and pain – and hope. That they had now decided that this was where they drew the line, even in the face of the administration's secret police, the Mukhabarat. Before there is a physical revolution, there is a mental and emotional one, which occurs in private: 'I will no longer suffer this.' Through Twitter, Facebook and other social media services, the online community of Egypt let one another know that they had reached that point, and did so in public, to some extent nailing their colours to the mast.

It is a mistake, though, to call this a 'Twitter revolution'. The country was seething with a sense of injustice, and had been for years. The poor of Egypt, without access to the digital communications media, were every bit as much a part of the revolution as their middle-class compatriots. The working class, who from 2006 onwards had been participating in strike actions in protest against the regime, were there, too, and their refusal to work in January heralded the beginning of the revolution. The long offline organization by activists was at least as impressive as that which took place in the final days online. Leaflets were distributed, guides to revolution that listed things you might need, places to meet, and how to deal with teargas. Many of them featured desperate pleas not to put the material online where it could be intercepted by the security forces.[1]

Social media have the effect of creating a powerful sense of mood, allowing a community to reflect upon itself. There is an effect – not always entirely beneficial – of amplification, as we look at the amount of support for our position and feel more assured. The Swiss research into crowd wisdom I mentioned in the last chapter has ascertained that this may cause crowds to make less good decisions with greater confidence, but in the case of revolution, perhaps that irrationality is necessary to drive immediate self-preservation into second place and assert instead an overriding need for change which requires drastic action. Some writers on rapid social change – including American academic Ted Gurr – have suggested that revolution occurs when the variance between the way we believe the world should be and how it actually is becomes too pronounced to ignore. Social media, spreading the narratives of Khaled Said and others, no doubt intensified and even speeded up this process, drawing more and more people into the discussion and letting them know they were not alone. But the conditions that lay beneath all this were ghastly and bleakly ubiquitous. The advent of a popular uprising requires a seed, which can be almost anything, and – to extend the metaphor – a growing medium. But the urge is there all along.

Social media are a great tool for spreading the word, and thus the seed – though they are far from being the only way – but the revolution was on the streets of Cairo, Suez and Alexandria, not behind computer screens. As Nadia Idle and Alex Nunns point out in their excellent introduction to *Tweets from Tahrir*, it's convenient to the West, with its decades-long complicity in Hosni Mubarak's regime, to imagine that all that was necessary to remove him was a few days of unrest organized through US-based websites. It would be more honest to acknowledge that Egypt's overnight sea-change was years in the making, and that while social media may have shaped it, even precipitated it, they did not make it. Like all revolutions, it happened because it could no longer be prevented.

The same is true of what happened in the UK. It came on like a sudden storm and grew into something utterly unexpected – except by any number of community workers who had been warning of something like it for months. By the end of August 2011 the riots were winding down in London, though elsewhere in the country it seemed they were just starting up. Sparked by the shooting by police of Mark Duggan in Tottenham, these thunderclap outbreaks of looting and violence had spread around the capital and around the country. They had their own Twitter hashtags – keywords that allow users of the service to access other messages using the same terms – creating an instant network of wreckers and thugs. But so, too, did the spontaneous, self-organizing clean-up crews, the Riot Wombles, named for the 1960s children's book series *The Wombles*, in which orange-skinned, pointy-nosed creatures living in burrows help the environment by collecting and re-using junk. Later studies seemed to show that more people used the social media for amelioration than did for mayhem.

And indeed, though the riots were initially seen as a phenomenon of 'feral youth' (I cannot tell you how much I object to the use of the term 'feral' to describe a human being; a brief look at the *OED* will tell you why), the subsequent trials skewed towards adult offenders, with the largest single age group being 18–20-year-olds.[2] Of a sample of 1,715 (alleged) rioters, 364 were 10–17 years of age, while 890 were 18–24. A further 318 were 25–34, with the rest older. Many rioters were also already, in the quaint phrase, well-known to law enforcement. The image popular with newspapers of untamed tweens in revolt during the riots seems less than entirely accurate.

At the time, an eerie unanimity appeared across the political spectrum: these were crimes without causes, a groundless wickedness to be condemned without hesitation or discussion. It was to be understood that seeking the origins of this phenomenon was futile, and any attempt to analyse what was going on amounted to an *apologia*. Although some journalists and commentators have now broken away from this line, our political class by and large has not. From the government and from the opposition the position was clear: these events were to be discussed without reference to the past or the present context. This was a lightning outbreak of immorality, something like a plague of demonic possession except that those involved had simply revealed themselves to be rotten from the outset.

This position was reinforced when the rioters, when interviewed, were unable to explain their actions. The BBC found two teenaged girls and asked why they were looting a shop. 'We're showing the police we can do what we want,' one said. The interviewer responded by asking why they were destroying a small local shop in their own community. 'It's the rich people,' she said, but seemed entirely at a loss to understand either the question or her own answer. 'They own shops. We're showing the rich we can do what we want.' Her friend didn't speak. (And to be honest: how on earth were they supposed to understand what was happening to and around them? The psychological mechanics of popular discontent and group violence are complex and obscure. Short of discovering some kind of rioting John Stuart Mill setting fire to a burning car, an autodidact of the social science of rage and bewilderment, the BBC was surely never going to get any kind of answer other than 'we're angry and upset'. Certainly, nothing the rioters themselves could have said would answer the retributive fury that was building all around them, unless they'd been able to produce evidence of grotesque abuse at the hands of police and merchants on a par with something from the bad days of Kosovo. That fury and the demands for heavy sentences are entirely understandable, if not necessarily wise as a matter of policy. What happened was ugly. But that is not the same as saying that the riots cannot or should not be understood.)

Our main parties have a vested interest in separating the riots from the social history of the UK. Margaret Thatcher famously told Britain that 'there is no such thing as society', and it's hard to miss the relevance of that dictum to what happened. The British style of policing relies heavily on consent, on a connection to other people and on a mass investment in the idea of community which is jeopardized by the hyper-individuality the

Thatcher era espoused. Tony Blair's Labour Party, and later Gordon Brown's, presided over the last decade and a half; if social conditions and the financial crisis are to blame for any of this, Labour – which courted business and finance even more assiduously than the Conservatives have traditionally done – cannot evade its share of responsibility for them.

The Cameron–Osborne response to the financial crisis, meanwhile, has seen bankers regain their explosively impressive bonuses while the institutions they control continue to refuse to lend to small businesses. (By way of an extreme comparison, consider the German response to the crisis: the former CEO of the bank IKB, whose handling of the bond market appears to have been honest if in the end massively over-trusting of the US ratings agencies Moody's and S&P, was sentenced to prison and asked to return his salary. That salary, incidentally, was €805,000, which is a lot of money, but barely makes a mark on the earnings of comparable UK CEOs.)

Both Labour and the Conservatives have also leaned on an idea of increasing prosperity as the natural order of things; like Icelanders before the 2007 crash, Britons have been encouraged to believe that they will grow wealthier each day, that credit will always be cheap, that the shops will always be full of discounted items and freebies, that a comfortably affluent lifestyle of increasing luxury is within reach of – even, is a natural right of – everyone in the country.

I don't see this background as irrelevant to what happened. The rioters were disengaged from their world to the point of destroying it for reasons they themselves could not express. They were alienated from themselves, too, heedless of consequences they knew must come, but somehow they didn't care or could not apply those consequences to themselves. They became, briefly, almost psychopathic, in that one of the distinguishing marks of psychopathy that can be measured in a magnetic resonance imaging scan is an inability to anticipate future suffering. So what happened to them? How did the nation lose its head?

In the 1930s US Depression there was a powerful sense that obeying the rules did you no good; being a law-biding citizen, working hard and saving, had turned out not to lead to the American Dream, which at the time was solidly middle class: a house in the suburbs with a white picket fence and a community of like-minded fellows around you, kids going to good schools and then on to college and growing more prosperous in the next generation, and any one of them might one day be President. The key was a notion of bettering oneself; but in the 1930s, the Dream was abruptly very far off, and a nightmare took over: no matter how hard you worked you might not make enough money to feed your family. You might slip down rather than climb up the social ladder. Certainly that white picket fence was nowhere in sight.

The point here is not absolute deprivation, though there was a fair measure of that, both in 1930s America and in 2011 UK, despite the cry that 'these kids have BlackBerries, they're not poor': as asinine a statement as I can imagine when there are people all around the world with cellphones who are otherwise living in conditions we would consider unthinkable. Rather, the issue is relative deprivation, the gap between the way people believe – or have been led to believe – their world will be, and the way it is. If you cannot get the things you have been told are natural to you, you will become angry, or, perhaps, in another cultural context, depressed and withdrawn: maybe that's part of why Japan, whose economy has already suffered a blow like the one we are now experiencing, produced its *hikikomori*. Be that as it may, in the UK situation at present, and unquestionably also in the US, where the Occupy camps are still going strong, there is a perceived issue of fairness. The concept is deeply rooted in us: there are experiments in Game Theory that show how deeply. One of them is called the Ultimatum Game.

In the Ultimatum Game, two players have to determine the split of a pot of money. One player offers a given split, and the other can accept or reject the proposal. If the second player rejects the split, neither one of them gets anything. Although the results can be variable, a surprising amount of the time the second player will reject a split that seems unfair even though the net gain of doing so is (inevitably) less than that of acceptance of even a bad deal. In other words, there is some evidence to show that people will reject an unfair settlement simply because it is unfair, rather than because it is not sufficiently advantageous. Turning the game around, there is a simpler version that does not technically qualify as a game, because the second player has no options within the structure. In the Dictator Game, the first player can simply dispose of the amount as they see fit. The second player can do nothing to affect this result. All the same, many of those cast as dictators do share the money.

Returning to the broken American Dream of the Depression era, the 1930s produced the gangster as we understand him now, and the expression of him in the media bled into the reality until the two were not separable. Cultural critic Robert Warshow described him in his screen incarnation as a creature bent on violence and crime as an end in itself, a man who does badness because it's what defines him. The gangster's salient feature, though, is that he won't accept – cannot accept – being part of a herd of persons who live without hope despite doing everything right. His response to the Depression is to rebel, to rewrite the rules in his own favour. He recognizes something fundamental about our capitalist democratic society, and something that is perhaps more obvious about the United States, which possesses a written constitution: we ourselves make the rules. They can be rewritten by us. Situations like the Depression are not, emphatically, inhuman. They are the product of human action, and it is against these humans, in the form of policemen and judges and bank managers, that the gangster – like the girl interviewed by the BBC – rebels. He chooses to stand above the rest, screaming defiance, and ultimately gets cut down by the larger group, or, at least, by the representatives of the supposed silent majority that has chosen the opposite course.

It's hardly an unfamiliar narrative in these recession days. And it makes sense, as well, in the context of the Arab Spring. An intolerable situation made people brave, or so numb that an ordinary greengrocer became a self-immolating martyr. The psychological effect of a societal dissonance was to make individuals behave – and think and feel – in a way that under less pressurized circumstances they would not have. The phenomenon is called 'deindividuation'. It is said to be a consequence both of the influence of wicked regimes and, in another way, of the anonymity and apparently consequence-free environment of the Internet.

~

The classic deindividuation study was done with Hallowe'en sweets: children who felt their individual activities could not be traced to them were likely to take more sweets from a bowl than those who knew they were observed and thus roped into the norms of sharing, generosity and moderation. It's obvious enough from one's own experience. But the most famous and interesting deindividuation story is the one they made the film about: the notorious Stanford Prison Experiment, which was conducted in 1971 by Philip Zimbardo. It has never been repeated because it went so well it nearly turned into a catastrophe. The strangest, saddest and bleakest thing I read in preparing this book was Zimbardo's account of what happened. His horror comes across as a fracture in his life, like a bereavement: 'I wish I could say that writing this book was a labor of love; it was not . . . it was emotionally painful . . . Time had dimmed my memory of the extent of creative evil in which many of the guards engaged, the extent of the suffering of many of the prisoners, and the extent of my passivity in allowing the abuses to continue for as long as they did.'

In the experiment, male students were selected to participate on the basis of having no negative personality traits – no narcissists, no sadists and so on. In other words, they were selected for not being dangerous monstrous bastards. They were then split into two groups, prisoners and guards. They were given uniforms and sent down to a basement level to live for two weeks in character. The experiment was halted after six days when it became apparent that the well-adjusted, hand-picked guards were becoming frighteningly violent with the prisoners. The ordinary, decent students had turned into dangerous, monstrous bastards.

Theorists highlight a number of factors: anonymity and participation in a group, diffusion of blame, hierarchy giving orders to subordinates whose defined job was not to think but to act. Students in the SPE apparently believed that if they stepped over the line, the experimenters would stop them before they went too far. Let me reiterate: these were people who should have known, without a shadow of doubt, where the line was and what 'too far' meant. They should not have needed a safety net to prevent them from administering a serious beating to a fellow student in an experiment. But they did. They had surrendered that aspect of the self to the rules of the game they were playing as they perceived it.

I cannot help but see deindividuation in the professional ethos I've discussed elsewhere in this book; in the claim that functionaries must act in accordance with decisions taken by higher-ups, that it's 'not their job' to make ethical decisions. I also wonder about people working in the banks during the sub-prime days. Reading journalist and former bond salesman Michael Lewis's extraordinary journeys through the US and European financial systems (*The Big Short* and *Boomerang*), it's hard not to think that those traders, many of whom knew on some level that the market could not possibly work this way for ever, were under the influence of a deindividuating situation in which they saw themselves as absolved of responsibility by the system in the same way as Zimbardo's students. It simply was not part of their assigned role to object, so they didn't.

The effect has been linked since the Stanford experiment with some of the really appalling moments in human conduct in the modern world, such as the Vietnam My Lai massacre and the mistreatment of prisoners at Abu Ghraib. One of the early projects that points to deindividuation – though it actually dealt with blind obedience – was performed by Stanley Milgram in 1963. Milgram put subjects in the position of thinking they were administering electric shocks to a test subject in another room. Under the guidance of experimenters, and despite the increasingly desperate pleas from a stooge in the other room claiming to be in mortal agony or even to be dying, 65 per cent continued the test to the very end, administering what was supposed to be a 450-volt shock to the (non-existent) test subject on the other end of the wire. In the shadow of the Nazi Holocaust, Milgram's experiments are telling and bleakly fascinating. With Milgram in mind, look again at Philip Zimbardo's reference to his own behaviour. One feels he was affected both by an internal version of Milgram's experiment in which he was both researcher and subject, and by the deindividuation affecting the test groups: they were anonymized and distanced by their roles as prisoners and guards, he by his as disinterested and objective observer.

So deindividuation is a huge phenomenon: a societal force, a shaper of revolutions and of horrors. It is also attributed to situations where individuals feel downward pressure and stress upon them that they cannot sustain; the self melts into the larger group as a defence against a situation that it does not understand and in which the individual feels there is no right course, no survival strategy. In other words, it's an aspect of how people living under regimes that have no compunction about torturing and killing dissenters cope, and how they eventually come out of the shadows and rebel, despite knowing objectively that many of them will probably die. They become part of something larger, and that larger entity is angry and cannot effectively be punished or destroyed.

The same force is also at work, apparently, in the way people act online. Anonymized and disconnected (in the face-to-face sense) from the people with whom they interact, Internet users can become spiteful and splenetic to a degree that would never be permitted in a physical social context, or, if it were, it would be profoundly uncomfortable and might devolve into violence. This can be seen as another aspect of the crowd phenomenon: self-reinforcing certainties unchecked by social brakes derived from actual presence.

French psychologist Gustave Le Bon proposed at the end of the nineteenth century that this kind of anonymity resulted automatically in a kind of lowest common denominator of human behaviour, a disinhibition. (Eben Moglen would no doubt counter that anonymity, and perhaps that very disinhibition, is a vital aspect of the liberty of the individual. If you feel there may be adverse consequences to expressing your opinion, your free speech is muffled and democracy suffers – as indeed does the wisdom of the crowd.) It seems that loss of contact with the world and of understanding of the self's place in it can lead to a kind of inability (or unwillingness, which in this context becomes the same thing) to regulate one's own behaviour. In the digital arena, where norms are either contested or not established, where there is an apparent anonymity, and where ultimately everyone is speaking not from their buttoned-up, outside-world self but from the unmoderated hearth, the private kingdom, the normal constraints seem not to apply.

It has to be acknowledged that there are profound differences of degree here. Those living under the kind of regime that was prevalent in the Middle East undergo an extreme version of this process, an absolute bewilderment that leads to the kind of wild, appalling demonstrations of pain that culminate in self-immolation. In the case of the UK riots, a growing sense of abandonment and contempt seems to have been a major factor, a hopelessness that I think does strongly mirror the US 1930s' experience, and will do so ever more if the situation worsens and persists, as now seems likely.

By comparison, the deindividuation of Internet use is mild, and perhaps somewhat differently constructed – but still very real. Net users feel anonymous because they are physically alone and can choose screen names and so on (and because the general awareness of how exposed a given user is on the Internet is quite low). The lack of a physical component means there are no obvious adverse consequences to anything that happens, which implies that there will be no blame. It's even possible that the constant barrage of legalese, far from restraining users, actually liberates them: if there are rules aplenty and structures to prevent you from doing things, that means that anything that is possible must be acceptable. Further, the world is formed neatly into teams, and the enemy is faceless not only because it is removed by distance and invisible, but also because it is structural: governmental or corporate. These are classic conditions for a low-level deindividuation.

The consequence appears to be a sort of ongoing digital nuisance: the kind of language you'd expect someone rather ill-tempered to use in heavy road traffic appearing in what ought to be the enlightened debating space of news website comments pages; cyberbullying; unlawful file-sharing. And yet it stands in stark contrast to the idea of social media as something positive, a medium allowing genuine connection and self-determination. Possibly this is because the situation is less monolithic and – once again – more patchworked. Some aspects of online life lead to deindividuation, and in those areas people behave badly. Others do not, and encourage and reward good behaviour.

But in any case, are social media really that important?

Aren't they just a replacement for physical encounters? And most significantly: can they really help us deal with massive problems?

~

The Internet is not a broadcast medium.

I never get tired of saying that. I keep having to say it because people of my own age and older grew up on the assumptions of a world of television, newspapers, film and so on which was essentially a one-way flow of information and ideas. The paradigm for media was a poster at a bus stop. You told the public what you were doing and then they knew about it. That was it. They could write to you, of course, but it was time-consuming and you weren't really expected to respond. More, the speed of events was perceived as being slower. Before email and fax, an urgent query would take a day to arrive (providing it was posted before the last collection) and the reply could not take less to return. In other words, the timescale for all but the most urgent correspondence was three days, and more likely a week. News, business and government moved – to outward appearances at least – more slowly. Data were harder to gather, and the effects of policy decisions could only really be estimated over a term of years. The public was not generally privy to government statistics in any case, and the UK's institutional culture regarded anything not specifically public as confidential. Information did not flow.

The Internet, however, is a mass communications platform: it allows the flow of information in all directions. And out of that quality have emerged the social media, which are also not for the most part hierarchical or top-down. Everyone can communicate with everyone. That's how they work and what they are. Participating in the social media is a very different activity from merely accessing websites or playing non-social online games. It involves interaction with other people, and they are a discriminating bunch. If you give nothing, you get nothing. If you engage at a low level, what comes back to you is by and large pretty unexciting. On the other hand, if you put some effort into social media, people respond rapidly with perceptions and favourite things of their own. Social media are reciprocal, and you can tell how you're doing because it will be evident in people's reactions to you. Social media are about connection rather than isolation: Twitter, Facebook and the rest are each in their own ways feedback structures.

Feedback, if you aren't quite sure, is a simple notion for something that can become fiendishly complex. Most people are aware of it now as a public relations term: companies and councils are forever seeking our 'feedback' on customer satisfaction forms. They then take our opinions of their work and (notionally) use those opinions to improve their service. Everyone benefits. Except, of course, that in many cases it feels to us on the outside that the feedback is simply ignored and the point of the exercise was not improvement but pacification.

Real feedback is the flow of information from the output of a system back into the earlier stages; when a microphone gets too close to a speaker, the output of the speaker is fed back into the amplifier through the mic. The noise gets louder and louder until either the mic is moved, the speaker or the amplifier is switched off or something explodes. In a more constructive setting, though, feedback can be a powerful force for positive change. The best example – as *Decision Tree* author Thomas Goetz observed in *Wired* recently – is probably those interactive road signs that tell you how fast you're going as you approach a pedestrian crossing or a school; you get information about your speed (which you already have, but the sign is external to your car dashboard and hence isn't part of the regular noise of driving, so you take notice of it) and you compare it to the limit. The result, across the board, is a 10 per cent reduction in speed which persists beyond the immediate vicinity of the sign – generally several miles beyond. There's no threat, no penalty, no physical restraint. The feedback itself, coupled with a low-level desire not to be a menace to kindergarteners, is enough.

Social media in particular, and digital technology more generally, are capable of doing exactly the same thing – providing relevant information in real time – in more diffuse human situations. That sounds like a small thing, but the effects are potentially huge, especially when that information is combined with a suggested action in response. In my first example of the road signs, the proposed action is obviously lowering your speed – but it can be something more sophisticated: an action that is itself a form of feedback into someone else's loop. In the case of the Middle East revolutions, users monitoring themselves and their fellows realized that the moment had arrived, that this time something really was going to happen, and then uncovered an array of possible actions in support. Those actions were themselves feedback to the regimes they focused on, urging a modified behaviour: compromise, resign or flee.

The most effective feedback systems, according to Goetz, are those that influence us subtly. The sweet spot is a fuzzy area between obnoxious and intrusive on the one hand and inconsequential on the other. Information supplied in this cosy band is the most likely to have the desired effect. In the context of social media, this is the more likely to occur because the feedback is actively solicited by the user. It's not an unwelcome irritant from a nagging external source, like the road signs – which I always find a bit finger-waggy – but simply a part of a pre-existing and continuing personal interaction. Lodged in the social network in this way, users are connected to group, place and person. That doesn't mean, as we know from the Arab Spring, that they retreat to a previous position, but rather that a new set of perceptions of reality are instated as norms. Under some circumstances, this will be a kind of reindividuation, a calming. In others, the collective mood will be of anger and discontent, and that will become a part of the individual until the perceived issues are resolved.

The social media site and the group of people associated with it become, in other words, the repository of a counter-culture – but do not create or define it. That is still done by people. The Riot Wombles weren't created by social media either; rather, the communications network allowed a local whimsy to reach out across the country and, using a childhood image that is widely known among people in the UK, take root in a variety of locations. Knowing that others were doing the same, and that the media were picking up on the story, and therefore that more people were coming to help, was a virtuous feedback loop.

By putting people in touch with others who feel the same way, digital communications technology compounds perceptions, facilitates the generation of movements, gives reinforcement to those who otherwise might feel alone. Above all, though, it allows us to understand in real time things that historically have taken place on slower scales, over months, years or decades. Websites such as They Work For You allow constituents to monitor the voting records of members of parliament day to day, and constituents unhappy with their representative's performance can say so immediately. Almost anything can now be observed as it takes place, rather than after the fact, and the heartbeat of nations, rather than playing out across timespans of generations, can be heard every morning and afternoon in the financial figures and the political reports. We are no longer disconnected from what's happening around us. We can see not only ourselves – courtesy of those road signs, and the systems that allow you to check your electricity consumption, your calorie intake, your use of the working day – but our nations.

Digital technology can also make us conscious of ourselves as parts of the systems that make up our society. This is not to say that we're all cogs in the machine. We are individuals, each of us interesting and special in ourselves, but we are also, consciously or not, parts in any number of systems – as with the shuttering of the *News of the World*. The paper's demise was partly triggered by communications from members of the public to advertisers: 'don't associate yourself with this; we are angry.' The message was heard loud and clear, and advertisers withdrew (demonstrating among other things that commodification does not render you powerless, though it may change the nature of your power). The interesting point is that there was at least a moderate consciousness in the public debate that targeting advertisers was a way to send a message to the paper. It was not simply a question of people disapproving of the brands' involvement with the *News of the World*. It was that in telling the brands of their disapproval, they could create a desired reaction: a conscious use of feedback. Being aware of our status gives us a degree of control over our environment.

In the social sciences there is a somewhat circular debate about agency, or, more plainly, how things happen in the human world. Do individuals have the power to change things? Or are we simply at the mercy of forces in the economy and in demographics that are so vast as to be imponderable? Are we capable of changing the course of events, or do events spring from interactions so complex and weighty that no one could hope to understand, let alone alter, the flow? Perhaps one of the most obvious examples is the question of whether revolutions are the product of heroic individuals working to undermine the established order, or whether they come as a consequence of giant structural forces that cannot be provoked, speeded or slowed. Vladimir Ilyich Lenin wrote that 'revolutions are not made, they come', but one might argue that he successfully initiated, transformed and perhaps ultimately betrayed one of the most extraordinary uprisings of the twentieth century.

In ordinary life, we tend at the moment to accept that there are structural forces that act upon us and which we cannot influence. We have been told repeatedly that the banking crisis, for example, was a structural problem, a great institutional madness in which the poor decisions of a few were somehow magnified to create a seismic collapse. But it's also true – and increasingly obvious – that we are part of these structural forces ourselves. We are bits of the group, and the changes in the group's structure are those forces we hear so much about.

~

The idea of the human being as part of a structure makes people profoundly uncomfortable. It plays to images of ant colonies and slavery, notions of the loss of self. That's cultural, though, and relatively recent. The industrial world's sense of what we are as humans has moved further and further over the last decades towards the idea of a single person as being complete. It's a posture that defines our politics – in the form of our freedoms – and our morality. Where previous generations might have responded, in line with the various touchstones by which they identified themselves and located themselves in the matrix of social and cosmological truths as they understood it, that the most significant unit was the family (Margaret Thatcher's infamous statement on the subject of social organization, which I mentioned earlier, was more properly: 'There is no such thing as society. There are individual men and women, and there are families'), the state, or the Church, we assume it is the singular human. Some cultures, including subcultures in the industrialized north-west, still feel more collective than not, but in the UK and US as well as elsewhere we generally make our rules and our decisions on the basis of individualism. It's an ethos that meshes well with the particularly brassy form of free market capitalism presently fashionable, which exalts the risk-taker, the money-maker and the creator of personal wealth over the steward, the good citizen and the bringer of wider prosperity.

The lineage of this combination goes back from the present day by way of Gordon Gekko, the fictional 1980s financial mogul portrayed by Michael Douglas in *Wall Street* – or through the real life equivalents of Gekko – to the controversial Russian–American writer Ayn Rand and her disciples in American public life (notably including Alan Greenspan, chairman of the US Federal Reserve from 1987 to 2006) to Ralph Waldo Emerson (the philosopher of self-reliance who grudged 'the dollar, the dime, the cent as I give to such men as do not belong to me and to whom I do not belong') and on into the diffuse origins of our capitalist world and the Protestant work ethic of which it has subsequently been stripped.

It is, however, not the only way of seeing things, or even necessarily the most persuasive. A single human being, after all, cannot reproduce; in fact, it's hard to determine a minimum viable population for human beings. Estimates range from the fifteen who resettled the island of Tristan da Cunha some time in the 1800s (the population today is somewhat below 300, with a high incidence of asthma derived most probably from three of the original colonists who had the condition) to a more robust 3,000, as proposed in a 2007 article in the journal *Biological Conservation*. Somewhere in that range, presumably, is a number that represents the smallest number of humans necessary to sustain the species and in a way, therefore, the minimum human unit. You could also look at the number of plants required to sustain breatheable air for a single person, the animal and vegetable ecosystem necessary to provide food, and the minimum amount of water and the means to recycle it. A human taken out of context is essentially a corpse.

While that discussion is interesting, and works to prise us away from the knee-jerk response, it doesn't really answer the question of what the basic building block of human society is. It's obvious we don't think of human life as being purely a question of genetic self-propagation. While we hold children in high regard, we don't generally feel that an individual, having reproduced, no longer has any point to their existence. Similarly, we would not acknowledge the identical twin (or for that matter the clone) of a given person as the actual individual. We would say that they were genetically identical, but still distinct. We would point to the minds and the experiences of two separate people. At some point in the development of the species, we became in effect two things at once: a physical self, which is replicated by sexual reproduction, and a mental self, an identity of ideas, which cannot directly reproduce in the sense that consciousness cannot be split and recombined, but which is composed of concepts that can absolutely spread by discussion, narrative and sharing. This mental self – however much it is bound to the physical one and emerges from it – is the one that we supplement with our digital devices and which we have extended beyond the body into journals, books, artworks and now digital technologies.

I don't wish to imply a literal dualism here. Absent some startling scientific evidence to the contrary, my assumption is that the mind is an artefact of the brain, a fizzing system of conscious cognition, unconscious drives and biological imperatives, all overlapping and intermingled to produce us. (I also don't mean to rule out the terrifying, splendid possibilities of advanced organ cloning and high technology to replace broken parts of a given brain. It's not that a mind is anchored irrevocably to a particular collection of cells, or that someone with a chip replacing an aspect of the brain would suddenly be non-human; rather, the mind emerges from the brain's encounter with the world. What happens thereafter is the adventure.)

That said, many scholars trace the development of the modern individual – and to a certain extent also the modern brain – from the arrival of the phonetic alphabet. According to Derrick de Kerckhove in *The Augmented Mind*, the adoption of silent reading, the final stage of the arrival of text, 'helped to turn speakers into thinkers and critics'. The word was fixed, and could be examined; and along with it, everything else, as well. Maryanne Wolf writes that 'The implications of cognitive automaticity for human intellectual development are potentially staggering. If we can recognise symbols at almost automatic speeds, we can allocate more time to mental processes that are continuously expanding when we read and write. The efficient reading brain,' Wolf explains, 'quite literally has more time to think.'

It may also be that the brain has trouble working on concepts for which it has no linguistic template. A 2004 study conducted by Peter Gordon of Columbia University showed that 'hunter-gatherers from the Pirahã tribe, whose language only contains words for the numbers one and two, were unable to reliably tell the difference between four objects placed in a row and five in the same configuration,'[3] suggesting that someone without language to describe a given concept may not be able to understand or learn that concept. Attempts to teach the Pirahã to count in Portuguese (they live in territory claimed by Brazil) were unsuccessful.

So does that mean there are two aspects of human life, one biological, which requires a large-ish pool to sustain itself, and one mental, which is the product of the brain's encounter with the world? It's not even clear that the modern mind can exist alone. The development of language requires a partner to communicate with and to act as a check; without someone to talk to, our grip on the meaning of words shifts with surprising rapidity. More, the individual is from birth engaged in dialogue, in an exchange of gesture and affection with parent or carer that is so much a thing of interplay and rhythm that some researchers have characterized it as 'communicative musicality'. This protoconversation, preceding the development of language, is our first experience of life, and we live it as part of a small community rather than as a lone individual.

Without language, in turn, some forms of abstract thought are difficult or impossible. 'Language' in this context need not be spoken; it can be a language of signs or text. A study of a deaf community in Nicaragua[4] compared two generations and found that members of the newer generation, whose system of sign language was more complex and expressive, were better able to pass what psychologists call a 'false belief' test. (In the test, subjects are shown a sequence of events in which two children are playing. One child puts a toy in a particular place and leaves the room. The other then moves the toy to a new location. The test question is: where will the first child look for the toy upon returning to the room? Children under four will answer with the location the toy is in now; older kids realize that the returning child can have no knowledge of the other's prank, and will look where the toy was when they left.) The implication of the Nicaragua study is that it is harder to develop a full sense of the existence of other, independent minds without a robust and complex system of language.

The modern thinking self, which understands itself to be separate from others and knows that their perspective differs from its own, is obtained to a great degree through language, and therefore to a great extent through discourse, meaning once more that to be a complete, rational human being in the sense of how we usually understand the words, you need people around you to interact with. Which means, in turn, that while we experience the world as individuals, we come to it as individuals who are part of a group. And increasingly, we can use our digital technologies to monitor that group and assess our position in it and relative to it in real time, taking decisions not based on what has already happened and cannot be undone, but on what is happening and what we actually want.

Feedback is a simple enough notion, and easy to implement, but it has profound consequences. That sense of complexity we experience, of a world out of control, doesn't come from digital technologies, but from the access they afford us, and the dawning realization that many of our actions have consequences far beyond the venue where we do them. The difficulty now lies in finding responses that produce the results we want; and there, too, feedback is helpful. Just as you visually check the position of your hand when trying to manipulate something very small, so we can guide our response with real-time feedback, and make sure it's achieving what we hope for.

～

And observe, you are put to a stern choice in this matter. You must either make a tool of the creature, or a man of him. You cannot make both. Men were not intended to work with the accuracy of tools, to be precise and perfect in all their actions. If you will have that precision out of them, and make their fingers measure degrees like cogwheels, and their arms strike curves like compasses, you must unhumanise them.

John Ruskin

One area of the digital realm I'm uncomfortable with is the design of our actual devices and their lack of uniqueness or narrative. John Ruskin argued in 1853 that machined perfection of form in physical objects was an assault on the human soul. The human was flawed, Ruskin said, and we should accept that and cherish it. For him, the precise lines of industrial processes were unwholesome, speaking of objects rather than people, and diminishing the value of man.

A hundred years later, machine-made items, endlessly replicable, were popularized in the austerity period following the Second World War. They were supposed to be democratic: art for everyone, not just for the wealthy. This was art the ordinary people could keep and inhabit: a concept iterated a thousand times being just as splendid as a one-off masterpiece. Art nouveau – the successor to Ruskin's Arts and Crafts movement – had by then itself been pilloried as a death of the individual. The influential architect Adolf Loos described in 1900 a perfect artisan dwelling place that echoed every aspect of its owner, leaving him essentially with nothing to do but die: he had been perfectly expressed by his home, so there could be nothing more to add to the story of his life.

Loos's thinking, like Ruskin's, embraced art and culture both, and his perception was that the removal of ornamentation was a sign of cultural progress. The process of purification in modernism was evidence of evolution, where art nouveau was 'erotic and degenerate'. Loos might well have approved of the seamlessness of our present technological devices: led by Apple, the makers of smartphones have eschewed physical ornamentation of any kind, reaching instead for industrial design. The original iPhone was a smooth aluminium and glass lozenge; the more recent model, the iPhone 4, is black plastic and glass. In a major concession, Apple has also produced the iPhone in white. Aside from the touch screen, there is one main button, a volume control, and an off switch. The phone absolutely cannot be physically customized; that is to say, opening it voids the warranty. It is as much an extension of Apple's identity into its users' as it is a personal item – and that is true of the software that operates it too, blending the technology of the device into a recognizably bland shopfront for selling content. The late Steve Jobs said in an interview that he didn't like to talk about design: 'it's not really how they look, it's how they work', and yes, the function of the iPhone absolutely overrides its physical form. But that, in itself, can be read as a message too: that existence alone is not important, that you should be judged on what you do. Worth is instrumental, not inherent.

Actions are important, of course, and this is not to mount an assault on Apple; Sir Jonathan Ives' designs are profoundly elegant, and the system inside is superb; a single iPhone, as a unique object, is a gorgeous and immensely useful tool. It's the spectacle of millions of units, each the same as the last, each not so much an identity as a vector for the transmission of identity in either direction, which becomes disturbing, and evokes Ruskin's concerns.

Each phone being identical is important because it means that (unlike with Google's competing Android platform) software developers can work in the knowledge that everyone will be running their apps on the same device. The screen will be the same size, the same accelerometer will be installed, the same chips. It also means that a lost or damaged phone can be replaced and – once the backed-up data is transferred – the new phone will to all intents and purposes be the old one. It's a practical issue, not obviously an ideological one. The upshot, though, is the same: we carry interchangeable devices, and we are encouraged to see their smoothness as a virtue and to think of their lack of identity as an identity in itself, or at least, to see identity – which you might also think of as a style of being – as something that can be assembled out of pre-made parts rather than expressed uniquely and organically. From Adolf Loos to Bruce Mau to Apple to us: does the homogeneity of pure design diminish the human? What does it mean that you buy your device from an Apple Store, which is an abstract entity in physical form, the physical instantiation of Apple's online presence and even its system self, rather than from a unique local vendor? If a given technology carries a message, does the design of our technology imply interchangeability and uniformity – and does that, in turn, imply it about us as individuals?

It sounds a rather fanciful question, but the anonymity of our technology is glaring when you consider how it might otherwise have been. In 1996 novelist William Gibson wrote in *Idoru* about artisan laptops:

> 'I like your computer,' she said. 'It looks like it was made by Indians or something.'
>
> Chia looked down at her sandbenders. Turned off the red switch. 'Coral,' she said. 'These are turquoise. The ones that look like ivory are the inside of a kind of nut. Renewable.'

'The rest is silver?'

'Aluminum,' Chia said. 'They melt old cans they dig up on the beach and cast it in sand molds. These panels are micarta. That's linen with this resin in it.'

The textureless lines of our technology lack any sense of play in their construction, of the uniqueness and history of Gibson's fictional devices. The exteriors of the Nexus S, the iPhone, the Kindle, the Vaio – all these are functional and industrial. There's no space in them for a sculptor's joke or a designer's concession to light or local materials. And while that may not seem important – after all, surely what's inside them matters far more – it continues a mood that permeates the industry as a whole, in which standardization is preferable because it makes the whole process easier – perhaps even makes it possible – for the company and its machines.

The human is secondary; even, actually, in terms of ergonomics. The structures of portable computers are not friendly to prolonged use by humans: they cause cramp, RSI and back pain. There have been occasional attempts to shift this: IBM briefly made a laptop with a fold-out keyboard of ergonomic design, but it was flimsy and the model was dropped. No one has ever made a laptop that did not put the screen at the wrong height for a human typing on the keyboard. Yes, of course, there are conflicting constraints of portability. But the ingenuity that has been applied to other seemingly insurmountable problems is absent. The designs are convenient for a non-human mass-production and distribution system, and that convenience is then packaged as being something desirable, something to be aspired to.

The same was true to an extent in the austerity years, but it's hard to argue with that in the context. Beauty of any sort was hard to come by in the fatigued post-war environment, and the understanding of it had been newly and appallingly altered by the discovery of the Nazi Holocaust. Theodor Adorno, the influential cultural critic, wrote in 1951 that to write lyric poetry after Auschwitz was impossible. The clean, unornamented lines of period furniture and houses were a reflection of that sense that embellishment and frivolous beauty were out of place. The functional cleanness of modern design bowed to a need, quite above and beyond the fact that there wasn't the time or the wealth to do anything else.

We've moved on from that problem into a new one. The successors of Marcel Breuer and Eileen Gray are IKEA and MFI, turning out replicas of revivals of copies and converting homes into airport lounges. Modernism isn't a design ethos any more, it's an economy of scale, and a marketing tool to sell the ordinary as something special, the sexless as erotic. A technological device without a specific, personalized identity has a subtext: it asserts the value of instrumentality. Its design is a reflection of its role. It's ironic that the iPhone and its competitors should come from one of the most identifiable and unique personalities of the modern age, Steve Jobs, who died in October 2011, and whose life has reshaped the digital landscape at almost every turn. The iPhone's inner self is like Jobs: versatile, adaptable and intriguing, but its exterior is everything its creator wasn't: sheer, stark, easily mass produced. The anonymity of these objects is part of what they are: interchangeable commodities whose uniqueness in so far as they possess any is created by what is done with them. Function is an identity. And that identity is something we are encouraged to incorporate into our perception of self, that anonymity is proposed as something to emulate. Whimsy and uniqueness are indulgences; handwork is just an awkward approximation of computer-assisted cutting. Precision is good, and the narrative of an object's creation in the hands of a workman is a bizarre sideshow, not really the point of the object.

Is it too much of a stretch to connect that idea – that what an item really is, really means, is a product of how it is used – with the sense of disconnection and hopelessness that organizations such as the Joseph Rowntree Foundation identify as part of the social problems that led to the UK riots? 'Through our research, we know that people in some places feel absolutely powerless . . . they believe their aspirations are frustrated and that whatever their effort they will not be recognised . . . [they] are worried about living in a culture that has increasingly defined status through material possessions . . .'[5] Does our technological culture tacitly propose that nothing is of value (as opposed to financial worth) of itself; its significance is determined not by its substance, but by what it can do? In which case if your prospects are not good, you are unlikely to achieve any value, or any discrete identity of your own, and the world has no place for you. In this picture, the specific self is without value: only the connection really means anything. Not that Apple and Google are responsible for this; rather that they incidentally lend strength to it, just as TV and film once contributed to the perception that smoking was a trait of the rebel.

You may argue that this issue is nebulous. But certainly, what our technological design lacks is the concept at the heart of this book: a sense of self. Our devices do not express who we are, except to brand us as belonging to a particular group of users, consumers and commodities. Loos has, for the moment, won his battle. The hand that assembled my desktop's components assembled a thousand like it and never made any impact on how they look or function; the designer who created it never touched the one I work on; the human narratives that could be in our technology are brushed away to make a perfectly artificial product with no history. We deny their origins, perhaps even are uncomfortable with them – the sweatshop labour, the mines where the coltan comes from – and we shut down a part of ourselves to avoid seeing. William Gibson's fictional sandbenders have history, and they reflect aspects of an unequal world. From the technology in the real life, you could imagine everything everywhere was like an Apple Store. We buy an illusion of silvery modernity and progress, a ghost of the designs of Le Corbusier stripped of his idealistic 'Open Hand' (a gesture of peace and reciprocity), over something that tells us the story itself and affords us the understanding of another life. The commercial culture surrounding our present style of technological design encourages us, however slightly, to choose not to see.

In other words, on some level – however slight – the design and manufacture of our devices deindividuate us and disengage us from the living world. In exchange for that deficit, though, we get access to the feedback system that is developing in the social Internet, to discussions and vibrant conversations that reaffirm who we are even as they challenge it.

The twentieth century was the century of mechanization, of speed and of industry. It was a time of rapid social change, confusing and bewildering alterations in the relationships between nations, between individuals and society, between individuals and one another. The fundamental tenets of Western capitalist civilization were questioned, reaffirmed, questioned, redefined and so on. Social order in the form of the Church, the legitimacy of the state and the notion of family were scrutinized and in some ways found wanting. Gender roles were reassessed, and the 'supermum', juggling job and family and finding a path through the whole thing, became the standard for women to aspire to – never mind that it was precisely this juggling act that men were and are notably unable to achieve. In the 1990s, the complexity of the post-Cold War world became apparent. Twenty-four-hour news arrived, the environmental crisis became increasingly evident and then was assailed as a confidence trick, the notion of peak oil was mooted again. The world became difficult to understand without the massive blanket of nuclear pressure to homogenize and override its many aspects. Simple things –

actions, beliefs, situations and perceptions which required no examination – were harder and harder to find. Even those cherished abstract systems, supposedly infinitely transferable, began to show holes as modern agricultural techniques applied without local knowledge in some 'third world' countries caused famine rather than feast, and not every model of industry proved instantly replicable in a new cultural context.

There's no question that the arrival of always-on digital technology has added in some ways to this sense of bombardment, in large part because it makes us available even when we are not out in public, in part because it connects those different cultural contexts, allowing them – forcing them? – to rub shoulders. However, looking at what digital technology does, and the changes its use causes in us, there's another way of seeing it: it's not the problem, it's the response.

Look again at the study Nicholas Carr points to which says that playing computer games and reading documents online foster an editorial and problem-solving faculty: what do those skills imply but an ability to cope with a world that was already becoming saturated with information, already out of control? The engaged use of digital technology teaches skills and creates architectures in the brain that are helpful in dealing with problems we already had when it became part of the world in the 1990s. Digital technology provides ways of using all the time we have, of being in more than one place at a time. It lets us adapt rapidly to changing situations: to call from the roadside to say we won't make a given appointment because we've broken down, or to exchange information in a more serious crisis such as the London riots. It's a way of managing time and space and of overcoming distance. It allows us to find people who are like us whom we otherwise would never know, which puts us back in a social context that we as humans actually do need, and which the nature of our society in the aftermath of the Enlightenment's application of doubt to its central pillars renders difficult. Digital brings its own problems – our weaknesses are adaptive, as well as our strengths – but it is a strategy we evolved to resolve a set of crises we already had, and which are still playing out, rather more than it is the cause of a new one.

Imagine for a moment that the sense data you experience all the time – your sight, hearing, sense of balance and so on – arrived ten minutes late. You wouldn't, for a start, be able to walk; the human method of locomotion requires that we fall forward and catch ourselves all the time. Balance is crucial (ask anyone who's ever had Labyrinthitis). You probably wouldn't be able to stand; even tiny variations in your posture would cause you to fall before you realized they'd taken place. Conversation and debate in real time would be almost impossible unless you were supremely gifted at synchronizing with the other person. It's not clear that you'd continue to think in the same way as you do now; gradually you would become isolated, your priorities would shift. In the modern world, you'd be able to continue to function as a human being by using a computer to relay messages to others, but until the 1990s you'd have been reduced to writing letters to communicate with others in a linear way. You might easily go mad.

And yet this is the situation in which our society has been up to this point. The feedback from our collective actions has been too slow to understand and too late to do anything about. The vast collective strength we have has been rendered almost useless by the slow speed of our senses. Only when we have been enraged or assailed, when the state of affairs has been so unequivocal that we've been able to recognize it and hold fast to that understanding, have we been able to bring to bear even a fraction of the strength we have. In other words, the giant has been blind.

Digitization changes that in a remarkable way: we are abruptly able to appreciate what's happening in something approximating real time. Our whole society is suddenly in the position of the motorist seeing the sign displaying his speed. We're not used to the flow of feedback information, so it feels too fast, too much, too raw, at least when we don't know what to do with it. Often, the statement of a problem arrives without a solution attached, and we don't yet have a developed instinct towards solving it; that is, after all, what we have been taught to expect from our governments, though their track record is less than perfect. Increasingly, however, solutions are presented: collective actions such as the Riot Wombles or protests like the Occupy movement. As we get better at understanding that the solutions must come from us, and at creating them from the ideas of a crowd, remarkable things are possible.

Several nations now consider Net access to be a human right, because the dialogue taking place online is adjudged sufficiently fundamental to the society we now have that deprival of it is a form of disenfranchisement. It makes for great tabloid headlines, and it strikes me as a contingent right rather than a fundamental one, but there's an element of truth in the position. To be out of the loop now is to be to some extent out of the greatest discussion ever conducted. It is to be unrepresented in the creation of a new public sphere, a space where new identities and self-perceptions are being made.

If the development of writing and the spread of literacy were part of the creation of the modern mind, allowing individual humans to see themselves as complete and separate from their environment and the institutions of their time, then the development of digital technology does something similar for our understanding of ourselves as part of a larger group entity. It's not that humanity is on the road to becoming a gestalt organism in which we are no more than unconscious cells, like the tiny individual animals that make up the body of a Portuguese man o' war. Rather, it's that we are aware of ourselves both as discrete persons, and as contributors to the interplay of forces that goes to make up the body sociopolitic. A fully functioning body of this kind can, of course, achieve remarkable things, such as the NHS, or the US space programme. It is a mistake to think of such involvement as a kind of appalling servitude; there's no implied diminution of the self in being a part of something greater; in fact, the evidence suggests that the reverse is true. It's entirely in keeping with being human and how human-ness developed. Certainly it may be necessary to meet the challenges we have set ourselves and which the wider world will set for us.

It may also be true that the arrival of digital text alters how we think about the world in general. A world constructed on static, printed text is a world of received truth, hierarchical arrangements of society and laws that are, if not unalterable, at least securely fixed. It requires radical social pressure to force those in power to change the rules. By contrast, a world where text is editable and fluid is a world where laws can be rewritten not only by parliaments, but at the behest of the general population. Regulations are no longer understood as divine edicts, but as the written product of other human beings subject to the approval and rewriting of us all. This produces a culture that can seem over-indulgent towards its own sense of entitlement, but it's also a culture that understands that law is made by consent, not decree, and that a political system constructed on the idea of representation in the seat of power should require representatives actually to be responsive to the desires and opinions of those for whom they stand rather than be benignly paternalistic.

What makes the biggest impact is perhaps the timescale of it all, not least because other timescales are also shortening. Just as medical research regularly uncovers possibilities that would have seemed miraculous even twenty years ago, so social change that was previously generational can be effected on a scale an individual human being can understand and appreciate – and aim for. Seeing one's own part in the pattern is not disempowering, but the reverse. And the ability to see where we're going – or at least where we are now – affords the chance, for the first time in human social history, to start making real decisions.

blindgiant.co.uk/chapter6

7

The Old, the Modern and the New

I'VE BEEN AROUND the UK publishing industry effectively for my entire life. I sat in on discussions about book jackets and paperback royalties and the rest from before I could walk. I have had a worm's eye view of some very interesting moments. Mercifully, I don't remember specifics, but I do have a sense of the arc of the modern publishing story, and it seems to me that it is a useful microcosm of the wider context as culture, politics and society have moved through three fairly distinct stages (albeit with my perpetual caveat that nothing is clear-cut any more, if it ever was, and there are pockets of the old in the new and vice versa) or styles of doing business which you could think of as personal, professional and participatory.

In the old days – by which I mean the time when my mother's corduroy trousers were my personal Pillars of Hercules, demarking the edges of the known world – publishing was a family industry. It was deeply embedded in local culture and social life, to the extent that publishers fretted that a given book might be too racy for the family shareholders, who would have to own up to printing something so filthy as *Lady Chatterley's Lover* to their friends at the bridge club. D.H. Lawrence's book was written in 1928, but was banned in the UK for over thirty years; even after that, you could still get ostracized for pushing the envelope of social acceptability. Publishing lived in pre-emptive fear of a collection of almost Wodehousian aunts and spinster sisters. The industry in Britain was essentially upper middle class, white, and based not just in London but in a particular area of the city, although Edinburgh also boasted a number of independent presses. It was premised on the taste and judgement of a vanishingly small number of people, who effectively defined 'good' writing for the rest. You could see the defining feature of this style of working as personality: the identity of a publishing house was defined by the managing editor, who was in today's term curating a selection of works that accorded with his (almost always) understanding of what was good and intelligent and worth putting out there.

Towards the end of the twentieth century, however, the operating environment changed. Publishing started getting treated as a business. Giants emerged and bought up the small houses, and a corporate culture was imported, although with only partial success. Publishing became a hybrid as the demands of business culture – making money, trimming excessive running costs, publishing on a regular schedule, making the maximum amount of money out of a given property – were grafted on to the long-lunch lifestyle of old publishing. Contracts, which in the 1960s could be a single page release, became lengthy legal documents. Serious marketing practices were brought in, and a publicity machine capable of some impressive hype was born. Celebrity biographies that might previously have been considered coarse and pointless were all the rage. The Net Book Agreement was killed so that huge chains – essentially the supermarkets – could take advantage of economies of scale and bulk purchase to sell books more cheaply.

But the relaxed culture proved resilient. Publishing is still partly what it was; when I mentioned my Aunt Theory recently in conversation, one publisher from a major imprint flinched slightly and said not much had changed in that regard. Where Hollywood studios spend millions on testing movies before release and working out the demographics of their audience, it's unusual for a print publisher to research who is buying a given book, or to test it in advance in any formal way. The focus group simply isn't a part of the landscape. Publishers were and are also unlikely to buy merchandizing rights, which movie studios will always do so that they can capitalize on every aspect of a film property – a lesson learned hard at the hands of one George Lucas, who waived his director's fee on *Star Wars* in exchange for the rights to the T-shirts and the toys, not, as he freely admits, because he thought they'd be a goldmine, but because he wanted to be able to publicize the film. As you might imagine, he more than recouped his loss leader.[1]

But the book trade has been, if not a little sniffy about that kind of exploitation, then at least less adventurous. There are working hours in publishing, but they are not measured in the way law firms budget the time of their fee earners and partners. When my wife was a commercial lawyer, her day was broken into a sequence of chargeable units, and she accounted for each unit at the end of every month so that she could bill her clients. A unit was six minutes. (Something to bear in mind if you should have cause to hire a lawyer: don't spend six minutes talking politely about the weather every time you call – it may appear on your bill.) This extreme version of payment by time – made possible by the mechanical clock, of course – imposes the professional imprint on the mind from the moment of waking to the last thought at night. Six minutes is a short enough period that no hole in the schedule need be wasted in idleness. All but the smallest gap can be converted into money. The day becomes a sequence of slots and increments to be managed, each fragment can be owned by or charged to someone, and the division between fragments is rigid and precise. Publishing – understandably, perhaps – hasn't gone that far. All the same, the ethos of the post-1990 house is professionalism.

While everyone was still struggling with the shift to mainstream business practice, another revolution took place. The flying saucer of digital technology crashed into the waving cornfield of the book world and set quite a lot of it on fire. It took a while for the industry to accept this was happening, because books were protected by their design and by the fact that the paper book is actually a refined and usable technology with much to recommend it. When my first novel *The Gone-Away World* came out in 2008, ebooks were still considered to be a possible but not definite future. It was hard to get anyone to pay any attention to them, although almost everyone would acknowledge that they might become something at some point. Perhaps in a decade or so. If the wind was blowing in the right direction. Now, of course, they've arrived, and the industry is playing a certain amount of catch-up; not just with the implications for the supply chain and the arrival of large, scary new kids on the publishing block in the form of Amazon, Google, Apple and others, but also with coming to understand that the heart and soul of the Internet is participation.

Publishing is traditionally a business which sells to other businesses – books go from publisher to wholesaler to bookseller. Actual publishers rarely dealt directly with consumers. Digital technology's arrival has inevitably meant a lot of walls coming crashing down, and suddenly, whether they want to or not, publishers are in a relationship with the general public, with all the strangeness, frustration and waywardness that entails. It is publishers who must deal with reported (and unstoppable) violations of intellectual property, and whose existing business habits are scattered to the four winds by the arrival of the Net. The most obvious example is probably hardback and paperback publication. Customarily, books are published in two or sometimes three formats: hardback at a premium price for those who just can't wait or who want a display edition for their shelves; and later paperback, which can be two releases: a soft-backed edition using pages printed to the same pattern as the hardback's, followed by a mass-market edition in a smaller size.

Where in all this does the ebook come in? At the same time as the hardback, cutting into paperback sales? If so, should it be at a hardback price or a more superficially rational level? Or later, forcing the market to wait and increasing the chances that people will pick up an unsanctioned copy from a file-sharing site?

At the same time, of course, not only are other companies getting in on the act, but the whole wide world now has access to the ability to put material on the Net and even get it printed and call itself a publisher. And it's true: being able to put together a document for public consumption and make it available does make you a publisher – in exactly the same way that owning an aeroplane makes you an aviator. All the same, the publishing skies are much more crowded, and the traditional top-down, broadcast pattern of publishing is being replaced – in some cases slowly and very much against the will of the main characters – by a more blurred distinction between publisher, commentator and consumer, and between publisher, wholesaler and retailer. What was once a clear set of relationships is now crosshatched with connections and interactions, as society at large knocks on the door of publishing's cultural village and demands to be let in, or worse, builds houses right outside without asking.

With this in mind, consider the broader history of the UK: until quite late in the twentieth century, we had a politics essentially amateur in nature. Aristocrats and middle-class intellectuals and working men (and, more rarely, women) campaigned and were sent to parliament to do what they could. They did not take a brief on each individual issue from their constituents, but went with an understanding of the ethos they were to represent – the ethos on which they had been elected. This was a genuine 'representative' process. Democracy was served by uniting electorate and MP in a mutually understood shared identity, though inevitably interpretations differed on specifics, and of course the current flowed in two directions: politicians imprinted their own identities on their parties and on the nation. The most extreme example must be Winston Churchill, whose diaries of his life are not merely a day-to-day account, but a self-portrait written with an eye to the creation of a historical narrative which still heavily influences our understanding of the events of his life. 'I was not the lion, but it fell to me to give the lion's roar,' Churchill said in a speech in 1954. Well, perhaps; but looking at the sequence of events surrounding Britain's entry into the Second World War one might also say that he roared the lion rather than vice versa.

At a certain point, however, the same transition that affected the publishing world touched our political class: they became professionalized. It was no longer enough that a politician compose their own speeches, make their own off-the-cuff remarks; Tony Blair's Labour Party was controlled centrally so that everyone was 'on-message' and everyone was reading from the same page. The party was to function in a unified fashion, and going off-piste was robustly discouraged. In government, the apparat continued to function in this way, and became so famously exacting in its use of 'spin' and publicity management techniques that it spawned the popular television show *The Thick of It*, whose dominant personality was a vituperative spin doctor cum political executioner rumoured to resemble Blair's Communications Director Alastair Campbell. The glossy, sound-bite politics of the spin era have been disparaged by almost everyone, but the style of superficial engagement works with conventional media and has not greatly altered.

More recently, digital technology has begun to make a mark on the political arena as well, as people realize they can reach out to their MPs and to government in general and make their voices heard. Websites allow those who might not under other circumstances have access to Hansard or their representative's voting record to see not only what positions an MP is taking but also how often they attend debates, and offer basic guidance on how to approach MPs. The web-based organization 38 Degrees has become a sort of clearing house for crowd-driven collective action. A system of electronic petitioning has been created as part of the government's digital presence, which carefully pledges that a petition with 100,000 signatures 'could' be debated by the House of Commons.[2]

Meanwhile, aside from the Occupy movement, which expresses the frustrations of many at the shortcomings of government, the perceived lack of responsiveness in our leadership has created numerous local and single-issue campaigns, rejectionist movements and new parties: during the 1990s the professional political class lamented the inertia and apathy of the electorate as evidenced by low turnouts at elections, and launched consultation exercises whose principal purpose always appeared to be to explain to objectors to any given policy why they were wrong, rather than actually holding out any genuine possibility of change. Now, though, the electorate increasingly expects participation, not just on election day but constantly. (And, interestingly, it is 'expects' rather than 'demands'; you demand what you don't have, but expect what you consider to be natural.) The ubiquity of communications media means that political information and participation can take place anywhere, at any time. Inevitably, there are suggestions that voting should be made possible online. If it is, at what point does parliament become superfluous?

We're nowhere near that moment yet, but consider: if you can poll the electorate electronically, and get a higher turnout than you would at a polling station, and if you can do so rapidly and easily and know that the culture of your country is such that people are actually paying attention to the issues, why would you bother to persist with representative democracy? (The tempting answer is: because people can't be trusted to balance the budget and respect international treaties or human rights law, and there is undeniably some truth in that. But at that point you have to acknowledge that you're living in a paternalistic republic, not a democracy.)

The participant culture can be difficult for those with a more conventional understanding of the flow of power and prestige to appreciate. Bloggers, Twitter power-users and the others who stand at the intersection of a large number of online lives can have a reach and heft that is hard to see until it materializes (in the words of author and blogger John Scalzi: 'The Internet is looking for an excuse to drop on your head'). Stephen Fry's access to this kind of power is more easily understood; he was a celebrity before Twitter existed, and because he is also a lover of all things technological and adept at communication and pithy commentary, that status has translated into a significant and engaged online following. Fry has to be careful what websites he recommends, lest the immediate response from around the world when he mentions something overwhelm smaller servers. And not just smaller ones: his appeal on behalf of a death row inmate in China briefly caused the Foreign Office web presence to go offline.

But traditional media, politicians and companies can be surprisingly rash when it comes to dealing with the indigenous powerhouses of the Internet. Sometimes, they just don't seem to recognize the magnitude of what they're dealing with. Recently, for example, a PR company contrived to offend the Bloggess, writer of the eponymous website, blogger on several sites apart from her own, and someone with a Twitter following of around 170,000. It's also worth noting that she follows around 15,000, which to my eye implies someone who communicates avidly and will therefore have generated influence and loyalty among those followers. Earlier, I touched on the semiotics of email addresses and the hidden information they provide if you know how to read them. This is much the same; if you had shown me the Bloggess's Twitter page and her website, I would have taken about eight seconds to respond that this was someone with the approximate reach on specific issues of a minor national newspaper in the UK, and probably a somewhat higher level of personal trust.

Having managed an initial misfire which went from waspish to profane in a single exchange, the PR company went right ahead into the minefield and told her she should be grateful for their attention. Whatever it was supposed to be, it sounded like the priesthood of the old media and cultural Church reprimanding a lowly acolyte of an insignificant splinter sect. That's not something anyone would be rash enough to do to the editor of a national newspaper, but for some reason it seemed like a good idea in this context. The result was – to anyone who knows how the digital world works – massively predictable. The Bloggess put the exchange online. She tweeted about it. And it became news. What looked like soft, disconnected power lined up behind her until she was the tip of a spear a few hundred thousand irritated people long. The PR company found its own brand and the names of its senior executives in the midst of a PR nightmare.

The incredible thing about this is not that it happens, but that it happens a lot. In another instance, author Neil Gaiman found himself embroiled in a battle of words with Matt Dean, a Republican in the Minnesota House of Representatives. The spat was covered internationally, and Dean was made to apologize – by his mother[3] – but not before he'd managed to be offensive about Gaiman's massive fan base and garner the kind of bad publicity his political opponents would have paid millions of dollars to arrange if only they could have. Looking at either of these sequences is like watching a cheap banana skin gag in slow motion – one of those where the clown picks himself up off the floor, congratulates himself on his stylish recovery, and walks through a sheet of plate glass into a vat of paint.

The stars of participant media are not like the stars of television shows. The love-hate, predatory aspect of the visual media celebrity culture is absent. The relationship is more friendly, more even-handed and more loyal than obsessive. Figures like the Bloggess are not just characters on the screen; the level of engagement is much higher. They are real people with whom their correspondents and readers strongly identify, whom they admire and whom they consider part of their social circle. They have extended their own hearths until they touch directly on the hearths of others, creating one enormous temporary psychological living room space. Or perhaps it's more than that, and they are perceived unconsciously as autonomous parts of an extended, digitally mediated self.

~

The political and cultural clash of these three styles is with us all the time. The unevenly distributed future is matched by an unerased past that continues to play out, occasionally breaking through the patina of recent history. Despite the political fondness – in my mind linked inextricably with John Major but adopted wholeheartedly by Tony Blair and now alas from time to time even by US President Barack Obama – for 'drawing a line' under uncomfortable issues, speaking the words does not make it so.

Broadly, it seems to me that the professional culture's fondness for systems was derived from a mistrust of the foregoing style of individual decision-making, whether that was ideological – an attempt to move away from the tendency to patronage, feather-bedding and 'jobs for the boys' – or a practical perception that gathering the expertise of an institution and bringing it to bear was a vital step in dealing with a world that increasingly required sophisticated competences. Michael Kuhn's book *100 Films and a Funeral* describes part of the method that allowed Polygram Filmed Entertainment to achieve such a remarkable string of successes between 1991 and 1999: no project was given final approval until every department was in sync and Kuhn could see that there were no misunderstandings about what a film was supposed to be, to whom it would appeal or how it was going to be sold. The entire journey was mapped out in advance – at least in broad brush – avoiding the classic disaster moment in movie production where the marketing team sees a film for the first time and knows that however perfect a statement of art or identity it may be, the audience is not large enough to support the money spent on it. The system collated the opinions and capabilities of Kuhn's team and the product speaks for itself.

In a social and administrative setting, creating a system that can be applied universally looks initially like justice. Making everything about a simple set of rules lets people know what to expect and ensures that everyone is treated equally (or perhaps not 'equally' but 'exactly the same').

Sadly, it also means that cases that don't fit the structures envisaged by those creating the system are shoehorned into spaces that aren't right. The notorious response of the uncaring bureaucrat in British comedy and drama – 'sorry, computer says no' – speaks to the reality that human life is inevitably messier than attempts to codify it can allow for. We knew that already; it's why Britain retains its system of precedent in legal matters rather than creating a written constitution. The map must be able to grow to become more and more detailed as the territory is revealed. All the same, the professional era – the modern era – was and is filled with expert systems: abstracted and codified sets of rules intended to be applicable everywhere. Governments, bureaucracies and corporations are all systems on this model; people working for them function within strictly set boundaries. The point of them, indeed, is that while you may use your judgement, you are not there to create a policy, but to implement a set of rules. Decisions have already been taken, were taken when the structure was designed. A person's whole responsibility within a system of this kind is to fill a role. To go beyond that – to attempt to influence outcomes – is frowned upon. And in a sense, this was in the twentieth century the only way to do it if individual and possibly biased judgement – and a resulting uneven implementation of the rules – were to be avoided.

The culture we created as a consequence, though, was – and still is in some ways – profoundly unattractive. What was supposed to be fairness can become callousness or, at the very least, can feel that way when read from the other side. 'There's nowhere on the form for that' is a truthful response that can also be a self-exculpation, an abdication of responsibility for a situation that may mean that someone loses a house or gets no medical care because the extenuating circumstance on which they wish to base a defence is not acknowledged by the narrow straitjacket of rules. Moreover, in the twentieth century we lost track of the reason for the existence of these systems and the fact that they were part of ourselves. We became alienated, not in the classic Marxist sense of being alienated from the product of physical labour, but from the technologies of the mind we generated to create a fair and effective living environment for ourselves. (Those systems – composed of people – also forgot their own function, so that, for example, banks have begun to use the financial system to maximize short term profit rather than concentrating on wise lending to create genuine growth. Things which were too important and obvious to codify have been set aside as the code as written has become the basis of behaviour. A form of fairydust economics has emerged where numbers in ledgers get larger while the actual world remains the same. Every so often, someone notices the discrepancy and the whole thing collapses.)

This, not incidentally, is another perfect setting for deindividuation: on one side, the functionary behind a wall of security glass following a script laid out with the intention that it should be applied no matter what the specific human story may be, told to remain emotionally disinvested as far as possible so as to avoid preferential treatment of one person over another – and needing to follow that advice to avoid being swamped by empathy for fellow human beings in distress. The functionary becomes a mixture of Zimbardo's prison guards and the experimenter himself, under siege from without while at the same time following an inflexible rubric set down by those higher up the hierarchical chain, people whose job description makes them responsible, but who in turn see themselves as serving the general public as a non-specific entity and believe or have been told that only strict adherence to a system can produce impartial fairness. Fairness is supposed to be vested in the code: no human can or should make the system fairer by exercising judgement. In other words, the whole thing creates a collective responsibility culminating in a blameless loop. Everyone assumes that it's not their place to take direct personal responsibility for what happens; that level of vested individual power is part of the previous almost feudal version of responsibility. The deindividuation is actually to a certain extent the desired outcome, though its negative consequences are not.

By contrast – or by reflection – the supplicants on the other side of the glass see themselves as discarded and unregarded by the bureaucratic team, feel pressure from bills or ill health, their identity expressed in customer numbers or taxpayer IDs rather than names, and believe they are treated not as individuals but as cases. What ought to be human fallibility tempered by a system designed to ensure fairness becomes a resource-allocation machine that can't handle the awkward shapes of genuine human suffering. A sense of hopelessness and despair prevails – and we're back in the 1930s. Under such pressure, deindividuation plays out as a loss of self and inhibition: actions that should be impossible become conceivable. The social contract is broken, because such systems work not only by fear of retribution but by promise of reward. Where the second is absent, the first is insufficient, even in the degree possible to Egyptian and Tunisian secret policemen. You can see this as the Ultimatum Game again: below a certain level of reward, players sometimes choose to void the game and receive nothing rather than accept a bad deal, even if doing that in practice requires time, effort and the acceptance of risk.

Digital media can potentially ameliorate the disconnection between the two sides if they are permitted to do so, and if we as constituents are up to the task. The system of rules is created to avoid having to decide on each individual case as it arises, something that would have been impossible before the advent of the digital crowd. Technologically, at least, it's now possible to put hard cases into a pool to be judged in real time by the population at large. As I said: at some point in the not so distant future, we will inevitably have to start asking why we still have representative government when we could have direct participation.

More prosaically, though, digital communication allows people to seek advice from those in a position to know the answers, and look for guidance from those who will process their applications or complaints. It matters less in the context of deindividuation that the advice they receive should solve their problems than that those problems be acknowledged and that they feel they are talking to a human being rather than a blank wall. The communication must be authentic rather than scripted, personal rather than professional. It must acknowledge them as participants rather than supplicants. It must be human – and it need not matter that it is electronically mediated, so long as it is kind. (The word 'kind' is worthy of a book in itself: the dual meaning of being of the same type as another person and being good to them bears exploration, especially in this context. We say 'be a person' and we mean 'do the thing you would wish done for you if positions were reversed.' Kind-ness is an issue of identity as much as of empathy.)

Another important consequence in the arrival of digital technology and its facilitation of feedback is that we can look at large systems and recognize them once more not only as part of ourselves, but also as components that can change. Our relationship with text has shifted; where once almost the only widely available text in Europe was the Bible, the immutable Word, now we are surrounded by millions of tiny, impermanent textual bites.

The Gospel of Matthew says 'It is written' as a statement of certainty; in the Book of Daniel, the writing on the wall spelled doom for Belshazzar; the Ten Commandments were written in stone. Culturally, for hundreds of years what was written was unalterable. After Gutenberg the monopoly of the Churches on text was broken and people began to express dissent; but still, what was written was written for ever, and carried a weight of authority. Even thirty years ago, what was in the papers carried additional legitimacy; and a large number of people still trust the *Encyclopaedia Britannica* over Wikipedia, despite a similar error-rate.

Now, though, we live in a world where text is fluid, where it responds to our instructions. Writing something down records it, but does not make it true or permanent. So why should we put up with a system we don't like simply because it's written somewhere? We are aware, more than ever, that what has been decided and contracted is simply that: an agreed statement. If we now disagree, that statement can be changed if people are willing to change it. Contracts and even laws are subject to renegotiation. That realization, incidentally, is something many companies and indeed governments – or the people who work in them – have failed to come to terms with in the context of the wider populace but seem able to take on board quite readily in relation to themselves. The UK parliament notably cannot bind a future parliament; the debts of sovereign nations are even now being reassessed and written down. The leaders of the US right trumpet the idea that 'corporations are people' but seemingly have not begun to consider the consequences of their constituents following this logic to its conclusion and demanding the right to act like corporations. It's too late for them to object, anyway: the franchise of rewriting has been extended to include everyone, but the aristocracy of the old regime have yet to acknowledge it.

Those debates to one side for now, the unfortunate side effects of the culture of expert systems make an important point as we begin to build new technologies that will create around themselves new economic ecosystems and institutions; it comes back to the feedback loop that embraces society, technology and the individual: the choices we make now about the technology we use and how we use it will affect the way our world looks in the future. Buying – whether it's with money or resources or with data – is voting: choices have consequences. Consequences do not fade away, and some become locked in. We have to learn to choose not just for the short term and the immediate bargain, but for the long game and the better outcome. In making or in endorsing new practices, we have to look at what they will create around themselves. We need to practise our choosing.

And more than that, we have to learn to code the change we want to see in the world.

~

Perhaps the most important corollary of the mutually influential relationship between technology and society is that, knowing it's there, we have some degree of choice about which direction to take. It's impossible to know in advance precisely how a given technology will influence the future, but we can attempt to create technologies and systems that are necessary for the kind of world we want to live in. More specifically, we have to create the technologies that are necessary for the institutions we believe we will need to support the way of life we desire.

By way of example: a favourite dream of proponents of the Internet as a great scholastic resource and a driver of education and literacy is the global digital library, a massive accessible collection of information in the form of texts, images and other media available from anywhere in the world. When the Google Book Settlement was in play, one of the arguments in favour (and it is, in my opinion, still the most powerful recommendation of that project, however much I disliked Google's approach to it) was that the resulting archive would be a moment akin to the arrival of the Gutenberg press. Google's mission to make the world's information searchable would dovetail with an absolutely undeniable positive: the creation of a library of extraordinary breadth and depth.

The problem with the Gutenberg comparison is control. When Johannes Gutenberg created his revolutionary press in the middle of the fifteenth century, the consequence was the breaking of the Church's monopoly on scholarship in the Christian world. The invention of movable type was a moment of massive decentralization. If information wants to be free, that was the first time that it ever saw daylight.

Creating a digital library owned by a private company in one country is not the same thing at all. It inevitably implies the possibility of a monopoly on that information emerging and, indeed, that was one of the profound objections raised in the fairness hearings surrounding the Google Book Settlement (though not the one on which the settlement was rejected). Because Google has, still, more goodwill than any other corporate giant, people tend to be less concerned about the possibility that it will suddenly 'turn evil' and require payment for access to such an archive. However, companies do not have solid identities. Granted, I've argued that people also are more fluid than we care to believe, but it's a sliding scale. Corporate entities are bought and sold, and sometimes bits of them are broken off. The last company so central to a vital communications service could arguably be said to be AT&T, which, under a 1982 agreement with the US Department of Justice to resolve an anti-trust case, shed its local operations, creating seven new companies known as 'Baby Bells'. (In any case it has to be acknowledged that part of Google's desire for the archive was to improve its own search software by improving the system's understanding of language.) If you imagine Google – or any media giant – in the same situation, divesting itself of such a digital archive, and that archive then being snapped up by a company with a less benign image, you begin to see the problem. The cost of academic journals in some cases can be thousands of pounds a year; what might EvilCorp Hypothetical Industries charge for access to the only complete digital library in the world?

Moreover, digital files controlled centrally are subject to curious dangers. In July 2009 users of Amazon's Kindle reading device who had purchased a particular edition of *1984* by George Orwell discovered that it had vanished overnight. The disappearance was the consequence of a copyright wrangle, but the precise grounds hardly mattered. That it should have been Orwell's book – in which a totalitarian government makes dissidents vanish by dropping them down a 'memory hole' – made the situation that much more bleakly ironic, but the basic truth was bad enough: a digital book could be removed from the Kindle device on instruction from a central location. Under what other circumstances might a text be pulled? If a book contained material that embarrassed the government, might it, too, disappear?

The question ought to be ridiculous, but the remarkable flexibility of any number of companies when it comes to government requests became obvious in the course of the Wikileaks revelations in late 2010 and early 2011. Bank of America, Western Union, MasterCard, VISA Europe and PayPal responded to pressure from the Obama administration and cut off funding to Wikileaks on request. Amazon dropped the site from its hosting service. Wikileaks is a troublesome organization and one that undertakes actions of which many people do not approve. The way in which it was assailed, however, should give anyone pause who believes that a digital archive will necessarily remain inviolate in the hands of a private company. (That said, I suppose we should be grateful the suggestions of some US legislators were ignored: at least one person suggested Julian Assange should be the target of a drone strike. He was at the time resident in central London.)

So, what to do? How do you preserve a text stored in a

mutable form? Obviously, you duplicate it and store the copies all over the place. Wikileaks, again, understood that the only way to be certain their trove of cables could not be sequestered or destroyed was to distribute it widely. The same logic applies to the global digital library; a real Gutenberg moment for the digital age is not the creation of a single database with a single gate-keeper, but the birth of any number of digital libraries accessible all over the world. For greater security of the contents, we'd also vary the format in which they were stored, making it harder for a virus to wreak havoc on them all. (You might argue that that brings its own problems of access, and it's true, but it is also true that it can be seen as insurance against the obsolescence of a given format. It's an interesting sidebar.)

The main debate comes back, in the end, to Marshall McLuhan: what is the message of a given technological choice? What does it mean to have a single digital library controlled from within the United States by a tech giant based in California, as opposed to having a vast number of libraries around the world, each of them containing the same media and each widely acces-sible? Which proposes democracy, and which leaves the door open to less amenable forms of governance? When we're struc-turing our technologies – and the systems that support them and grow from them – we have to choose, over and over again, the path that emphasizes the society we want.

It isn't possible – at least, it's not humanly possible, and not technologically possible *yet* – to map perfectly the consequences of an attempt to incentivize or disincentivize a given behaviour. Governments attempt it constantly using tax regulation, and the results are rarely if ever what was intended. Part of the under-standing regarding the bank bailouts in the UK was that the banks would start lending to businesses again to encourage growth, but that isn't happening either. Incentives that seem clear-cut can be more complex when you put them in context. For example, returning to *Freakonomics* for a moment: capital punishment is supposed to be a deterrent to serious crime. However, according to Levitt and Dubner, the annual execution rate among death row detainees in New York — and let's not forget that a percentage of these will be innocent of the crime of which they are accused, so there's a measurable chance that if you commit a crime, someone else will die for it — is 2 per cent. That compares favourably with the 7 per cent annual chance of dying just because a person is a member of the Black Gangster Disciple Nation crack gang. (And that's before you factor in the point I made earlier, that a system of social controls relies on positives as well as negatives, and many of those who commit serious crimes may well have crossed that Rubicon already, feeling that society has no path for them.)

Getting incentives flowing in the right direction is hard. Levitt and Dubner also cite a study that showed mechanics allowing cars that failed a clean air standard to pass because lenient mechanics got repeat business: great for the car business, good for drivers whose need or desire for their car outweighs their under-standing of pollution and its negative consequences, but bad for the economy because those negatives are probably more expensive and bad for public health (which obviously is also an economic factor).

That said, the other thing you can learn from reading *Freakonomics* is that looking hard at the information in an intelligent way will help you track down situations where the incentives are all wrong. And a digital era attitude to how systems work, one that says that no model is perfect first time, but that a model can be made better and better by refinement, might be able to make it work. It would probably require that we as human beings learn to function intelligently as a group rather than in our own individual short-term favour, something else that becomes easier as digital technology allows you to appreciate your place in a larger tapestry, and why it's better for you to accept a short-term loss in quest for a longer term gain.

Fundamentally, in reaching for a better world, we have to code for it: we have to create the technologies that will foster the culture and institutions that will produce it, and legislate for the climate that will allow it. It is not enough to cross our fingers and hope, now that we no longer have to.

~

Choice is a new experience for us in the context of social change. We have until now been part of a process of change prompted by climatic shifts and migrations, famines, warlords and technological advances: not an inexorable progress towards a 'higher form' of social life, but a sort of ragged wandering. Furthermore, in case it isn't obvious, the traits that are evolutionarily successful are not always those that we would desire for our societies. In biological evolution, a shining example of the cruelty of the selfish gene is the chicken. All but flightless, also tasty and nutritious, the chicken is the ideal domesticated bird. In consequence, the reported global chicken population in 2003 was 24 billion, making it the most successful avian in biological history. Any given chicken, of course, can expect to be eaten at any time, and a vast number of them live in appalling conditions in factory farms. The DNA doesn't care as long as they breed.

Similarly, if there is a process akin to evolution that applies to societies, it does not necessarily select for mass happiness. If the population's unhappiness makes them more likely to survive hard conditions or destroy a competitor, that will do fine. Nor, indeed, is such a process a guarantee of our own society's survivability. We could be a dead-end. Nonetheless, accounts of history have tended – sometimes unconsciously, sometimes with reference to a teleological theory like Marx's historical materialism in which all roads eventually lead to perfect socialism – to suggest a kind of upward progress, and that notion is lodged in the popular consciousness. Francis Fukuyama proposed the end of history in 1992, suggesting that henceforth all change would be technological: the advent of liberal democracy meant the end of sociopolitical evolution. But it's not clear why that should be the case. The neatness of teleological ideas of history and the future makes me suspect them; and then, too, they're so self-congratulatory: we're better in every way than those who came before us.

It seems more likely to me that human social change to this point has been a drift, a series of actions and reactions, mostly without any sense of what the outcome of a given choice would be. Our grasp of what's going on is still fragmentary, but we can increasingly spot correlations and trends, and, importantly, we can spot them while they're happening rather than long after. Not all of them are immensely sophisticated; some are almost embarrassingly biological. For example, a recent study by researchers at Cornell University analysed half a billion postings from 2.5 million Twitter users, and established a common emotional shape to their days, varying by day of the week. In other words, there appears to be a predictable pattern of positivity at certain times of day, negativity at others, which extends across the eighty-four countries represented in the data.[4] It's simple enough, but consider for a moment what it may mean to someone who is trying to sell you something. A study of different kinds of people will reveal whether they buy when they're happy because they feel confident or when they're feeling tired and cranky because it cheers them up. Advertising that reaches the right person at the right moment will be more effective, especially in a connected world where purchase can happen at almost the moment of desire. Cross-referenced with a closer understanding of the kind of person someone is gleaned from their social media information, and a database of like and dislike matches, perhaps a credit score, and you have a slightly alarming persuasion engine which knows when and where we are most vulnerable to an 'impulse purchase', or can guess how to get a more stolid soul to choose 'yes' in the longer term.

Leaving aside the obnoxiousness of a system that can get you to fill your house with consumer junk you might have decided you didn't need if left alone, we're presently painfully well acquainted with the macro-effects of irrational and over-aspirational decisions taken under the tutelage of corporate institutions such as credit card companies and banks who were perhaps looking to their own bottom line rather more than to the best possible advice for the individual. The wrong kind of successful persuasion could leave us with even more ghastly financial wreckage.

At this moment, there is a kind of arms race taking place as we learn more about ourselves and what influences us – and we, as individuals, are definitely not in the lead. The world's big companies, and most particularly those that control or have access to Internet data, presently know more about how we buy than we do, because, as in Google's case, or Facebook's or Amazon's, the business of their day-to-day function entails the gathering of huge amounts of raw data which they have the know-how to collate. That's to say that they know more about what influences us to buy, how we make the final 'yes' decision, and conversely what's likely to prevent us from doing so. They know that people do, ridiculously, buy more items priced at 99p than they would items priced at £1 (in behavioural economics, the phenomenon is called 'left-digit bias'). They know that we take undue notice of anchor prices and indeed of random numbers that look similar to prices in assessing whether something gives good value. They formulate ways of saving such as Amazon Prime, which for a single annual payment gives you 'free' one-day delivery – a bargain that results in people buying more and more from Amazon to offset the fee, so that what appears to be to the company's disadvantage ultimately works out in Amazon's favour.

Like casinos, large corporate entities have studied the numbers and the ways in which people respond to them. These are not

con tricks – they're not even necessarily against our direct interests, although sometimes they can be – but they are hacks for the
human mind, ways of manipulating us into particular decisions
we otherwise might not make. They are also, in a way, deliberate
underminings of the core principle of the free market, which
derives its legitimacy from the idea that informed self-interest
on aggregate sets appropriate prices for items. The key word is
'informed'; the point of behavioural economics – or, rather, of its
somewhat buccaneering corporate applications – is to skew our
perception of the purchase to the advantage of the company. The
overall consequence of that is to tilt the construction of our society away from what it should be if we were making the rational
decisions classical economics imagines we would, and towards
something else.

Governments, too, are looking to the technologies of 'nudging' to push us towards certain behaviours and away from others,
trying, perhaps, to push back the ghost of the classical Greek
orator Isocrates: 'Democracy destroys itself because it abuses its
right to freedom and equality. Because it teaches its citizens to
consider audacity as a right, lawlessness as a freedom, abrasive
speech as equality, and anarchy as progress.' But the idea of
nudging really means subconsciously influencing the voting
population to things they might otherwise not choose, rather
than arguing the case directly. There's a very fine line here:
the feedback system of road signs that tell you your speed is,
obviously, a hint to slow down, but it is overt and leaves you
with a clear choice. The classic example of 'nudging' is making a
decision 'opt out' rather than 'opt in' – organ donation, for
instance, or indeed the original Google Book Settlement. In a
governmental context it's an Orwellian style of dictatorship that,
by presenting heavily skewed choices or options that involve
irritating effort versus others that do not and avoiding genuinely
difficult balanced choices between two possible courses of action,
effectively makes the population practise docility until it becomes

nicely habitual. Like cross-subsidization, 'libertarian paternalism' is the quiet death of genuine choice, the creation of a society in which a class of supposed experts rules over a common herd. It also throws away any hope of using the power of the crowd to make good decisions, because it supplies the crowd with bad basic information.

But information about our behaviour is also, increasingly, available to us. It is possible to become what some psychologists call 'test-conscious': aware of the tricks, and therefore while not immune to them at least capable of understanding that they are being played and looking for ways of compensating. Once again, we're discussing a kind of feedback, and once again, it comes from our new ability to watch ourselves in the digital mirror at various different levels – as individuals or as large groups. We can learn to use our knowledge of what will influence us to nudge ourselves towards good decisions, thus creating a virtuous cycle. We need, ultimately, to favour the creation of systems around us that foster informed, intelligent decisions, not the ones that increase the profit margin of companies at the expense of our own good outcomes or bow automatically to the will of a government that may or may not know what it's doing. In the shorter term, we need to learn to make good choices even though we are also irrational, and to educate and train ourselves in the habit of decision.

By way of example: Dan Ariely describes the pricing structure of US subscriptions to the *Economist* magazine – $59 for Internet-only, $125 for a print-only subscription, and $125 for a combined sub – and breaks it down as follows: 'most people don't know what they want unless they see it in context . . . the *Economist*'s marketers offered us a no-brainer: relative to the print option, the print-and-Internet option looks clearly superior.' But the only reason the combination option looks so strong is the presence of the print-only option. In fact, that comparison is the sole reason for the existence of the print-only option. It's there to make you think the combination is a bargain. Consider it again without the print option: $59 for an Internet subscription, or $125 for a print–and–Internet combination. Even having gone through the whole process openly, do you suddenly find the choice slightly different? I have read and re-read that section in Ariely's book. I have used the example repeatedly to friends and in professional discussions of ebook pricing. And yet to me, as I type this, the equation has still changed. Abruptly, the combination option seems more expensive than it did at the beginning of this paragraph.

Perhaps the most important thing is not to get good at making decisions, but to remember to want the opportunity to do so. On 13 July 2011 *New Scientist* magazine carried an item on Prodcast, a software system created by Microsoft to help you decide when to buy technological goods. The logic is unassailable: new technological gizmos decrease in price over time and eventually are replaced. There is therefore a sort of perfect window where they're as cheap as they're going to get without being outmoded (although 'outmoded' is a harsh description for a fully functional item that is fractionally slower than the newer version or takes slightly lower resolution pictures). Prodcast tells you when to strike, while other expert systems advise on what and where to buy.

Taken together, these systems seem to imply that human intervention in the decision is rather unnecessary. The same idea resonates in Eric Schmidt's assessment of Google's ability to predict what a user is thinking and in Amazon's recommendations: the concept is that the system knows what you will think before you think it, but of course it's somewhat self-fulfilling, like the old trick of telling someone not to think about purple elephants. It goes beyond advertising, which to me has a sense of being broadcast; it's an offer of a specific product driven by an analysis of you. The next step in the seamless interaction of the system and your environment is a kind of checklist: *Are you sure you don't*

want object x? Well, no, I suppose I'm not sure I don't want it . . .
Maybe I do . . . And indeed, my online supermarket does exactly
that: before I can check out, I have to run a gauntlet of helpful
suggestions of things I may have forgotten and things I haven't
tried but which the software is offering me on the basis of an
analysis of purchasing patterns across the board.

One step beyond that is the creation of a bank account to
which the software has access. You could set up a robot that
would check all three variables against whether you had sufficient funds, and place an order if you did, and your shiny new
product would arrive before you even realized that you wanted
it. It would probably send you an email to let you know the item
was ordered, so that you didn't accidentally buy one in the
meantime. Life without the stress of discovering your own
amusements; new things just arriving for you to play with. If we
follow this road, will we lose, instead of decision-making ability,
the habit of volition? Long-term prison inmates eventually
lose the habit of opening doors for themselves. Instead they stand
and wait for a warden to unlock the door and tell them to step
through. It starts to look a little like the nightmare scenario, but
it's a consequence of choice. If we ever arrive at that place, we
will have chosen it. It's not inherent in the technology – but it
may be an aspect of our culture. The problem with that, of
course, is that the choice is clouded and concealed. We don't see
it for what it is – although we are perhaps beginning to.

Practically speaking, it's possible to build a strong habit of
choice. It's like learning to fasten your seat belt when you get in
the car. You just do it, over and over, until it becomes part of the
business of starting the engine. (In fact, of course, what you're
doing is strengthening the relevant neural pathways in your brain
– turning neuroplasticity to your own advantage.) In the real
world, it might be hard to find evenly balanced decisions with
trees of branching possibility to practise on, but, coming right
back to the beginning of this book, we know that decision-

making skills are among those emphasized by frequent interaction with digital technology. Both computer games and web use require anticipation, problem-solving and decision. So if you're already working and playing digitally, you're solving part of the problem. (Games, obviously, want to present you with hard choices to keep you interested, and deciding whether to click through a link in an article to the deeper information beyond is, as Nicholas Carr describes it, a split-second change in cognition during which you weigh what you're presently reading against an assessment of the interest and value of what you are likely to find beyond the link.)

US writer and thinker Howard Rheingold, who chronicled the rise of the WELL in the early days of the Internet, also wrote a checklist for lucid dreaming. Lucid dreams are dreams in which the sleeper is aware that they are dreaming and can control their actions and environment. The trick is to reach that point without also waking yourself up. Rheingold gives three easy ways of spotting a dream: physical laws don't work; text changes when you read it twice or is illegible; switches and mechanisms that ought to function do nothing. He advises would-be lucid dreamers to check these things frequently throughout the day so that they do it naturally, and hence while dreaming.

The concept lends itself well to training oneself to good habits of decision-making. Each time you're confronted with a situation that seems to call for choice, check your assumptions. Look at the options in front of you, and remove the ones that seem out of place, like the *Economist*'s print-only option. Now ask yourself whether the options available accord with what you actually want and what you feel able to pay in terms of time or effort or money – or personal data. At each stage, demand more of yourself. Don't simply wait for time, the system or circumstance to make the choice for you. (This last is particularly important as businesses in all areas confront the digital challenge; there's a natural caution that urges us to watch and wait and see what it all looks like 'when it's calmed down'. The problem with that is that it cedes the act of creation of the new landscape to others who have different priorities. Once again looking at the publishing trade, the digital giants – Amazon, Apple and Google – have different priorities and business models from those of conventional publishers. A 'wait and see' strategy hands control of the book's new era to entities that need different things from the existing publishing industry. The hard truth is: get involved, or get sidelined. The future is not set. It's being made right now.)

Broadly, the 'choice habit' looks a bit like this:

1 What are the overt costs and benefits?
2 What are the hidden costs? Under what circumstances if any will this become a disaster?
3 What will the effects of this choice be on the wider world?
4 What assumptions have I made in framing this choice in this way? Are there other ways of dealing with the same situation that might be better?

It's quite interesting to run different decisions through the list. For example: *Should I accept an interest-only, negative-amortizing, adjustable-rate sub-prime mortgage?*

Rendered in English, that's a loan secured on your house on which you have the option of adding your interest payments to the capital sum as you go along. If it sounds barking mad, that is because it is, as far as I can tell, the worst type of loan created during the sub-prime lending boom, designed in essence for people who could not afford to borrow what they were being offered. It is a loan whose purpose is not to serve the borrower but to form part of a package of loans that can then be securitized and sold on: a loan-as-commodity. It stumbles a bit on question 1, looks utterly alarming on question 2, and brain-shatteringly scary if you can actually answer question 3. (In which case, you can join the five or six people who dared to ask hard questions in the run-up to the collapse and make a lot of money.) The answer to question 4 would probably be: *Yes, you need to consider a different property or a rental.*

I'm not proposing that this is magic, just that a real decision process, robustly applied, will at least reveal the nature of the choice in front of you. It works equally well on the *Economist*'s pricing scheme, by the way: question 4 has you re-examining the different price bands and asking, if you're really being serious about it, why the print-only option is included at all.

It's a longish list, and it requires some brainpower to apply it, but habit makes this kind of thing very rapid – as with the example of starting your car. In that case, the sequence goes something like: seat belt, got everything, know destination, start car, mirrors and road, signal, move – and takes a few seconds. Obviously, a choice-under-pressure list looks different, as we've already seen. But in context, part of the point of choice is that you have to construct your own priority list; that very action is an important aspect of deciding where you assign value. And once you begin to use a list like this, you shape your life around the idea that you make your own decisions and it becomes self-reinforcing; feedback once again.

Something else emerges from this discussion about us as human individuals: we're not fixed, stable intellects riding along peering at the world through the lenses of our eyes like the pilots of people-shaped spacecraft. We are affected constantly by what's going on around us. Whether our flexibility is based in neuro-plasticity or in less dramatic aspects of the brain, we have to start acknowledging that we are mutable, persuadable and vulnerable to clever distortions, and that very often what we want to be is a matter of constant effort rather than attaining a given state and then forgetting about it. Being human isn't like hanging your hat on a hook and leaving it there, it's like walking in a high wind: you have to keep paying attention. You have to be engaged with the world.

Perhaps more, though, you are mutable, and that is good. Your habits and opinions are not written in your brain or your DNA like carvings on stone tablet, although some of your predispositions probably are. Steven Pinker again: 'When identical twins who were separated at birth are tested in adulthood, their political attitudes turn out to be similar.' Our brains are to a certain extent set, but within limits they are changeable, trainable. So we need to learn to treat our identities as something we make, at least in part, and be sensitive to the possibility that others are using that mutability as a tool to manipulate our actions – while at the same time taking advantage of it to become more who we wish to be. What we can't change will take care of itself. What we can is up to us.

blindgiant.co.uk/chapter7

PART III

8

Engagement

A FEW YEARS ago, a friend of mine was studying for an art history qualification (I forget which kind). She had among other things to absorb the entirety of a wonderful book about Italian art in the Baroque period called *Patrons and Painters*. I had almost no knowledge of the topic, and yet somehow I had to help, at least to glean enough so that I could test her knowledge. I started at the index, looking for a way in that would allow me to find a meaningful path through a foreign land, and noticed that one name occurred a great deal: that of Consul Joseph Smith.

Smith was a collector and a patron; actually, you could say that he was *the* patron. He knew everyone. He occurs a great deal in Francis Haskell's book because he's a pivotal figure, which makes him ubiquitous and therefore useless as a first stepping stone. There's simply too much of him to absorb without a background. However, in skimming the main entry on Joseph Smith I found someone who was, to me, more interesting: Giustiniana Wynne.

Giustiniana Wynne was the daughter of a Greek adventuress and an English noble. She attracted – most probably, she sought out and fought for – the attention of some of the most important players in the game of art in Venice during her lifetime. Joseph Smith courted her, lost her, and was so hurt by the rejection that he fell out with his rival and pupil, Andrea Memmo. Memmo subsequently became a significant patron in his own right.

Giustiniana eventually married the Austrian ambassador; Memmo, incidentally a friend of Casanova and an enthusiastic sampler of life's pleasures, had long since moved on. I don't know whether it was he or Giustiniana who terminated the affair; they seem to have been well-matched. In any case, the ambassador, Count Rosenberg, was apparently a man who enjoyed less cerebral activities such as hunting; his wife aspired, in Haskell's words, to the company of the learned. The final relevant entry in the book has her, older and more respectable but still a force to be reckoned with, keeping company (romantic or simply intellectual is unclear) with Angelo Querini, the 'last important patron to emerge in Venice'. Giustiniana was witness to, and binds together, some of the most interesting developments in art and philosophy of the period.

When I began to trace the story of Giustiniana Wynne through Venice, I became deeply and delightedly engaged. Maryanne Wolf, in *Proust and the Squid*, describes it perfectly in relation to reading a passage from (of course) Proust:

> As your brain's systems integrated all the visual, auditory, semantic, syntactic and inferential information . . . you, the reader, automatically began to connect [it] with your own thinking and insights . . . Reading is a neuronally and intellectually circuitous act, enriched as much by the unpredictable indirections of a reader's inferences and thoughts, as by the direct message to the eye from the text.

I knew that, given time and information, I could come to understand the culture and the people Francis Haskell was describing by following the traces of this one remarkable woman, Giustiniana Wynne, through their lives. I was also interested, excited and moved by the small fragments of her life I encountered. I took sides in fights and wished her well in her later, more tranquil years. She, in turn, showed me who was important and what they cared about. Haskell passes on her account of Angelo Querini's house at Alticchiero, now destroyed:

the building is not sumptuous, nor is the furniture lavish of choice; but – far better – the arrangement is as simple and convenient as possible.' On the tables are busts of ancient and modern philosophers, among them Voltaire and Rousseau by Houdon, and the influence of both men is felt throughout the villa and gardens. No precautions are taken against theft. Only at Tahiti and Alticchiero, exclaims Mme Rosenberg, can such trust in human nature be found.

Giustiniana Wynne was a telescope through which I could see another world.

This sense of engagement is key: I found something that I could relate to and process. I have always needed context to remember and understand things. At school, I found the lists and tables of mathematics impossibly hard because I was required to learn them by rote without understanding why they worked or why I needed them. I could not engage with pure figures and operations: they slid off the surface of my mind and left me groping for them in the dark. Tell me, on the other hand, about Pythagoras, and explain the importance of his work, and I can retain and understand his geometry. As Wolf observes, in my uptake of Giustiniana's world, what was already in my head was as important as what was on the page: it is the encounter between the two that is the relevant experience. It is not important, in this context, whether the engagement is taking place between two flesh and blood human beings, two or more human beings mediated by the Internet, or one human being and the text of a book written by another. There is an interaction taking place, not a straight dump of information from source to brain.

That should hearten anyone who fears that the increasing reliance in digital society on Dr Johnson's secondary sort of knowledge – the knowledge of where to find something – is destroying the idea of scholarship and excellence. Johnson's secondary knowledge actually comes in two parts, the tacit part being 'knowing where to put information in your own mental map when you've found it, and knowing what to do with it'. Expertise is not merely knowledge, and it is not supplanted by access: it is the ability to incorporate information at a high level, to work with it and manipulate it – to engage with it fully.

More than that, though, engagement is the key to authenticity. With it, something meaningful is happening, whether you're watching an animated cartoon or discussing ontology with a famous metaphysician. Without it, you could be standing in the midst of wonder and see nothing. The classic image from American movies of recent decades is the dad on his mobile phone when he should be paying attention to his children, but you can equally easily find the phenomenon in people who can't stop discussing their favourite topic when they're walking through a rainforest, or those to whom one aspect of life is so utterly all-important that everything must be seen in its light, be that taxation, Marxism, God or sex.

But what was happening in my head was not the straightforward 'deep reading' experience Nicholas Carr is concerned we are losing. That encounter – while it is also a powerful engagement – is supposedly more narrow. In deep reading, there is a single stream of information from text to brain that excites what I would call engagement. It is not a question of binding together disparate narratives and creating a fresh perspective, but of connecting one's own thoughts to those of an author. It is, as it were, monogamous, although Carr also mentions that the act of reading paper differs from reading on screen because there are measurable sense data that differ starkly, which seems to undermine his point. If the business of reading is partly supplemented by subsidiary information like that, then it isn't entirely devoid of additional streams after all – though, granted, there is a difference between sense information and cognition.

Rather than being like deep reading, the business of understanding the story of Giustiniana Wynne was – subjectively, at least – more akin to the process of writing, or to reading a string of different documents to try to appreciate a news story from a variety of angles. It was inherently an act of synthesis, of editing, of judgement and creation. I was putting together a narrative. Rather than relying on a linear history with a single viewpoint, I was assembling a new understanding from a selection of incidents. You could argue – in the context of news stories, particularly – that this is a much better way of getting to an accurate perception of events than accepting the account of a single narrator. It's the skill at the heart of digital reading in my experience: assemblage reading, a kind of internal storytelling in which a series of perspectives including one's own is merged to produce a new understanding that embraces a string of other narratives and accepts them as primary but single-perspective and tries to assemble an over-arching, inter-subjective picture. It's what we did ('we' being everyone on Twitter and other social media sites) as we tried to fathom what was happening in Egypt in spring 2011, following the stories of people we had never met and weaving them together.

The position of the reader in these two different ways of engaging is key to understanding how digital and plain text differ: in Carr's deep reading, the reader is active, but still essentially a docile audience. In the read/write creation of a narrative from fragments, the reader is a participant – and that is at the heart of the digital age. The nature of our digital technologies as they presently exist fosters this way of being: a creative, synthetic approach to information and the world rather than an obedient, consuming one. As the growth of literacy allowed human beings to examine themselves as if from without and ushered in a new human mind – and brain – which hinged on that ability, so perhaps the digital technologies bring a more critical, creative, and engaged self to the fore.

~

Engagement is not a substitute for deep reading – at least, I'm not proposing that it fills the gap Carr feels is left in our brain's plastic architecture and function by a diminished amount of time spent reading in the conventional sense, although it may, in fact, be what is replacing it in many situations – but it is a measure of whether or not an interaction is authentic. If you are engaged, either with a person or an object, you are paying attention to them, learning from them and about them, incorporating your encounter into your understanding of the world. If you're not doing that, your interaction is cursory at best. In a social context you may offend them, and you're unlikely to remember much about them. If what you're not engaging with is the nail you're banging into a piece of wood, it's entirely likely you'll hit your thumb with a hammer.

Obviously, when you're dealing with a person, it isn't simply a question of learning about them to gain access to information about the world. When we try to find out about someone socially – What movies do you like? Can you dance? What kind of work do you do? – we're looking for places where we can bring our own experience and identity into contact with that of someone else. We're in a species of dance, probing the edges of our agreements, looking to learn, to discover commonality or points of enjoyable difference. This kind of engagement is the interaction and meeting of two identities effectively communicated.

The key factor is that what separates real from counterfeit is not physical presence, but the actual interaction of mental and emotional patterns. Granted, you can't have a real fight or real sex with someone without a physical component – yet – but if you have an hour-long conversation in the flesh and come away with no memory of the detail, no sense of who the other person was, and no real change to yourself as a consequence of the interaction, it's hard to see how you can feel that you've had a real encounter. On the other hand, if you have an hour-long conversation online that moves and challenges you, and that experience becomes a part of who you are, the engagement clearly is important and the interaction is real. More challenging is what would have happened if you'd had that same conversation in the flesh. Would it have been more intense, more engaged? It's impossible to say. Yes, our non-verbal communication is hugely important, so you would receive additional cues and information. On the other hand, would it have taken a different course? Would a sexual dynamic have occluded intellectual honesty and resulted in a lousy cognitive engagement, an encounter filled with partial deception ending in a physical encounter? Does that qualify as more genuine?

I'm far from being the first person to identify and emphasize the value of the engaged state. Robert Pirsig's novel *Zen and the Art of Motorcycle Maintenance* discusses something very similar. Pirsig identifies moments of disengagement as 'quality traps'. When you make a poor decision, force a screw and strip the thread because you were in a hurry and not really concentrating, that's a quality trap. The smooth focus that Pirsig proposes we should all try to inhabit all the time has been lost, and the consequence of a heedless, careless interaction with the world is frustration.

Psychologist Mihaly Csikszentmihalyi also wrote extensively about what I would identify as the deep engagement of creative work in *Flow*: 'When all a person's relevant skills are needed to cope with the challenges of a situation, that person's attention is completely absorbed . . . All the attention is concentrated on the relevant stimuli . . . one of the most universal and distinctive features of optimal experience takes place: people become so involved in what they are doing that the activity becomes spontaneous, almost automatic . . .' But importantly, 'Although the flow experience appears to be effortless . . . it requires . . . highly disciplined mental activity. It does not happen without the application of skilled performance.'

Csikszentmihalyi's 'flow' is almost certainly the most concentrated sort of engagement; I don't propose that we all constantly push ourselves to the level of focus required to drive a Formula

One car or write a novel. In any case, judging by my own experience, that state is not something that can be maintained at all times and nor is it entirely desirable to do so; the absoluteness of it makes it a perilous friend if you're walking through a crowded marketplace or driving a car (unless that activity is what you're concentrating on). I find that when I'm working at that level I lack what fighter pilots call 'situational awareness'; more colloquially, I could keep working through a small earthquake so long as the power to my computer remained uninterrupted, and if the power did fail I might well just go and find a pen.

But the basic tenet of focus, of the application of the attention of the mind to a task, an activity, is the same. It's what differentiates interactions that are real and worthwhile from those that are essentially a waste of time, or, at least, the kind of thing with which our days are filled and which we generally forget: tying shoelaces, brushing teeth and so on. We don't engage with those activities in general because we don't see that they have value; they're mechanical actions rather than ones we need to get to grips with and understand. (As a matter of interest, engaging properly with either one of those examples yields fascinating information: shoelaces lead backwards into history and sideways into fashion and the mathematics of knots, and tooth-brushing touches biology, chemistry, advertising, body mechanics . . . Pirsig would probably say that was the point: an open appreciation of the world around yields understanding and wonder.)

Engagement is also important because it is in part a determinator of whether we grant someone the privileges of the hearth. That's more than simply a question of whether you allow them into your house; it's a question about whether you'd give them a key to your house. Granting someone access to the hearth – to the place where we play and where our families live – is a gesture of trust and an acceptance of them into a different order of our personal understanding of the world. Inside the hearth circle, there is a code of behaviour, a reciprocal relationship of guest and host, of co-equals, and of mutual obligation. It goes beyond 'Netiquette', the much debated code of online politesse. Hearth rules are exacting yet soft, more understandings than codified laws, requiring attention and even empathy.

In *Predictably Irrational*, Dan Ariely describes an example that intrigues me. At a day care centre in Israel, there was apparently a problem with tardy parents. The centre, in an attempt to ameliorate this, imposed a fine for lateness. Not only did this not solve the problem, it actually exacerbated it: the change from social obligation – hearth rules – to commercial transaction made parents much more willing to show up late, because now there was a straightforward cost that could be met by paying the fine rather than a sense of anti-social behaviour. The host–guest relationship was annulled and replaced with a simple transactional one, in which transformation, people in cooperation became representatives of two separate financial interests bound in a contractual relationship. In the new situation, the only obligation upon the parents was to pay their bills, after which it was up to them to extract the most good from the service. What had been cooperation between individuals on an informal, hearth basis in which everyone knew what was and was not acceptable, but it was not codified, became tension between (fractionally deindividuated) representatives of two teams. Reversing the process seems to be very difficult; when the fine was discontinued, behaviour got even worse: now there was neither a social penalty nor a financial one, so parents just turned up when they wanted to.

The lesson is that hearth rules and social obligations are a more powerful, if more diffuse, way of defining boundaries than we might usually expect. In a strictly professional setting, people will perform the minimum necessary action to satisfy obligations. By contrast, social obligations under the rules of the hearth require a higher standard of compliance: essentially, doing the job to a standard you yourself would be happy with. Hearth rules also tap into the curiously powerful phenomenon of gift-giving, which according to research that appeared in *Science* magazine in 2007 is itself inherently pleasurable: 'even mandatory, tax-like transfers to a charity elicit neural activity in areas linked to reward processing. Moreover, neural responses to the charity's financial gains predict voluntary giving. However, consistent with warm glow, neural activity further increases when people make transfers voluntarily. Both pure altruism and warm-glow motives appear to determine the hedonic consequences of financial transfers to the public good.'[1] If you're covered by the rules of the hearth, of gifting and personal connection, you're protected somewhat from the predatory side of human nature and benefit from what appears to be a hard-wired (if contextual and conditional) generosity.

~

Given that the hearth provides that kind of protection, it might seem that taking advantage of hearth rules was an ideal online strategy for content owners, and in a way that's true; but if you come at it from that perspective, authenticity will start to be a problem. To borrow from Csikszentmihalyi once more – he's talking about the emancipation of consciousness, but it applies equally here – engagement 'cannot be institutionalised. As soon as it becomes part of a set of rules and norms, it ceases to be effective.' You can't, in other words, fake it. You have to be real.

One of the best examples of people who understand this is Cory Doctorow. Doctorow communicates freely and personally with a huge following, uses social media aptly and elegantly and in such a way that it's clear he is genuinely interested in the conversations in which he participates. He makes digital versions of his novels available to download on his website without digital rights management restrictions, on the basis that obscurity is a greater enemy of a writer than piracy. He also asks those who download his work free to buy physical books as presents or archive copies if they like them. A large number do exactly that.

People feel that they're part of Doctorow's social circle; default would not be a matter of taking money from a faceless corporate entity, but rather from the man himself, with whom many have interacted, and who has trusted them with the keys to his hearth.

In doing this, Doctorow shifts the ground of his work from a straightforward commercial enterprise to one that is bound up with social responsibility and personal obligation. In a limited but entirely genuine way, he opens his doors, offers himself as host, and his readers and visitors accept a role as guest, and obey the imperative of the hearth by reciprocating. At the same time, of course, his request that readers buy physical books as gifts as a way of recompensing him for free downloads plays to the pleasure of giving. It's a virtuous circle, and one that is sufficiently powerful that I feel a measure of unhappiness at breaking it down like this: clinical analysis is not 100 per cent compatible with the ethos of the hearth, belonging to a cooler tradition. On the other hand, while I have met Cory and read his writing (I bought a paper copy) I haven't yet got to know him, so I don't feel entirely within the hearth circle yet, and therefore perhaps I'm not really transgressing.

Both sides of the copyright debates online could profitably pay attention to this example. On the commercial side, we need to understand that there is literally nothing worse than a harsh deterrent that cannot by definition be enforced. It shifts the positions to their most adversarial – prompting deindividuation and increasing the likelihood that people will ignore the rules – but as in the case of the day care centre or indeed the capital punishment debate it fails to provide a sufficient reason not to act. The present strategy in the content industries is so counter-productive as to be almost painful to watch: a desperate attempt to turn back the clock to the pre-digital age by making digital files less copyable and the penalties for copying them more unpleasant, thereby throwing away any goodwill and creating the worst kind of system of faceless aggression and impersonal disengagement, while inevitably being unable to punch hard enough to make a difference to the availability of unsanctioned file copies of content. Governments and parliaments have so far quite rightly refused to allow constant warrantless surveillance in the name of television companies. (It was at once uplifting and depressing to see the resistance to the Stop Online Piracy Act in the United States in early 2012 – the former, because a digitally coordinated populace used the machinery of the conventional democratic state to oppose a ridiculous law; the latter because they did so to preserve the digital status quo rather than, for example, to demand the repeal of the more alarming aspects of recent anti-terror legislation which have rolled back historically hard-won freedoms in the name of questionable increases in national security.) Once again, I come back to the point that there has to be a limit on enforcement strategies, because the alternative is an Orwellian state. That being so, the 'crushing litigation' strategy is over before it begins, and we would do better to recognize that and move on.

In the meantime, while many would argue – rightly – that file-sharing can popularize a product and make the creator's name, it has to be said that it can also run together with wasteful and ungenerous behaviour. Developer GAMEized created an app for iPhone called *FingerKicks*. The initial indications were that the game was doing well. Two weeks after the initial release, players using the software, measured through Apple's GameCenter – the online gaming hub built into the phone's operating system – numbered around 16,000. Legitimate downloads, though, were only 1,200; the other players were all using copies that hadn't been paid for. The game was priced at 99 cents. Needless to say, the company did not recoup its investment.

One way to solve this problem is simply to adopt a different pricing model – for example, one which allows free download but requires payment to play or to access the full product – a subscription or an incremental payment strategy. While that works, it also dodges the issue – it's not a nudge, but an armlock, and it hints at a society where anything which isn't nailed down will be appropriated. It's easy to laugh at developers, or writers or musicians, who say that after a certain point they'll just do something else – but it might be kinder and wiser to wonder at what point they might in fact do so – or, more immediately, at what point they will simply have to turn their talents away from that particular way of working to another where they can actually make money, creating a sort of tragedy of the commons in which a hostile environment deprives us of content – artworks, music, novels, television – we really want. This discussion fragments with depressing speed into mirror-image counterpoints, one side claiming that creatives are financially better off under the digital models, the other side responding that they are not. I suspect that both are true in different situations, but once again, the more important thing is that the outcome of the encounter between philosophies is not set. We can still influence – by ingenuity and entrepreneurship and by legislation and debate – the shape of the cultural market in years to come.

The tragedy of the commons, incidentally, is worth revisiting in connection with this discussion, not least because it brings a dose of reality to all concerned. In the classic version, a shared resource is gradually destroyed by the collective actions of the group. Because no one takes time to maintain it, and everyone seeks to extract the maximum benefit from it, the resource is eventually depleted past the point where it can recover, and the community as a whole suffers. I vastly prefer this way of looking at the issue to the ridiculously shrill approach still taken in many copyright advocacy infomercials, which use the term 'piracy'. Piracy is robbery with violence, often segueing into murder, rape and kidnapping. It is one of the most frightening crimes in the world. Using the same term to describe a twelve-year-old swapping music with friends, even thousands of songs, is evidence of a loss of perspective so astounding that it invites and deserves the derision it receives. Unsanctioned file-sharing is not piracy, it's littering. Each individual action is of no consequence whatsoever, but the overall result is akin to what GAMEized have experienced: a product can become popular and yet there's no benefit whatsoever to the maker. There is, therefore, no financial motive to make anything similar (or at least, not with a similar pricing model) again, and considerable impediments to doing so, as the process of developing an app or generating content is expensive and labour-intensive. The creative environment is stifled.

The same applies to books, music and film; the maker puts a great deal of time and self into a project. To find that people are prepared to take it and use it enthusiastically, but balk at paying even a modest fee, is massively dispiriting and sets up the stark divide between maker and user once more, creating an oppositional, hostile relationship of mistrust. At some point, the Ultimatum Game once again becomes relevant: sooner or later, it's simply so upsetting to be part of the situation that people quit. People generally think that doesn't happen, but I've actually done it: I left the movie industry because I couldn't, in the end, put up with what felt like a corrosive working environment. It was making me too unhappy. I wrote *The Gone-Away World* as a sort of last gasp at writing: if it hadn't been well received, I would probably have gone back to university to train as a lawyer. The only way I can see to deal with this situation is to de-professionalize the relationship, creating an environment that fosters engagement between consumers and creators. I don't mean that the relationship cannot involve financial transaction; rather it seems to me that content creators and content owners must have an appreciable identity, a presence that can be encountered and understood in terms of its place in the world and the people who are a part of it. Companies can do this too; there's no *a priori* reason why a company's ethos cannot be strong and welcoming rather than abstract and seemingly uncaring. The time when a company was an expression of a single individual has mostly gone, but if an organization can develop a coherent, consistent and responsive identity it can be trusted and engaged with.

Google and Apple both benefited from a perception of a unique and positive character in their early days; Microsoft, by contrast, suffers from the opposite. All are now encountering resistance because their responses cannot be sufficiently substantive to satisfy the demand for engagement. Like politicians, they have to be wary of what they say, and their hedges and plays for time read like what they are. A personal friend who hedges is doubly unattractive; honesty and openness, on appropriate topics, are part of the hearth relationship. (The first time I saw a strategy like this given life was years ago, in an article about a US realtor. He had chosen to blog his days, including his mistakes. His competition thought he was mad, but his customers enjoyed the openness. They knew he made mistakes – everyone does – and now they knew what those mistakes were. Similarly, in the confrontation between the unnamed PR company and the Bloggess, the company could at any time have reversed its fortunes with an appropriate apology, turning enmity into appreciation. Quite often in life we are more impressed by those who deal well with mistakes than we are by those who claim to make none.)

For many industries and institutions, publishing included, this kind of venture – enjoyable though it would be, I don't propose that everyone admit to their blunders – will mean a change of attitude regarding the place of the end-user. For most publishing companies, consumers have historically been someone else's problem. Communicating with individuals was an unnecessary chore best left to booksellers. Once again, it's the broadcast mentality. Now, however, it seems to me that there's an opportunity to use the heritage of each imprint as an independent house to engage with the readership, to create or reveal the identity and history of the various companies – many of which are genuinely fascinating and moving – and allow a natural engagement wherein people united by a particular sense of taste can find and follow a publisher with interests and styles that meet it.

The alternative is not good. In this environment, not having an identity – or, rather, not being able or willing to engage – equates with being rude or evil. It's actually not that different from human face-to-face communication in that regard. As I noted before, we use a huge number of non-verbal signals to communicate alongside speech, all vital in reassuring an interlocutor that we are engaged, interested, paying attention and sane. Try fixing your eyes on someone's ear instead of letting them move around the face and the room, and watch them work to attract your attention. Stare right past them and wait for them to ask outright if you're 'still with them'. If you don't respond with an affirmation and then moderate your behaviour, they will rapidly become upset. If you really stick to it (and by the way, messing with your non-verbal communication is surprisingly hard) they will conclude either that you're really angry with them or that you're insane or unwell. Kinesic interviewing uses the same knowledge in reverse to force a rapport between interviewer and subject, mirroring posture, rhythm, even breathing.

We are, both online and off, unnerved in the extreme by entities that don't respond to normal human patterns in a reliable way. Something that appears human but doesn't perform like one is alarming to us – like a waxwork. In 1970 robotics researcher Masahiro Mori suggested that there is an 'uncanny valley' – a zone of simulation where something too closely resembles a person but does not perfectly counterfeit one, and is as a consequence more disturbing than it would be if it were clearly non-human. Whether or not the physical version of this idea holds water, the psychological one surely does. That which pretends to human identity but does not respond humanly is deeply unsettling and unwelcome.

Coming back to the discussion of commercial engagement: models that favour the blurring of the line between Us and

Them and encourage community over separation seem to me inevitable. Call it participation, call it hybridization, companies and organizations need to be open to the possibility of connection, to present themselves as what and who they are, without the armour of process and form, to avoid being cast at best as Other and at worst as inimical. The benefit of this flows – perhaps predictably – in all directions: companies get a better relationship with their consumers, which they need because the digital age has transferred power from the holders of rivalrous and excludable goods to the holders of the means of mass duplication; and consumers (which ultimately means everyone) get to move through a world of real relationships and interactions rather than scripted encounters with people functioning as robots (and perhaps, it occurs to me, transforming themselves into inhabitants of the uncanny valley: a human functioning machinically appearing like a robot trying and failing to be a person).

In my experience of the interaction, dealing with companies through social media in situations where the contact is informal, 'de-professionalized', is hugely liberating for both sides. Instead of an adversarial discussion of a problem, both sides feel able to concede more and arrive at a solution. Everyone goes that extra mile, and the guarantee of good conduct is not the commercial relationship but the personal one.

~

There is a story about Pablo Picasso – I have no notion of whether it's true – that puts the issue of what is authentic under the microscope.

There had been (the story goes) a series of high-profile forgeries of Picasso's work, and an auction house asked him to come in and verify that the paintings they were about to put on sale were genuine. The great artist agreed, and on the appointed day arrived with a close friend with whom he was staying while he was in town. Brought to the room where his paintings were laid out, Picasso ran his hand along the trestle table and sighed.

'This one is real,' he said at last. 'This one also. This, though . . . this is not. It is a fake. And not a very good one. This is real, and this, this and this. That is not.' And so on, down the line, and each time he added to the pile of forgeries the auctioneer's face grew a little sadder and more strained. Finally, he picked up one particular piece, and his friend stopped him.

'But Pablo,' the friend said, 'I saw you paint that one myself!'

Picasso shrugged. 'I can fake a Picasso as well as anyone,' he said.

All right: it's a great story. Let's assume for a moment that it all took place as I've recorded it here. Taking it as given that some of the pictures so identified were actually fakes, their chain of connection is fundamentally broken; the artist did not conceive them in his mind, execute them with the skill of decades with his own hands. There is none of his sweat in the works. Then there are the other ones, which he did paint, but which he regards as dross. The connection is there, but he asserts that it is broken at the final stage: he was not himself engaged with the work as he was doing it, was not in the flow state, and the result is at best second rate, at worst lacking in the markers of Picasso's particular genius.

But the most interesting thing is the possibility that Picasso identified as real some paintings he had not himself executed but which he felt were good enough to carry his name. He asserted ownership, even authorship, of these. Does that make them Picassos? Or something else? The narrative connection to him is strong, characterful and interesting. Someone with that kind of money might pay a lot – though perhaps not as much as they'd pay for a Picasso by Picasso – for one of those, not because it's a good imitation, but because the artist felt it shared identity with him to the point where he was prepared to claim it, perhaps even envied it. He saw himself in it. Someone had engaged with his work so perfectly that they were able, in whatever limited way, to produce a painting that had more of the quality of his good work than paintings he himself painted on bad days. That person was more closely connected to Pablo Picasso than any number of people who touched his life more directly, and he understood that and in a curious way endorsed it. He recognized the connection to himself and felt it possessed authenticity.

The punchline in the joke, though, comes from the fact that without really thinking it through, we're apt to feel that a forgery cannot, by definition, have any real connection with the painter whose work is being forged. Walter Benjamin's point about a physical history comes back again: the forged painting has no narrative of presence, no path of creation by the hand of Picasso. The physical connection is missing, and touch matters. The sense of touch, immanent and profound, is immensely persuasive to us as a guarantee of reality, even where there is no particular information to be had from it. A physical connection is disproportionately impressive to us. We make pilgrimages, religious or not, to bring ourselves into the physical presence of items we admire and wish to associate ourselves with. The physical history of an object is important.

By way of illustration: I bought, a few years ago, a black vinyl laptop bag with a garish orange silk patch on it. I have subsequently mistreated this bag woefully, so that the orange patch is smeared with the grime from various European train stations and one or two more far-flung sorts of dirt. It looks like a prop from a zombie movie. If I asked you whether you want to touch it, you would almost certainly look at me as if I were proposing something slightly disgusting.

Except.

Except that before the orange silk patch was stitched on to a bag, it was the re-entry parachute for a Soyuz Space Capsule. It went into orbit, and fell to earth again, bringing its passengers safely back home. It is the closest I will ever get to space, and it is not in a museum or a cabinet and I will not object if you lay hands on it, for a moment, and think about what remains one of the most remarkable journeys an object can make.

And suddenly, you would at least consider it.

We remain culturally and perhaps also in terms of our construction predisposed to be influenced by our senses, by physical proximity and by presence. We are hybrids: creatures both cognitive and immanent, thoughtful and sensual. I think that beneath the fear of the inauthentic, and in particular the fear of inauthenticity in the digital world – at least in part – is the simple fact that much of our life as human beings is about physical experiences. We're not instinctively ready to accept realities that can be understood only through cognition. Things and people that are apprehended in the mind but at the same time are objectively real are relatively recent in the lives of our cultures; until now, that category was reserved for stories, legends, hallucinations and dreams.

In general, we experience the world fairly directly. Information from our senses hits our consciousness without passing through our thoughts. It is mediated by the brain; the unconscious does a lot of filtering and assemblage so that what we experience is more like a movie than a lousy, jagged home video with bad sound and uncertain camera work. More scientifically: your vision is surprisingly limited in scope. You see colour mostly in the middle of your field of vision; your brain helpfully colours in objects outside this area. There's a blind spot in your eye where the optic nerve touches the retina (draw a cross on the pads of your first two fingers, and close one eye; starting six inches away, keep looking at one cross, and move your fingers away from your face; the other cross will disappear, along with the tip of your finger). Your brain interferes in the direct feed, making the world clearer – but all the same, the basic experiences that we have all the time, and through which we perceive everything we will ever experience (unless technology reaches the point of being able to feed sense data directly into your head), come to us without conscious thought. A great part of us is not modern, not textual, and mistrusts what is only written rather than seen or experienced.

And our thoughts and experiences are physical. The neuro-modulator oxytocin, released during birth, is connected with bonding; it's sometimes thought of as the 'love hormone'. Testosterone affects aggression as well as libido. Problems with dopamine and serotonin are implicated in addiction and depression. There is a quiet controversy cooking at the moment over the effect of Omega 3 oils on personality; a prison study in 2002 seemed to show that low levels of Omega 3 were linked with poor impulse control and violent behaviour: 'Prisoners given nutritional supplements committed 35% fewer violent incidences than those given the placebo.' A larger study at HM Young Offenders' Institution in Polmont will report soon.[2]

By way of contrast, Steven Pinker references various studies pointing to 'genetic and neurological mechanisms' that underlie violence across human societies; in other words, a violent disposition may be a product of genes or environment, and while neither necessarily absolves an individual of criminal behaviour, both propose a physical root of what might appear to be a psychological phenomenon. Perhaps more unnerving in the field of embodied cognition (exactly what it sounds like: thinking in the body), people asked to generate random numbers produce smaller ones if they're looking down and to the left, larger ones when looking up and to the right.[3] Even cognition is not entirely separate from physical action (although the researchers in this study propose that the effect occurs because the subjects learned numbers from left to right as children, and 'see' a range of numbers going from low left to top right; if so, it's an artefact of the way we live).

All of which is to make two points: first, that it is unsurprising that we are suspicious of the authenticity of situations that don't directly involve the body. We rely on our physical self for so much more than we are generally aware of, and it shapes us profoundly, but that is not to say that our resistance to primarily cognitive modes of communication is reasonable or helpful. We do better to differentiate between interactions on their merits than on the basis of a perception of what is and is not real that is rooted in that part of us born before the advent of the written word.

Second, the power of sense experience and the body to move the mind – and the apparent strength of the argument that some aspects of personality are predetermined – seems to me to give us a healthy resistance to being overwhelmed by the digital side. We feel balanced between the cognitive, the sensory and the physical, but actually we exist in the overlap of them all. Cognition and sense are not opposed, but complementary and interwoven. As we move forward into the digital world, and engage with one another in mediated situations, as we use the cognitive more and more, we may need to nourish our irrational, immanent side, to make sure it keeps up with our modern, textual, cognitive selves – but I don't see that as more difficult than any of the other balances we have to learn to strike in our complex, modern lives.

blindgiant.co.uk/chapter8

9

Being Human in a Digital World (Or Any Other)

IN THE PADDOCK in the middle of a structure the size of an aircraft hangar, a woman pours out her heart to a guy in a blue aviator jacket. (It looks like a Buzz Rickson's L2-A, the kind of thing men like Neil Armstrong wore when they were test-flying planes in the 1950s.) Listening to this lady is probably a great deal like being a priest hearing confession; her brief speech is a litany of self-accusation. She has come in desperation. It has taken two days to get here, because she had to ride her horse all the way. She left the children with her husband and came alone because she wanted quality time with the horse, to soothe him and be with him. The reason she had to go through all this, and why she needs to be here in the first place: he will not, under any circumstances, travel in or even enter a horse-box. Attempting to force him into one triggers a spasm of fear and fury that frightens her. He is at other times a sweet-natured horse. She doesn't know what to do. She can't live like this. If he won't load – if he cannot learn to brave the box – he will have to be sold.

'Sold' sticks in her mouth. She looks down at the sand. People become very, very attached to their horses; failure of the relationship on this level is genuinely traumatic. And there's a tacit, grisly question of who would buy a non-loader, and what would happen to him. If things don't change, the outlook isn't good.

'Well, let's see if we can do something about that,' the guy in the aviator jacket says.

They lead the horse into the paddock. He's not small, but he is, as promised, utterly benign. He looks around, perhaps a bit wary, but mostly just curious. From where he's standing, he can see the bright circle of the paddock bounded by a high metal fence, and beyond that maybe also the faces of a couple of thousand people arranged on bleachers all around to see this demonstration. If so, the audience doesn't seem to bother him. Everyone is being very, very quiet – these are horse people, and this is serious for them. They don't want to spook the animal, because it's not fair to him and could cause a serious problem for the trainer. The owner leaves the paddock, and the big guy scratches the horse between the eyes for a moment. What he absolutely does not do is whisper to the horse. He has been called a horse whisperer, and while that title is probably useful, it's also starkly at odds with what he believes and wants everyone here to learn: he doesn't talk to horses. He listens to them.

Monty Roberts is an American classic: silver-haired and broad-shouldered, light on his feet, commanding and charismatic. At the moment he's wearing a cloth cap in addition to the aviator jacket, a piece of traditional British trainer gear. On other occasions, he sports a Stetson. Roberts, though, is not a cowboy in the conventional sense. He abhors violence in general, and in particular in the context of training horses. 'Violence is never the answer,' he says, over and over, in interviews and articles and during his demonstrations.

When Roberts is sure the horse is relaxed, he signals to his team and they reverse a horsebox to the paddock gate, and one of the assistant trainers leads the horse towards the box. Roberts holds up a wrist in a plastic splint and explains that he got kicked a few weeks ago and has been told not to take risks with his arm while it heals. You have the impression that he listens to that advice maybe 60 per cent of the time, dropping to 20 per cent if no one's looking and zero if there's something that really needs doing and nobody else can do it. Right now, though, he's playing it safe and letting the much younger trainer test the horse's resistance to loading.

And that resistance turns out to be pretty absolute. The horse stops dead a few metres from the box and won't go any further, becoming more and more unhappy with each attempt to persuade him, and ultimately trying with growing urgency to escape. Before the urgency can turn into real terror, Roberts calls a halt.

'That's where we used to try pushing him in with brooms,' the owner says from the side.

In my mind, that conjures images of a mob from a Hammer horror movie poking at the horse with agricultural implements as if he were Christopher Lee in a black cloak. If Roberts finds the idea unusual or annoying, it doesn't show.

'How did that work out?' he asks.

'It was awful,' the owner says.

Roberts doesn't reproach her. He nods in a way that acknowledges that anyone can make a mistake, especially under pressure, and she's here now and that's a much better choice than brooms. He starts to work with the horse. He sends him away first, running him around the paddock enough times so that he covers three-eighths of a mile. That's a crucial number in the Roberts universe; predators in the wild are sprinters, so a horse that has run that distance and survived has outlasted the enemy and can stop and relax. Everything Roberts does, he says, he learned from watching horses themselves. This isn't training in the conventional sense; it's communication.

When the horse slows and drops his head, Roberts tells the audience, it means he wants to come and form some sort of understanding with the only other animal in the paddock. It's all a negotiation. If he can't run away, can he form a relationship with the human which does not involve being eaten? The range of options is primal, and Roberts describes it in primal terms: big cats jump up, on to the back of a prey animal, looking for the throat. Wolves attack low, looking for the legs or the belly. A saddle, in this simple, savage lexicon, is 'where the cats go'. Taking a saddle for the first time is stressful because instinct says something on your back is about to kill you. The girth strap is 'where the dogs go', and means evisceration. We listen. And then, bang on time, the horse comes in off the paddock fence.

Roberts makes himself small, curving his back and drawing his arms in tight to his body, and turns away. Eye contact is a threat, so he doesn't let it happen. The horse takes a few steps closer. Roberts doesn't seem to notice. He's still, and calm, and not interested. The horse comes closer, and still, Roberts waits. Finally, the horse nudges him on the shoulder: 'Hey, you!' Roberts makes a fuss of him, very quietly, scratches his forehead again, then takes a step away. The horse follows as if on a rein. Roberts keeps walking, and the horse follows. They go around the paddock a few times, Roberts abruptly changing direction, zig-zagging, and the horse follows.

Inevitably, because the paddock is not large, Roberts eventually arrives near the horsebox. He slows. The horse slows too, peering at the old enemy. Roberts makes no move towards the horsebox, wanders off again, and the horse ambles after him. Then he goes back. Then away. Each time they get a little closer to the box, and each time the horse spends some time checking it out. Roberts walks towards the box, and the horse comes too. Roberts walks up the ramp. The horse stops. Roberts stops, reverses the horse away from the ramp and away. They loop around the paddock, then come back. This time, the horse puts his front hooves on the ramp. He doesn't like it very much, but he wants to follow Roberts. He pokes at the ramp, and it clanks. Roberts repeats the reverse, and comes back for a third time.

When the horse follows him all the way up the ramp and into the horsebox, Roberts barely seems to notice. He turns right around and walks out again. The crowd, on the other hand, has absolutely noticed. Many of them have been down this road, and they know that what they've just seen is spectacular, bordering on spooky. The owner has her hand over her mouth. This simply doesn't happen with non-loaders. It's so unlikely that even though his methods are reproducible – and reproduced successfully by thousands of trainers and owners around the world – people still accuse Roberts of fakery.

Roberts walks the horse around the paddock, back into the box without breaking step. This time they stay for a while. The horse investigates the box a bit. Whatever he thought was in there clearly isn't.

Roberts walks him out again, then once more round the paddock, and this time the horse doesn't even need to be led. He's in the habit. When Roberts stops, the horse walks past him, right up the ramp and into the box, turns around and peers out, as if to ask what all this fuss was ever really about. The whole process has taken less than half an hour.

Roberts makes everyone wait until the horse is well away before they applaud, but I imagine you can hear the sound from the next county.

Monty Roberts is at pains to say that what he does isn't magic. He hasn't used a Blacksmith's Word. He's just made a connection with a confused animal. It's something that – demonstrably – anyone can do, given the appropriate training and practice. The part of what he does that is more difficult to teach is the human side: he works an audience with the same facility he displays with horses, a trick that is even more impressive because he can actually do both at once. He's also keen to point out that the horses he works with in his shows in the UK are horses he has never seen before, and they're not suddenly turned into something different by what he does. Put them in a stress situation and miscommunicate and they can go right back to where they were. The conversion from non-loader to self-loader requires maintenance at home, an ongoing reassurance and instruction in the simple body language horses use among themselves and understand.

It seems to me that we are like a horse – and like Monty Roberts – at the same time.

~

Roberts's achievement is not leading. It looks that way because the horse ends up following him around the paddock, but looks are deceptive. What he's done is the ultimate in a very handy digital skill: following. He's derived his method of helping horses to understand what's required of them – and that is what he does – by following their lead. He watched the interactions of wild horses, taught himself the body language and the pattern of their engagements, and worked out how to insert himself into the loop. The result is absolutely remarkable.

And – up to a point – it's possible to do something similar with the self. We know an ever-increasing amount about our own behaviour, and as I've tried to point out, much of it is irrational. There's no particular need to be worried about that, unless you have constructed your way of life on the notion that humans are at root a profoundly rational bunch – in which case, to be honest, I have to question your skills of observation. But it's also true that as information on how we as individuals and as groups behave becomes more widely available and understood, we are apt to find those behaviours being used to lead us about by the nose – unless we make an effort to take charge of ourselves. At the same time, to get along with digital technology – to use its advantages in beating the modern malaises we created it to defy, without in turn being changed in directions we would not choose, or perhaps worse simply made unhappy – we need to be aware of how we live and use our tools.

The following list may make some people a bit uncomfortable, because it includes things that are not generally thought of as serious or important. That's partly because the rational/ professional ethos that most of us grew up with defines 'serious' and 'important' things as those that are instrumental and effective in making money and achieving concrete results, and doesn't make a lot of space for play, or for the hearth. In fact, its area of competence is bounded by those things, so it tends to dismiss them. As that ethos increasingly tries to claim our attention through the extended hearth, so we have to push back and assert their importance. (It's like the pressure suits doctors wear in biohazard zones, which are inflated from within so that any puncture will cause air to flow out rather than letting infectious agents in.)

The idea that you might choose a path that meant you got less rather than more stuff done is alien to many of us, but the need to do more is where the sense of time slipping away comes from. There is, after all, a finite limit to the amount one person can do in one day, and it's not clear that doing more makes you happier. Sometimes, happiness is about sitting still for . . .

How long would you say? Ten minutes? An hour? A day?

Carlo Petrini, founder of the Slow Food movement in Italy, told Carl Honoré: 'Being Slow means that you control the rhythms of your own life. You decide how fast you have to go in any given context . . . What we are fighting for is the right to determine our own tempos.' It seems to me that you cannot possibly know what your tempo should be if you're always flat out. You have no idea what you, yourself, look like at another speed. We as individuals and as a society have to choose who we want to be. Refusing to do so is no longer a neutral posture, if it ever was. We are surrounded by forces that will influence us, some of them actively working to do so using information and tools created by interactions with massive numbers of individuals, constantly being refined. Being inert means being washed away by this current, and trusting that governments, and large technology companies and the institutions that hire them to influence us, know better than we do how the world should be and have our best interests at heart.

Like most people, I suspect, I don't believe that's the case; the pace, priorities and nature of modern life in the industrialized world create an environment that is not ultimately a human paradise. The unease people report as information overload or future shock is not a product of digital technology; it predates even the mobile telephone. It comes from the way we live, the division of time and the emphasis on getting more done, and our naïve (in the sense of inexperienced rather than careless or foolish) use of abstract systems in the form of government bureaucracy and commercial companies to take advantage of our collective strength and to attempt to ensure fairness; we have come to see these systems as external objects, and are only now beginning to understand them as re-editable products. Digital technology is one of the coping strategies we have evolved to deal with a sense of disconnection, of being out of control; a treatment for the symptom rather than the disease, but which has enabled us to see our own reflection and to understand the situation.

Technology is not born pure, however: it is the result of a commercial design process. In other words, there was a demand for something to manage time and space, to connect us, and the society we have gave us mobile phones and the Internet. The revolution was – as all revolutions are – hijacked before it was born. The technologies of reconnection have been incorporated into the structure of the world and have become in some ways part of the problem, but how we use them and respond to them is up to us.

We're not used to thinking that we can change the big things. We habitually accept that governments and leaders will behave badly, that companies will offend and receive risible fines or no punishment at all, that prices will rise and what appear to be deals will come with strings. We accept this last so absolutely that we become suspicious if we can't identify a catch. And yet these are contingent truths, truths that are created by our collective actions rather than being inherent in the world. We have come to see ourselves as separate from our environment and the technologies of the mind we have created to reduce the number of impossible decisions we have to make in a day. We have seen and to some extent continue to see our governments and our corporations, even the nations of which we are a part, as something bigger than us: huge, alien, imponderable forces that crush us and which we cannot stop. It isn't true, and we're remembering that.

If the revolutions in the Middle East, or the Velvet Revolutions of the late 1980s and early 1990s, or even the bleak, depressing events in the UK in the summer of 2011 show us anything at all, it is that government takes place by consent, because these things are made up of individual people. We know this: we have come to an understanding that our law is text, and that text can be edited. What we now have to accept is the responsibility that goes with that. It's not enough to say 'I want': that just gets you bills you can't pay and a raft of purchases you could have done without, whether you're an individual or a state. We have instead to make the wise choice, which is hard. And that requires a way of understanding the world, a culture of being present for the big decisions – a culture of engaging.

And that is the habit we need to acquire above all others: the habit of paying attention, of making our own decisions and interrogating the choices with which we are presented: ask *why* the *Economist* pricing system includes the redundant print-only option at the same price as the combined print-and-digital package, and you're on your way to the kind of behaviour that will improve the way we live. Ask the question online, and compare your perceptions with those of others, and you begin to construct a wise crowd. Keep doing it, day after day, and that's the start of a society that can work as a democracy, rather than one that merely exhibits the trappings but functions as an oligarchy. And as we know, habits are more than just behaviour: they change the brain. These changes are a part of (and perhaps the actual physical expression and location of) expertise as we develop it. Neuroplastic changes are less than absolute; there are limits to their depth and scope – even constant use of the Internet will not turn you into a machine any more than endless free-diving will turn you into a seal, although both may make you different, and therefore separate you from people who live a more balanced life.

But within that limit, we can collectively and individually become experts in living intelligently and well, if we try. There are skills we can develop – simple ones which we already possess to some extent, not involved ones which require great commitments of time and energy and thought – that will help. John Gabrieli, an expert in cognition, memory and emotion at MIT, recently found that the brain naturally enters a preparatory state before taking in information, and measured a 30 per cent improvement in memory when the state was observed over when it was not. The preparatory state was surprising: in MRIs taken by Gabrieli and his team, the parahippocampal place area, a region of the brain known to be highly active during learning, seemed to be very placid. Gabrieli speculated that this might be a 'clearing of the decks' before taking on a heavy load of information[1] – presumably cleaning out the working memory, ditching any current cognitive load so as to be able to take on more. If so, it's all the more important, when you really need to engage with something, that you be able to ditch any other concerns and concentrate on one subject without others interfering.

In other words, your brain takes time out to have tea and a biscuit before starting work. There may well be real value in doing nothing for a moment (ten minutes, or an hour – or more). Perhaps predictably, given the way we live, Gabrieli's observation has led some to wonder whether it might be possible to trigger the preparatory state artificially, by using electrodes to stimulate a given area of the brain – or with drugs. No doubt something in this area is achievable, but why bother? If the ability is present in us already, we just need to practise it.

Back to Monty Roberts: if you don't train a horse to move in all the available directions on command, the ones you leave out will become its escape route. Some riders don't like to teach their horses to walk backwards. That's what they'll do when they're unhappy, Roberts replies, because backwards belongs to them, not you. In the digital context, and the wider world, I think the same is true. You have to own your own directions. Addiction counsellors, I understand, will tell you much the same thing, albeit rather more pithily: 'You have to own your own shit.' This means doing things to retain a perspective on what is humanly important, and connecting with the simple, human, analogue self, while at the same time taking ownership of the extended self and the digital technologies we use. Digital is not an enemy; it is a powerful tool. The question is not whether the tool is wicked, but whose tool it is, and part of the way to make sure it's ours is to know that it is just another aspect of life rather than a replacement for everything.

~

The way we experience life breaks down into a variety of perceptions and understandings. We make assumptions because that's how we live. We model the world because it's too vast to know in detail and because we learn, as we get older, to focus our attention on matters that are of immediate relevance and screen out those that are not. It always seems to me that creative people are the ones who are able to see, or indeed cannot avoid seeing, multiple interpretations of the same situation, from the prosaic (a businessman walking home with a newspaper under one arm) to the unlikely (a weary detective bringing his last case home with him) to the positively baroque (the last of the Knights Templar carrying the original pages of the Virgin Mary's diary).

In any case, our assumptions are often fairly sound and we can work happily within them, but in some cases they betray us. A perception of the world that is accepted by everyone around us seems the most obvious and likely, until we check it and it turns out to be simply untrue (a topical example might be the sub-prime crisis. Everyone knew the bonds based on sub-prime loans were okay, because the ratings agencies said they were Triple-A. Then people like Michael Burry looked at the fine print and saw that in fact the situation was not okay at all). In the less dramatic everyday world, we learn to accept external perceptions of time – the digital clock and the chargeable unit – which can come to dominate not only our working hours but our entire lives. The single sense of time that is set by our employers and the people around us, by a general rush and bustle that implies somehow that if one is not too busy one must be slacking, can be offset by engaging with other perceptions of time. So, for example, you could:

1 Read a novel

Yes, well, I would say that, but it works. My advice would be to get hold of a copy of *Heart of Darkness* by Joseph Conrad. It's short, which makes it feel approachable, but the prose is stacked and demanding. It requires your attention; you won't be able to read it at all if you aren't concentrating. Obscurantism – the deliberate act of making a text more difficult than it needs to be in order to force the reader to pay attention – was a policy of the German critical theorist Theodor Adorno. Adorno was one of the banes of my life at university, and I cursed him for his ridiculous posture on clarity. Of course, I remember more about his work than most of the other people I had to study, and recently I found out why: obscurantism actually works. To my enduring irritation, it turns out that making something hard to read – for example by using a nasty typeface – makes you pay more attention to it: 'You can't skim material in a hard-to-read font, so putting text in a hard-to-read font will force you to read more carefully.'[2] (I'm curious as to how this tallies with Nicholas Carr's concern about deep reading: does it force the state, or jolt you out of it to parse difficult sentences? And if the latter, how does the outcome – greater uptake of information and greater engagement – square with Carr's position that the absence of deep reading entails a lesser interaction with the material?)

Reading books will also, of course, re-establish the reading skill in your brain, if you're concerned that you're becoming too focused on the creative, participatory style of reading we do online, or if you are simply eager for a rest and want someone else to drive the narrative train for a while. Read linearly, in the old-fashioned way, and trust the author to take you where you need to go. It may even be better to read a novel that is plot-centred rather than one that wants you to stop and consider its deeper meaning all the time. Follow the path of the story rather than trying to define it. Let the text be fixed for a few hours – but let yourself be a bit more fluid. Engage with the book, allowing it to change you, or, at least, to transport you. The experience is immersive, to the point where you can miss your stop, so I find it's often better to read on the sofa, but it's certainly a good way to rid yourself of a dull commute.

Reading is the definitive activity of the age that created the brain we have. It is also a path to empathy, and therefore to connection; it is central to who we have been and to many of the beliefs we hold to be a core part of us. To whatever extent we are being changed by digital technology, reading is one of the principal ways of retaining a connection to the present way of being human, and the skill of following someone else's linear narrative, which is as important as being able to construct one's own. We need to be able to choose which one is more appropriate in a given setting, just as, in some contexts, a pencil is better than a laptop, or vice versa.

If you really want to push your sense of time in a new direction, though:

2 Bake sourdough bread

Sourdough is not like the fast yeast you can buy at most super-markets, or even the more traditional live baker's yeast: you take a couple of weeks to get a sourdough starter up and running, because you let the natural yeast in the air and the flour grow. Then, when you make the dough, it takes longer to rise than ready-bake yeast loaves. Dried yeast tends to be a single fast-growing variety, not terribly flavoursome. Sourdough is a gallery of strange yeast beasties, and you have to give them some time to do their thing. The end product is splendid, though; it's like the difference between orange squash and freshly squeezed orange juice. Making sourdough is about as far from the efficiency of the chargeable unit as you can get: you're working to a pre-modern schedule, not an industrial one. The dough is ready when it's ready, and you have to get used to checking on the starter, then putting it back. If you're like me, your mouse-finger will twitch: you'll want to use the 'Hurry' button or the fast forward, skip to when you can do the next bit. Sourdough time would delight Einstein; it's relative. It isn't precise, professional time or digital clock time. It's biological time.

In making sourdough, you're also stimulating your fingers and your nose. You're acquiring a new skill – good for keeping older brains young. You may find you are applying decision-making and problem-solving, too; both have definitely featured in my bread-making. So now you're hanging digitally acquired skills – those aspects of your brain are apparently trained by working with digital technology, remember – on an analogue peg. Look:

your life just got integrated. (Cool.) And you've joined a community. You are part of a line of bakers which begins so long ago they had no concept of the clock or the calendar and comes all the way to the present. There almost has not been a period in human history in which we did not make bread. At some point, it is likely that almost every generation of your family – unless you are a king or a queen – did this same thing. You are also part of a contemporary community of bread-fiends who will help you out when things go wrong, and who will come to you for advice. The easiest way to find them, of course, is online, which binds a profoundly non-digital experience to your electronic desktop, and vice versa. Distinctions between on- and offline become blurry, because the technology and the social world both want them to.

Having carved out a sense of time as something malleable rather than something rushing past:

3 Learn to dance

Dancing is a string of sensations and created instincts, practised possibilities. Once again, it's a skill that must be learned, which improves physical coordination and gives you a sense of your physical body. It works with balance, with timing, with touch and hearing – it's immanent and to some extent irreducible. It is a pursuit you do in the time and place where you are doing it. You really do, in every sense, have to be there. It is an activity which after a certain point can drop you into a profound and almost meditative calm. You can't do it while texting, while emailing, or even while worrying about work. It is a single-focus activity, which excludes fretting, stressing and multi-tasking. There is only one positive outcome – good dancing – and a negative one is easy to spot. It also counts as play, in that it is a pointless activity with no obvious reward other than itself. The act of dancing belongs to you and your dance partner alone. More than that, though, some dances – especially one of my favourites, the Argentine tango – teach following and engagement at a high level, and even decision-making. You simply can't do them unless you are really, significantly paying attention to the dance and the person you are dancing with.

In tango, each step is led by one partner and followed by the other, and the lead-follow relationship can be inverted during the dance by a skilled pair. Tango is one of the most sophisticated non-verbal dialogues I've come across. It's easy to do badly, with the physical equivalent of poor grammar and shouting (awkwardness and shoving). It's much more difficult (and rewarding) to do well, with subtle cues and elegant phrases. With some styles of dance, you might be tempted to skim-read your partner's intention – salsa and Ceroc are both led, but led in patterns, so that you indicate to your partner which of a variety of moves you propose, and you're then on track for that sequence and can relax – but with tango, that option is closed. Like Theodor Adorno's infuriating prose, tango demands your attention. You're making decisions about where to go and what sort of dance this is, and choosing your own responses to the music and your partner's cues.

As with tango, so too with some martial arts. The focus on following and understanding has to be enormous. Like Monty Roberts, a martial artist (or a tanguero) must learn how a given person works through movement. The notion of following is at the heart of t'ai chi, the Chinese soft-form martial art which most people regard as a form of moving yoga or interpretive dance practised by the elderly. In fact, t'ai chi can be as much a combat style as aikido or karate. The key to its use is the ability to move with your opponent, maintaining contact with them so as to be able to feel the lines of resistance in their body and the tipping point of their balance. The t'ai chi practitioner in turn should be almost completely relaxed (one of the training manuals proposes that a master's arms should be like iron bars hinged with elastic) so that an attempt to throw them or control their balance can be nullified – not by resistance, but absorption. I tried for six years to lock the elbow of one of my teachers, and never managed it once. It was like trying to put handcuffs on a trout. By contrast, he seemed to know where I was going to move before I had consciously decided it myself, reading the transfer of weight in my feet through the contact with my wrist or shoulder, or even simply the position of my hips.

This kind of following is different from the kind needed to make social media interactions authentic – it's physical, obviously – but the attitude of mind, the decision to pay attention, the openness to subtle signals from a partner, and the preparedness to accept those directions and move in synchrony, are the same. If you follow well, you open yourself to the world, to social engagement and to new information and changes in direction.

Armed with all that:

4 Learn to play on your computer (or your phone)

Of course. Why? Well, aside from the simple answer that computer games are fun – even if you don't think of yourself as that sort of person, the sheer variety and ingenuity of the games milieu almost guarantees there's something out there for you, from quirky, cartoonish fun to strange, almost lyrical things that are half test of skill and half artform – games are at the heart of electronic life. The grammar of the digital world, not just literally, in the sense of human language, but in terms of design and style, derives in many cases from games. More, sophisticated games require a sophisticated pattern of enquiry, hypothesis, testing and re-envisioning of the game reality; essentially, learning how to learn about and affect the world you are interacting with.

As Steven Johnson points out in *Everything Bad is Good for You*, this is the basic scientific method, but it's also the basic skill for understanding and acting in our own world, whose levers and rewards are often unclear. Games teach decision-making, of course – prioritization under stress, logistics, even blind guessing, because sometimes you just have to – but they also can be enormously relaxing. (Say after me: 'There's nothing wrong with just playing.') The simple, constrained universes of basic games, where the victory conditions are known, the problems are finite and predictable, and the rewards arrive in reliable patterns, are a great way to dump a boatload of worry for half an hour. That may even be why some people end up devoting too much time to them, because they're just easier to handle than the real world. Used in moderation, however, that simplicity is a blessing.

At the same time, learning to play in the digital world makes you comfortable with the technology, brings it into your life rather than making it an external and possibly inimical force, while at the same time teaching you another useful skill: recognizing when to ignore it. When the time comes to put the game down, you put it down and walk away. Of course you do – it's just a game. And that habit is worth a mint, because you can, with a little tweaking, do the same with intrusive phone calls and emails. Yes, that can wait until tomorrow. No, I do not need to talk to that person. Anyone who needs me knows how to find me, so I'm switching off. You don't have to run from technology to own it; in fact, the faster you run, the faster it comes up behind you.

These days, games can also be social. Some of them are based around social networks. Others require cooperation; once again, something that isn't always necessary or encouraged in the offline world. In shared online universes, you meet and then play alongside people almost immediately, which requires a measure of trust and cooperation. It can also mean taking charge or following orders, and engaging with and understanding the position of another person in a short space of time. Which brings up the wider sense of the word 'play' I used earlier: the human social life, the non-professional, non-reward-based side of who we are and what we do.

Take some time to colonize the digital space with your life. Make it belong to you. Social networks, as I've said, are not just great piles of people blithering at one another and talking inconsequential nonsense. Of course, those conversations take place, but those conversations take place everywhere, from train carriages to pubs to the green rooms of theatres. You don't have to listen to them. Services like Twitter, which allow a rapid progression from initial contact to interesting conversation, are opportunities to encounter other people and take in their thoughts; that is, after all, all they are in the Twitter context: thoughts written down and passed to you. Allow yourself to find the people who are not like you, or to discover that people with whom you share one interest have wildly different perceptions on other issues.

Obviously, you'll have to consider carefully which services to use and what to put on them; you'll have to ask how much of your data – your extended self – you want to make available to the wider world and the companies that study that kind of available information. But unless you propose to live entirely on cash, generate your own heat and power, and grow your own food, that's going to happen to some extent. It seems better to me to be in the mix, getting a sense of how it's all happening, and influencing the pattern. Find and make use of online tools that illuminate how you behave and what effect it has – there's a search engine now that will tell you how to buy equivalent products to the obvious high street and designer brands that have a far smaller carbon footprint – but the specific tools may be less important than the business of being in the digitally mediated conversations that are taking place all the time now, which follow events and form opinions and ultimately protest or endorse what has been done.

Once you're present in the online stew, you can find the arenas you care about and discover how to make a difference to that specific issue – or create a way. That's the whole point: not that there are pre-existing discussions you can sign up to, but that together we can create tools which actually have an effect. 38 Degrees, the re-taskable online campaigning organization, is an evolving prototype, but the more people choose to involve themselves, the more significant the movement becomes. Be aware of received wisdom, bias towards people who agree with you and away from those who share uncomfortable truths, and try to form an opinion based on your own understanding rather than a desire to be in the majority or aligned with the most charismatic. Learn to be a helpful, engaged part of the smart crowd.

For centuries, the idea of democracy has relied on a public sphere of debate that would inform the decisions and understanding of the electorate, but the existence of such an area has been uncertain at best. Now it's there, and you can choose to be part of it.

Learn that you are one of many, and understand that that is not a statement of insignificance, but the reverse.

blindgiant.co.uk/chapter9

10

Coda

A T THE BEGINNING of the twentieth century, Great Britain was still the dominant power in the world. Women did not get the vote here until 1918, and even then the franchise was only extended to the over-thirties. In 1901 – the year Queen Victoria died – the life expectancy of a male child was forty-five (a girl could hope for four years more). A new invention, the telephone, was spreading across the UK, with the first municipal exchange opening in Glasgow.

Since then, the franchise has been extended to anyone over the age of eighteen. Two world wars, the arrival of labour-saving devices such as the washing machine, and the stalwart campaigning of the feminist movement have changed the face of British society, although in the fine detail equality is still shaky. Our attitudes to religion, gender roles, the nature of family life, the definition of marriage, the place of children, the position of the UK in the roster of nations, the way we eat, and the value of traditions have all changed, and will continue to do so. The medical definition of death itself has shifted in our favour. It would be insane – and rather worrying – if we didn't feel that the world was changing around us. It is. The touchstones on which my parents' generation relied to locate themselves in the world have faded. The 'job for life' is now so rare that it barely occurs in political discourse. Who we trust, what we value, and what we know about ourselves are constantly revised. So many things we were taught to believe were fixed turn out to be in motion.

The digital world offers ways to locate one's self in a broad context, a web of connections and understandings, flexible, adaptable and supportive. As old ways of finding a place fade away, new ones arise – new ones that I find hugely hopeful. Which is good, because it only gets stranger from here.

In 2008 Yukiyasu Kamitani of ATR Computational Neuroscience Laboratories in Kyoto, Japan, demonstrated a new use for functional magnetic resonance imaging. An MRI scanner is the big, metal cylinder that in one particularly memorable episode of the medical drama *House* sucks the metallic ink from the tattooed skin of a patient. It provides an image of the invisible parts of the human body, like an X-ray. The technique is notable because it provides good images of soft tissue, which is much harder to see on X-rays, and does not make use of ionizing radiation, too much of which can cause cancer. This new use, however, was rather more than just notable. To me, at least, it's staggering.

According to *New Scientist* magazine, 'Software developed by Kamitani's team analyses the scans to find patterns of activity [in the brain] that are associated with certain pixels being blacked out. It then uses this information to discover signature patterns of brain activity for each pixel.' In other words, Kamitani was able to take an image of what a test subject was looking at directly from the brain.

The images extracted in 2008 were simple 10 x 10 characters, blocky and awkward as the numerals on an early digital watch. They were live, rather than remembered, and were derived from the visual cortex. This wasn't mind-reading, it was more like stealing cable television from the trunk under the road. The next step is to find out whether it's possible to refine the image, or to derive an image of something someone is thinking of, rather than directly apprehending. Kamitani himself acknowledges that this leads directly into some stark issues of privacy and law.

My first reaction is to worry about the justice system; under what circumstances might a court be permitted to order the accused to submit to a scan of this kind? And how reliable would it be? Would there be a scientific way of telling the difference between the memory of an imagined scene and a genuinely remembered one? Would it be a matter of interpretation? How long would it take the tabloid press to demand that certain people – alleged or convicted sex offenders, say, or terror suspects – be 'trawled' for recollections of recent criminal activity? And if them, why not random passengers at air terminals? And if, on being trawled for dangerous intent, you happened to think of something else you felt guilty about, should that then be admissible in court?

Lest you think me fanciful, one project bringing this kind of technology to security (the Human Monitoring and Authentication using Biodynamic Indicators and Behavioural Analysis) already exists. In the UK, the historic 'right to remain silent' has already been watered down so that a jury may draw adverse inference from a refusal to answer questions. It's also an offence – punishable by two years in prison – to refuse to give up the key to encrypted data. The path to court-mandated scanning is open.

Even if the technique only ever allows for images to be derived from the present activity of the visual cortex, a more sophisti-cated iteration with colour images and better definition raises the possibility of a person becoming, effectively, a CCTV camera. Might it be possible to achieve something similar with sound? In which case a human may become a live surveillance device. Or, perhaps equally disturbing: a machine might read the visual cortex of people in the street to determine which of a variety of advertisements they choose to spend time looking at. Combined with facial recognition and already existing software to deter-mine age, gender and ethnicity (or even simply attempt to connect them with existing social network profiles) the system might gather data for more targeted selling – even targeted ads further up the street. And those are the obvious applications and consequences; the more rarefied ones – such as, perhaps: what might such a system learn about our unconscious triggers, our emotional states? How far might politics be manipulated by the live collection of data from the electorate during the election season? – will come upon us unawares.

And that's just one technology. The first consumer biohack is on its way. Body Architect Lucy McRae and biochemist Sheref Mansy are creating swallowable perfume. According to the press release: 'Fragrance molecules are excreted through the skin's surface during perspiration, leaving tiny golden droplets on the skin that emanate a unique odor. The potency of scent is determined by each individual's acclimatization to temperatures, to stress, exercise, or sexual arousal.' In other words, it's a pill that speckles your skin with gold and causes you to produce 'a genetically unique scent about who we are'.

Tiny though this change may be, it's an example of something that could become a fad – or a powerful tool – in the near future: rewriting our bodies to make them do something new. There are other possibilities. A 2006 article[1] in *Wired* magazine by Quinn Norton discussed the implantation of a rare earth magnet under the skin of the ring finger. The magnet responded to the presence of electromagnetic fields, allowing Norton to sense them. If that sounds useless, consider running your hand along a plaster wall and knowing where an electrical cable was sited. Once again, neuroplasticity allows us to integrate new senses (and new variations on old ones) with surprising rapidity.

It's been suggested recently that we have simply integrated Internet access into our maps of ourselves. As when writing was developed (and contrary to the fears of Socrates) we haven't lost the capacity to remember things. Instead, it appears that we only try to remember things automatically if we know we may not be able to retrieve them from a machine.[2] If we think we will be able to find the data without retaining it ourselves, we don't bother to learn it. If that's true, it could be seen as an extension of the same phenomenon Maryanne Wolf describes: we're saving brain power and energy for the real thinking. But if so, what thinking? What exactly do we need all this time for? At a certain point, we may have to stop and decide what ration of biological to prosthetic memory we want.

Kevin Warwick, Professor of Cybernetics at the University of Reading, has gone further in the hope of connecting the human nervous system directly to a machine, allowing paralysed patients to control and feel a prosthetic limb – or even enhance the human experience with new senses. Warwick was successfully given an implant that allowed bi-directional flow of information between machines and the human nervous system. He used an ultra-sonic sensor to navigate blindfold, operated a robotic hand using his brain via the Internet, and ultimately was linked directly to his wife, Irena, so that he was physically aware when she moved her arm.

In the extreme version of this technology, would it be possible to create a literal external memory store, so that we never forgot anything at all (so long as the external hardware remained intact)? One has to wonder, as well, what might be possible with a combination of Warwick's technology and Kamitani's direct mind-to-mind live streaming from the visual cortex? Or even the sharing of surface thoughts? What might be the effect on society of casual blurring of the lines between individuals? Would we remain individual at all? Would we grow together, losing our sense of being discrete from one another – or would it be more like having a constant Twitter feed in one's head, a background murmur of opinion from which relevant information could be searched at will? At that point, we're in the Happy Valley – or the grip of a ghastly Orwellian nightmare. It all depends, of course, on how we allow it to take shape.

I'm not proposing that all these things will happen, or that all of them are even possible. The point is that they are not flat-out ridiculous. We will push the boundaries of what it means to be human, what it means to be an individual, what it means to be alive. We will continue to challenge our preconceptions. This is our world: we are reaching for these things, and day by day some of them get a little closer, even as others are consigned to the rubbish bin of scientific progress. These improbable notions or others like them will produce the next big societal shake-up, but if we choose to engage with them rather than simply letting that technology evolve in the dark without reference to what we believe is important, we may yet be able to help design the world that comes.

When I started writing this book, I was concerned in the first place to unpick the idea that digital technology was responsible for all our ills. I felt that that was at best a superficial explanation for what ails us, and at worst a fig leaf for the failings of the way we do business and the relationship between work and home life in the industrial world. I feel that even more strongly now, and I do not believe in the end that the influence of computers and the Internet on the structure of our brains is malign; I think we are being changed, within limits, by the way we live, and I'm excited that we've noticed and can decide how we feel about it. I do accept, though, that some people may not be able to control their interactions with the technology, and I am concerned that the sheer power of the increasingly sophisticated tools of manipulation that are made available by digitization and its presence in our lives is not generally understood. I can see a possible social future that divides us tacitly into those who control the nudge, and those who are nudged, but I'm not sure, to be honest, that that is any different from how we live now, and the more we are aware of it, the more we can resist – if we want to.

And in the end, it comes down to that: if we do find ourselves living in an ugly, unkind world where we could have had a bright one, it will for the first time be not because we could not have known what was happening to us, but because we chose to remain blind to possibilities where we could have chosen to see.

blindgiant.co.uk/chapter10

Acknowledgements

Non-fiction is different from a novel. It's a different experience, a different process and, I suspect, it uses different bits of the brain. My habit in general is to design countries, cultural and religious movements, cities and people to suit my needs; here I've had to rely on reality. I'm still amazed that anyone cares what I think about a world I did not personally make up. My first acknowledgement must go to you: thanks for reading.

Thanks are also due to Roland Philipps, who commissioned this book and persuaded me I could actually write it, and to the team at John Murray who made it into a reality. Patrick Walsh and the gang at C&W (as ever) picked me up when I fell. Nice work, people!

My gratitude is also due to all those who gave permission for use of quotes, in particular to William Gibson, who not only granted permission for the use of the brief section from *Idoru*, but also is probably responsible in some convoluted way for my being interested in all this in the first place.

More formally, I should doff my cap to acknowledge the quotes I have used as follows: *Flow: The Classic Work on How to Achieve Happiness* by Mihaly Csikszentmihalyi, published by Rider. Used by permission of The Random House Group Limited; *The Lucifer Effect: How Good People Turn Evil* by Philip Zimbardo, published by Rider Books. Reprinted by permission of The Random House Group Limited; *Proust and the Squid* by Maryanne Wolf, used by the kind permission of Icon Books; *The*

Shallows by Nicholas Carr, used by permission of Atlantic Books; *The Blank Slate* by Steven Pinker, used by permission of Penguin Books Ltd; *On Human Communication: A Review, a Survey, and a Criticism* by Colin Cherry (third edition), published by The MIT Press; *Patrons and Painters* by Francis Haskell © Yale University 1980, used by permission of Yale University Press.

Loz Kaye and Andrew Robinson gladly agreed that I should quote my interviews with them despite knowing I might be holding them up only in order to object to their positions. That alone should inspire you to consider their ideas even if you think you disagree with everything they say.

Richard Stallman took time out to engage in an email dialogue regarding copyright and other aspects of what I would term Intellectual Property, a usage he regards – not without justification – as a loose and misleading conflation of different concepts.

Susan Greenfield was kind enough to talk to me regarding her worries about digital technology. I accept, obviously, her deep understanding of the brain, though I disagree with her on social and political grounds. She's a person of profound intelligence, and I consider myself lucky to have had her perspective.

Finally, I could never do any of this without Clare.

Notes

Chapter 1: Past and Present

1. Twitter's Response to WikiLeaks Subpoena Should Be the Industry
   Standard, 10 January 2011
   http://www.wired.com/threatlevel/2011/01/twitter/
2. TEDxSantaCruz: Roger McNamee – Disruption and Engagement, 9
   July 2011
   http://www.youtube.com/watch?v=aR6jLD1USW0&feature=
   youtube

Chapter 2: Information Overload

1. Mobile Effect on Sleep, 21 January 2008
   http://www.nhs.uk/news/2007/January08/Pages/Sleepandmobile
   phones.aspx
2. Here's the Guy who Unwittingly Live-tweeted the Raid on Bin
   Laden, 2 May 2011
   http://eu.techcrunch.com/2011/05/02/heres-the-guy-who-unwit
   tingly-live-tweeted-the-raid-on-bin-laden/
3. Shaking Hands with Saddam Hussein: the U.S. tilts toward Iraq,
   1980–1984, 25 February 2003
   http://www.gwu.edu/~nsarchiv/NSAEBB/NSAEBB82/

Chapter 3: Peak Digital

1. Letter dated 23 October 2003 from the Secretary-General addressed to the President of the Security Council
   http://www.un.org/Docs/journal/asp/ws.asp?m=S/2003/1027
2. Raj Patel: The Value of Nothing–the $200 Hamburger, 5 February 2010
   http://www.youtube.com/watch?v=oagmlbhobnY

Chapter 4: The Plastic Brain

1. Navigation-related Structural Change in the Hippocampi of Taxi Drivers, 10 November 1999
   http://www.pnas.org/content/97/8/4398.full
2. *Discover* magazine: The Brain on Sonar – How Blind People Find their Way around with Echoes, 25 May 2011
   http://blogs.discovermagazine.com/notrocketscience/2011/05/25/the-brain-on-sonar-%E2%80%93-how-blind-people-find-their-way-around-with-echoes/
3. Reading Fiction 'Improves Empathy', study finds, 7 September 2011
   http://www.guardian.co.uk/books/2011/sep/07/reading-fiction-empathy-study
4. Some Preliminary Experiments on Vision without Inversion of the Retinal Image – Dr George M. Stratton, University of California (read at the Third International Congress for Psychology, Munich, August, 1896.)
   http://www.cns.nyu.edu/~nava/courses/psych_and_brain/pdfs/Stratton_1896.pdf
5. *Journal of Mental Health*: Online information, Extreme Communities and Internet Therapy: Is the Internet Good for our Mental Health? August 2007
   http://mindfull.spc.org/vaughan/Bell_2007_JMH.pdf
6. *New Scientist*: Why Facebook is Good for You, 6 March 2009
   http://www.newscientist.com/article/mg20126986.200-why-facebook-is-good-for-you.html
7. The Carter Center: Tune Out, Stay In; An Epidemic of Young Japanese Pulling Back from the World has Deep Roots, 20 August 2011
   http://www.cartercenter.org/news/documents/doc599.html

8. *Science* magazine: Searching for the Google Effect on People's Memory – John Bohannon, 15 July 2011
http://www.sciencemag.org/content/333/6040/277.full

9. MailOnline: Swine Flu Jab Link to Killer Nerve Disease: Leaked Letter Reveals Concern of Neurologists over 25 Deaths in America – Jo Macfarlane, 15 August 2009
http://www.dailymail.co.uk/news/article-1206807/Swine-flu-jab-link-killer-nerve-disease-Leaked-letter-reveals-concern-neurologists-25-deaths-America.html

10. Health Day News: Last Year's H1N1 Flu Vaccine Was Safe, study finds – Steven Reinberg, 2 February 2011
http://www.wunderground.com/DisplayHealthDay.asp?id=649531

11. Science Fiction is the Most Valuable Art Ever. Discuss, 5 September 2011
http://damiengwalter.com/2011/09/05/science-fiction-is-the-most-valuable-art-ever-discuss/

Chapter 5: Work, Play and Sacred Space

1. *New York Times*: Four Nerds and a Cry to Arms Against Facebook, 11 May 2010
http://www.nytimes.com/2010/05/12/nyregion/12about.html

2. Did You Say 'Intellectual Property'? It's a Seductive Mirage – Richard M. Stallman, 20 September 2011
http://www.gnu.org/philosophy/not-ipr.xhtml

3. Wikipedia: The Ones Who Walk Away from Omelas – a 1973 short story by Ursula K. Le Guin
http://en.wikipedia.org/wiki/The_Ones_Who_Walk_Away_from_Omelas

4. *Guardian*: The *Sun* drops World Cup Sweepstake as Bloggers Cry Foul – Mark Sweeney, 16 June 2010
http://www.guardian.co.uk/media/2010/jun/16/sun-world-cup-sweepstake-blogs

5. Lovelace: the Origin – Sydney Padua, 19 April 2009
http://sydneypadua.com/2dgoggles/lovelace-the-origin-2/

6. Reading Fiction 'Improves Empathy', study finds, 7 September 2011
http://www.guardian.co.uk/books/2011/sep/07/reading-fiction-empathy-study

7. *New Scientist*: Your Clever Body: Thinking from Head to Toe – David Robson, 21 October 2011
   http://www.newscientist.com/article/mg21228341.500-your-clever-body-thinking-from-head-to-toe.html?full=true

8. View from the Crow's Nest – Nick Harkaway, 29 September 2010
   http://www.futurebook.net/content/view-crows-nest

9. Tesco-opted – George Monbiot, 10 August 2009
   http://www.monbiot.com/2009/08/10/tesco-opted/

10. You Are Not Facebook's Customer – Douglas Rushkoff, 26 September 2011
    http://www.rushkoff.com/blog/2011/9/26/you-are-not-facebooks-customer.html

11. How Social Influence can Undermine the Wisdom of Crowd Effect – edited by Burton H. Singer, University of Florida, 13 April 2011
    http://www.pnas.org/content/early/2011/05/10/1008636108.abstract

Chapter 6: Tahrir and London

1. Egyptian Activists' Action Plan – translated by Alexis Madrigal, 27 January 2011
   http://www.theatlantic.com/international/archive/2011/01/egyptian-activists-action-plan-translated/70388/

2. BBC News online: Analysis: the riots data so far – Dominic Casciani, 15 September 2011
   http://www.bbc.co.uk/news/uk-14931987

3. *New Scientist*: Language may Shape Human Thought – Celeste Biever, 19 August 2004
   http://www.newscientist.com/article/dn6303-language-may-shape-human-thought.html

4. *New Scientist*: Language may be Key to Theory of Mind – Anil Ananthaswamy, 23 June 2009
   http://www.newscientist.com/article/dn17352-language-may-be-key-to-theory-of-mind.html

5. The Riots: What are the Lessons from the JRF's Work in Communities? – John Low, 7 September 2011
   http://www.jrf.org.uk/publications/riots-what-are-the-lessons

Chapter 7: The Old, the Modern and the New

1. YouTube: How George Lucas Got the Rights to the *Star Wars* Sequels
   – George Lucas, 6 Nov 2009
   http://www.youtube.com/watch?v=dPJ2gQdKXqk
2. HM Government: How e-petitions work – Directgov, undated
   http://epetitions.direct.gov.uk/how-it-works
3. Weasel-necked Pencils. Part I Hope the Last – Neil Gaiman, 5 May 2011
   http://journal.neilgaiman.com/2011/05/weasel-necked-pencils-part-i-hope-last.html
4. *Discover* magazine: Twitter as a Giant Global Mood Ring – Ed Yong,
   29 September 2011
   http://blogs.discovermagazine.com/notrocketscience/2011/09/29/twitter-as-a-giant-global-mood-ring/

Chapter 8: Engagement

1. Neural Responses to Taxation and Voluntary Giving Reveal Motives
   for Charitable Donations – William T. Harbaugh, Ulrich Mayr, Daniel
   R. Burghart, 15 June 2007
   http://www.sciencemag.org/content/316/5831/1622.full
2. News Focus: The Theory? Diet Causes Violence. The Lab? Prison –
   John Bohannon, 25 September 2009
   http://www.ifbb.org.uk/files/Science-25-9-09.PDF
3. *New Scientist*: Your Clever Body: thinking from Head to Toe – David
   Robson, 21 October 2011
   http://www.newscientist.com/article/mg21228341.500-your-clever-body-thinking-from-head-to-toe.html

Chapter 9: Being Human in a Digital World (Or Any Other)

1. *New Scientist*: Natural Brain State is Primed to Learn – Jessica Hamzelou,
   19 August 2011
   http://www.newscientist.com/article/mg21228341.500-your-clever-body-thinking-from-head-to-toe.html
2. *New York Times*: Come On, I Thought I Knew That! – Benedict
   Carey, 18 April 2011

http://www.nytimes.com/2011/04/19/health/19mind.html?_r=3&
pagewanted=all

Chapter 10: Coda

1. A Sixth Sense for a Wired World – Quinn Norton, 7 June 2006
   http://www.wired.com/gadgets/mods/news/2006/06/71087?current
   Page=all
2. Google Effects on Memory: Cognitive Consequences of Having
   Information at our Fingertips – Betsy Sparrow, Jenny Liu, Daniel M.
   Wegner, 2 May 11
   http://www.sciencemag.org/content/early/2011/07/13/science.
   1207745#aff-2

Index

273